Agen
The Hung

Agency in
The Hunger Games

Desire, Intent
and Action in the Novels

KAYLA ANN

McFarland & Company, Inc., Publishers

Jefferson, North Carolina

This book has undergone peer review.

LIBRARY OF CONGRESS CATALOGUING-IN-PUBLICATION DATA

Names: Ann, Kayla, 1994– author.
Title: Agency in the Hunger Games : desire, intent and action
in the novels / Kayla Ann.
Description: Jefferson : McFarland & Company, Inc., Publishers, 2020 |
Includes bibliographical references and index.
Identifiers: LCCN 2019058440 | ISBN 9781476674162
(paperback : acid free paper) ∞ | ISBN 9781476639147 (ebook)
Subjects: LCSH: Collins, Suzanne. Hunger Games. | Agent (Philosophy)
in literature | Young adult fiction, American—History and criticism.
Classification: LCC PS3603.O4558 Z525 2020 | DDC 813/.6—dc23
LC record available at https://lccn.loc.gov/2019058440

BRITISH LIBRARY CATALOGUING DATA ARE AVAILABLE

ISBN (print) 978-1-4766-7416-2
ISBN (ebook) 978-1-4766-3914-7

Front cover image © 2020 clarst5/Shutterstock

Printed in the United States of America

*McFarland & Company, Inc., Publishers
Box 611, Jefferson, North Carolina 28640
www.mcfarlandpub.com*

To my husband, mother,
step-father, and grandparents,
thank you for being my allies in the arena
and for your continued support

Acknowledgments

First and foremost, I give all glory to God. It is through Him that I have the ability to write and the desire to grow in scholarly pursuits.

Secondly, I would like to thank the multitude of people, my prep team, who constantly stood beside me, assisting me in this endeavor. To my parents, Licia and Ben, who read so many early drafts of various chapters and sections that did not even make it into these pages, thank you for your time, effort, and feedback that helped me produce a better book. To my husband, Jacob, who supplied me with tea and snacks and constantly encouraged me when my brain felt stuck, thank you for the support that made this book a reality. To my grandparents, Linda and Grover, I never would have thought that I could succeed in publishing a book if not for your consistent love and inspiration. Thank you for pushing me to always follow my goals, even when they seem like impossibilities. To my grandfather, Robert Weaver, who read my entire book from cover to cover, offering grammatical and contextual feedback on every page, thank you, this project would be severely lacking without your input.

Thirdly, I want to acknowledge those who sat on my thesis committee, Dr. Erika Travis, Dr. Derek Updegraff, and Professor Isaacs, who helped develop the early stages of ideas that later evolved into this book. Their invaluable suggestions heightened the quality of my work and urged me to dig deeper into my analysis of *The Hunger Games* series. I also need to thank Dr. Toni Kirk who was the first person to help me pursue the idea of analyzing and dissecting issues revolving around human agency.

Fourthly, this project would not have been possible without the incredible editors at McFarland. In particular, I want to say thank you to Dylan Lightfoot who walked with me during the initial stages of this book and Layla Milholen who saw it through to completion.

Lastly, I want to thank Suzanne Collins for creating such an intriguing and compelling world within her trilogy. Her presentation of characters has encouraged me to view my own world in new and enlightened ways.

Table of Contents

Preface

Welcome, Fellow Tribute

I first read *The Hunger Games* trilogy while still in high school like the majority of the series' demographic. Mimicking Gale's brilliance at captivating his prey, the novels swiftly ensnared my fascination with its compelling first-person narrative, substantial plotline, and dark themes running throughout the trilogy. I had no way of knowing that years later, I would be dedicating months and even years to researching and rereading the trilogy time and time again, picking clean the pages with the same dedication that Katniss has as she picks clean the bones of a squirrel in the arena. With every reread, I would pick up on some new tidbit of information that I had previously overlooked: moments of foreshadowing, allegories I had missed, flashes of epiphanies sparking in my mind like the flames of Cinna's fashion creations. Inspired by these revelations, I committed myself to the task of better understanding Suzanne Collins' well-received trilogy through the academic lenses of accomplished scholars.

As if called by Claudius Templesmith to attend the mid–Game Feast, I eagerly devoured literature conducted on the series. As I read essays, journals, and books about the trilogy, I could not help but notice a startling gap. While *The Hunger Games* trilogy has garnered a substantial amount of scholarship, it is not yet all-inclusive in its reach, particularly in the popular sphere of research written specifically for *The Hunger Games'* fan base. Within the novels, there is an intense representation of human agency[1] that is challenged and developed by major and minor characters alike that has not yet been presented to the popular audience as its own individualized topic.

Scholars of various backgrounds and focuses have examined a variety of topics within the series looking at characters, themes, historical allusions and so much more.[2] As is popular to do with literature in the twenty-first century, many academics analyze gender within the novels. For instance, Jennifer Mitchell looks at the ways in which members of each gender blur traditional gender characteristics, queering female and male characters alike. As a whole,

1

most scholars readily agree that Katniss rejects gender norms. Instead, Katniss "learns to parody gender,"[3] "bends feminine norms when she must,"[4] and "defies segregation."[5] Additionally, the motif[6] of the body strikes the fancy of many scholars who note its importance such as Valerie E. Frankel, Susan Tan, Christian Van Dyke, Gretchen Koenig, Brian McDonald, and Amy Montz. These scholars make up only a sample of authors who discuss the ways in which the Capitol objectifies, modifies, and makes alien the bodies of the tributes—specifically Katniss' body. Many of these scholars examine the negative ways in which the Capitol "desecrate[s] and defile[s] the bodies of others without restraint."[7] At times, even District 13 attempts to use Katniss' body to accomplish its own agenda. Therefore, many scholars have discussed the ways in which Katniss' personal agency has been restricted by those around her.

On the other hand, few scholars concede the ways in which Katniss reclaims and exercises her own agency within the same events as discussed by the previous scholars. Susan Tan, author of "'Burn with us': Sacrificing Childhood," argues that both Katniss and Peeta "demonstrate that their bodies are no longer sites of punishment, denying the Capitol the ability to exercise power through them."[8] Indeed, Tan claims that Katniss begins her path toward rebellion in discovering her agency in relation to the body. Additionally, both Michael Macaluso and Cori McKenzie, co-authors of "Exploiting the Gaps in the Fence: Power, Agency, and Rebellion in *The Hunger Games*," discuss the ways in which the Capitol's power over the individual is not absolute. There are "gaps" in both physical and metaphorical fences that allow the Capitol's citizens to exercise agency.[9]

While some academics, such as those mentioned above, do discuss agency, very few focus their discussion solely on how individual characters implement or grapple with agency and how their struggles relate to the twenty-first century reader.[10] For instance, many scholars of young adult dystopian literature may discuss morality, but they will do so by looking at the unethical ruling authority within the texts more often than at the individual. Contrarily, this book looks directly at how an individual's moral and ethical convictions affect his/her ability to exercise successful agency against corrupt authority. A handful of scholars such as David R. Dreyer, Joseph J. Foy, and Tom Henthorne discuss the topic of morality within the trilogies; however, their research is not intended to relate specifically back to individual agency. Likewise, as authors explore various topics such as trauma, identity, and power, very few ever relate their conclusion to the discussion of agency with the popular reader in mind. The longer I researched, the larger this gap became. There is a need for a book that discusses these complex topics in a way that is accessible for the regular *Hunger Games* enthusiast. Consequently, I discovered a need to discuss agency within the text in an unprecedented way, by looking directly at individual agency, how it is gained, exercised, lost, and reclaimed and how this discussion ultimately relates back to the twenty-first century reader.

The purpose of this book is to build on previous scholarship with the direct intent of focusing the discussion on the evolution of personal agency as displayed by various characters in a way that is both enlightening and understandable for fellow *Hunger Games* enthusiasts like yourself who desire to understand your favorite series at a deeper level. I argue that it is this focus on agency that highlights the importance and appeal of this series for its readers. Agency, often associated first and foremost with the ability to act, is a core concern of mankind who fears the removal of their rights. While other novels, particularly dystopian novels, deal with topics of control and agency, *The Hunger Games* series is uniquely situated in its appeal to both young and adult readers alike to discuss agency. With its wide range of readers, *The Hunger Games* series is worth additional study, particularly for the adolescent and young adult reader as the trilogy touches on topics of gender, power, control, morality, individuality, sacrifice, and more, all within the same context of agency. Adolescents on the cusp of adulthood, and even adults in the midst of their maturity, feel the weight of wanting to change their societies and the subsequent burden of feeling powerless. The discussion of agency within this book works to enlighten and encourage young adult readers of the current century who feel that they lack a sense of agency to affect change in their own lives and apart from themselves.

Since the tragic events of September 11, 2001, there has been a spike in dystopian literature geared toward the young adult. Literature such as Suzanne Collins' *The Hunger Games* series accurately addresses the social climate of anxiety that currently surrounds and permeates young adult everyday life in the twenty-first century. This book displays how readers, through Collins' characters, can find the strength to enact their own agency even within a restrictive society. It is no surprise, then, that readers crave a trilogy such as *The Hunger Games* in which not only the main protagonist, but even minor characters, are able to achieve agency within a society intent on destroying individuality. This book invites fellow tributes such as yourself to dive into the text in ways you may never have considered and to explore how Katniss, Peeta, Gale, Haymitch, Cinna, Prim, Finnick, Mags, Johanna, and Beetee experience their own struggles for agency and rebel against impossible odds, suggesting that agency is obtainable regardless of the encompassing society or authority. Through analyzing not only Katniss, Gale, and Peeta, but also a handful of "minor" characters, this analysis differs from all previous popular research and offers something new for its readers. And so, I invite you to join me, to fasten on your Mockingjay pins as we delve into the world of Panem and explore the various representations of agency.

Introduction:
"Here's some advice. Stay alive"[1]

In the summer of 2017, I traveled to the forests of Big Bear, California, with minimal hiking experience and a wonky knee. Surrounded by tall pine trees and expansive evergreens, with the sounds of birdcalls and squirrels in the air, the overwhelming desire struck me to whistle Rue's four notes. As I struggle with even the most basic whistle, it took me several tries before I could perform an adequate imitation of Rue's notes. I waited, hopeful that perhaps some bird would delight me with an answer, but no Mockingjays picked up the simple tune to repeat back to me in a glorious melody. Instead, all I received was the shrill of a nearby bird that sounded a lot more like my alarm clock back home and a couple of bug bites. As I think back now, I realize that maybe it was a good thing I did not hear the Mockingjay's response to my whistle. After all, if I had, then it would mean that all other sorts of muttations—jabberjays with their heart-wrenching cries, monkeys with their sharp teeth, and genetically-enhanced wolves with the eyes of my enemies—might also exist and appear before me.[2] Yet, on that hiking trail covered by black ants so large you would have thought they were engineered by Capitol scientists, I could not help but be disappointed by the lack of a response. Part of me craved to hear Rue's melody—a melody that later transformed into a battle cry—bounce among the trees of Big Bear. But why? To answer that question, we must look at why the series itself has become so renowned.

Suzanne Collins published *The Hunger Games* in 2008, the first installment of her well-known trilogy that director Gary Ross would later adapt into film. In 2012, the Girl on Fire had outsold the Boy Who Lived—Harry Potter. By this time, the novels had lit an unquenchable fire that only on-screen adaptions could satisfy. Jennifer Lawrence starred as the fierce yet surprisingly loving Katniss Everdeen with Josh Hutcherson and Liam Hemsworth as her co-stars. By 2017, *The Hunger Games* franchise had brought in $4.3 billion combining book and box office sales.[3] Katniss' claim, made during the 74th annual Hunger Games, proved prophetic: "No one will forget me.

Not my look, not my name. Katniss. The girl who was on fire."[4] Indeed, in no time at all, posters and action figures all around the globe displayed Katniss' image within the homes of *The Hunger Games* fans—revealing that both young and adult readers love Katniss Everdeen as she only continues to grow in popularity. Through her books, Collins entertains audiences with Katniss' snarky attitude, causes them to feel sympathy for the love between Katniss and Prim, and encourages them with Katniss' ability to stand strong and resilient against all odds—which never seem to be in her favor regardless of Effie's wishes. In response, readers eagerly consume the books, movies, and even outside literature on the series. Again, I propose the question: Why? Why do readers crave this trilogy? Why did I desire to hear the mockingjays' music in the pines and evergreens of Big Bear?

Scholars have filled pages in the pursuit of understanding why twenty-first century readers hunger for the dark and brutal stories of Panem that Collins fills with sporadic bursts of radiant beauty and enduring hope. Books and collections such as *Of Bread, Blood, and the Hunger Games*, *The Hunger Games and Philosophy*, *Space and Place in the Hunger Games*, and *Approaching the Hunger Games Trilogy* have analyzed the various components of the trilogy through scholarly lenses. Within these works, scholars look at "big picture" ideas concerning gender, politics, power, and identity in the quest to further discern the source of the trilogy's acclaim. Other published works, including *Guide to the Hunger Games*, *The Panem Companion*, and *The Girl Who Was on Fire*, also delve into the world of Panem, exploring the beloved trilogy and attempting to understand why it has developed such popularity. Tim Challies, book reviewer, claims that it is the trilogy's extraordinary themes of good versus evil, the underdog, and love that attract readers.[5] Jeff Goins, an award-winning blogger, insists that the edgy writing style is more practical and appealing for a society focused on youth culture.[6] Made clear from the ample collection of writings on *The Hunger Games*, there is something irresistible about Collins' trilogy. As such, this book offers yet another understanding as to why *The Hunger Games* so successfully leaves all competition smoldering in the ash.

Undoubtedly, the trilogy attracts readers with its intense themes, daring writing style, and strong female protagonist; however, there is another key factor to consider. Mankind longs for a sense of control and power over their actions and lives. We strive for free will over fated circumstances. There is no better arena to explore power struggles, both individually and communally, than within a dystopian society and the society of Panem is definitively dystopic. Many scholars have argued that various genres apply themselves to *The Hunger Games* trilogy. For instance, Katniss' experiences with self-growth in maturity can lend itself to viewing the novels as a *Bildungsroman*—a coming-of-age-story—the almost magical properties of the mockingjays suggest fantasy or magical realism, and the incorporation of technology harkens to the science fiction genre.

While varied genres label *The Hunger Games* trilogy, at its core, the novels are dystopian texts. The overwhelming use of propaganda, constant surveillance, encouraged fear of the natural world, and dehumanization tactics along with the absence of family devotion serve to identify the series as dystopian. Additionally, Katniss fulfills the role of dystopian protagonist in her struggle to escape the confines of an oppressive society, recognition of a corrupt authority, questioning the systems of both the Capitol and District 13, and, ultimately, coming to reveal the flaws of each. For decades, the purpose of dystopian literature has been to enlighten and challenge its readers by presenting itself as a warped mirror image of the current society or the direction in which that society is headed. In other words, dystopias serve as reflections and as eventual warnings. For *The Hunger Games*, this reflection forces readers to consider the importance behind their actions, when they act, how they act, and, most importantly, why they act. It warns twenty-first century readers to consider the consequences and the power associated with their decisions regardless of age. Within the series, characters are not only fighting for physical survival, but they are also battling for the right to exercise and maintain individual aspects of human agency.

Before we engage the series itself or any of these ideas any further, it is important for there to be a clear understanding of what is meant by this term *agency*. At its core, agency is the individual's ability to perform intentional actions based on his or her own beliefs and desires. However, this is a simplified definition. According to philosophical scholars such as Markus Schlosser, Gilad Feldman, and Amartya Sen, numerous constructs and outside forces affect and influence agency, which the individual then executes in various degrees based on such constructs. Agency, in the sense of the above-simplified definition, is not unique to humans as animals too can act on their instinctual desires. Contrarily, agency, as intended in this discussion, is solely humanistic in the ways that agency connects to free will, well-being, and moral responsibility. Indeed, the presence of morality is the distinctive feature that separates animalistic agency and human agency. While an animal might be free to choose to hunt, a human has the innate knowledge of when or when not to kill. Henceforth, humanity demands morality, as will be seen in our later discussions of how agents act or react to their inner code of conduct.

The term "agent" or "agents" refers to an individual or a group of individuals with the capacity and intent to act (most often physically although inaction can also prove crucial to individual development). Furthermore, agency applies not only to an individual, but can be shared between a collective group of individuals with shared goals. Shared Agency occurs between two or more agents and Collective Agency occurs when a group of more than three accomplishes the desired action intentionally, such as District 12's three-fingered salute to Katniss Everdeen and Peeta Mellark on the Reaping Day before the 75th Annual Quarter Quell. Their uniformed salute signaled an exercise of action against an unjust system, made stronger through numbers. Agency is innate within all individuals as it depicts the control that one has over one's own actions. Throughout *The Hunger Games*, matters concerning human agency abound, drawing in readers who seek to discover a way to control and exert power over their own actions within the twenty-first century.

However, agency cannot yet be understood without first discussing the implications of free will as agency can only exist when agents are capable of both choosing and effecting a specific action (or inaction). Free will is constantly under the influence of external and internal constraints such as society, environment, genes, and desires.[7] In dystopian literature, the oppressive authority often restricts an individual's movements and desires, attempting to reprogram the individual to fulfill the needs of the government instead of their own. This can be seen in the ways that the Capitol reduces its citizens to production values by categorizing each district based on what it can create or offer the Capitol. As such, the ability to enact agency is crucial for the dystopian protagonist's triumph over the totalitarian authority. Consider Katniss' hunting activities. Through such illegal actions, Katniss actively works against the Capitol's power. However, she also abides by the Capitol's laws in not flaunting her possession of contraband—bows and arrows. Katniss exercises limited agency—a type of agency in which the agent (Katniss) can act based on intentions (to provide for her family) but is still limited by internal or external constraints (the Capitol's ever watchful eye). Contrarily, total agency is the ability to act intentionally based on desires while working either within or against such constraints. Since free will is the ability to act in whatever manner the agent chooses and well-being is his/her goal, then agency is an agent's ability to act in a way most advantageous for him/herself.

Or, at least it would be, if an individual's actions affected only his/her own well-being, and not the well-being of those around the individual. Instead, the well-being of others affects how agents act as they must reflect on how their actions will affect and influence another. An agent must then base his/her actions on his/her beliefs about moral responsibility. Amartya Sen, an Indian economist and philosopher, distinctly asserts, "A person's agency aspect cannot be understood without taking note of his or her aims … [and] the person's conception of good."[8] In fact, an individual's moral responsibility might cause the agent to act in direct opposition toward his/her well-being.

For instance, both Peeta Mellark and Mags display a sacrificial nature that often neglects their own well-being for the sake of another's survival or protection. Another philosopher, Andrew Eshleman, argues that a person's "status as morally responsible agent" is a distinctively human feature.[9] Therefore, when taking the above scholars into consideration, agency is uniquely humanistic in the agent's ability to act freely, based on desires of well-being, and influenced by their sense of "good" and moral responsibility. Of course, this brings up the problematic discussion of what is "good." While many would argue that the line between good and evil is a clear one, through our discussion it will become evident that this line is in fact blurry and often on the move.

In essence, this book intends to take a hard look at the presence of agency (in *The Hunger Games*) and how these examples both reflect current society and provide warnings to its readers. In writing the series, Suzanne Collins responds to and addresses current societal issues, warning against what our future may evolve into. *The Hunger Games*, like many dystopian texts, is a product of the author's environment. With first-hand experiences of military history as the daughter of an Air Force pilot and historian, Suzanne Collins was brought up on war stories. Collins' father, Michael Collins, believed in "educating his children about war" and in turn, Suzanne Collins incorporates her knowledge of the violent consequences of war within her narratives.[10] Refusing to shy away from the brutal, graphic nature of war, Collins displays dark themes using adolescents as her main characters. Her lack of censorship, especially concerning children, caused her series to end up in the Top 10 Censored Books of 2012.[11] In fact, according to the American Library Association, *The Hunger Games* became the third most challenged book in the United States as "unsuited to age group and violence, anti-ethnic, anti-family and occult/satanic."[12] Such comments are common criticism of most young adult dystopian literature as critics attempt to shield younger minds from the reality that they live within.

However, Collins insists on the necessity of children learning how to cope with harsh truths, rather than being continuously misled by the adults in their lives. In an interview, Collins elaborates on this idea, saying, "We think we're sheltering them, but what we're doing is putting them at a disadvantage."[13] Collins depicts realistic and horrific situations within her narrative for the intended purpose of enlightening her readers and preparing them for the reality that surrounds them. Through her main protagonist Katniss Everdeen, along with other supporting characters, Collins probes realistic and problematic issues that arise in twenty-first century society such as an individual's ability to maintain and exercise agency regardless of internal or external influences. Indeed, it is this focus on the complex nature of agency that sets Collins' trilogy apart from all other twenty-first century young literature. Collins' complicated illustration of human agency is what grasps readers' attention as they read *The Hunger Games* series and, ultimately, is what caused my desire to hear the Mockingjays' song while in the forests of Big Bear.

Therefore, this book evaluates the incorporation of agency within the dystopian society of Panem as presented in *The Hunger Games* trilogy and how characters such as Katniss, Peeta, Gale, Haymitch, Cinna, Prim, Finnick, Johanna, Mags, and Beetee represent realistic complications that arise with human agency. Through this analysis, readers of the series will come to view Collins' trilogy as far more than just a young adult series intended to entertain. Rather, *The Hunger Games* series is the battle cry of a generation that strives to regain control over their own chaotic societies. In working alongside established literature, I further the current discussion surrounding the trilogy by presenting new interpretations for future fans and scholars, such as yourself, to build upon. In the following chapters, I write under the assumption that readers are at least familiar with all three novels. For those who are not, or for those who need a refresher, I have included terminology, along with a character list, in Appendix A at the back of the book. In addition, those interested in the scholarship mentioned above or within the following chapters, can find additional information and suggested readings in Appendix B.

Chapter One opens this analysis of human agency by addressing the overabundance of bodily imagery throughout the trilogy. The emphasis on the body originates from the fact that it is through the body that dystopian governments, and often our own, first attempt to suppress its citizens, and it is the primary avenue for individuals to first establish agency. Engaging with reputable scholarship on the body, with renewed focus on Michel Foucault's[14] discussion of docile bodies, Chapter One examines Katniss' reclamation of agency through the control of her body. Collins' narrative echoes traditional dystopian texts in which the oppressive government robs the individual of agency. However, once Katniss is in the Games, Collins rejects traditional dystopias by allowing Katniss to realize the limited quantities of agency she can gain through the presentation of her body and the reclamation of the bodies of others. We ask, can an individual truly retain agency if their actions are controlled by another? This epiphany influences Katniss' acceptance of the Mockingjay persona. In this chapter, we investigate whether the Girl on Fire truly desired her wings. Through this examination of Katniss, we explore ideas of limited versus free agency and the discovery of agency through the physical body.

Chapter Two examines Katniss' actions within the 74th Hunger Games and the Quarter Quell, her role as Mockingjay, and the moral complications that are born from rebellion and war. Both Games require the deaths of others in order to ensure her own and Peeta's survival, resulting in an outbreak of questionable actions, forcing readers to consider moral conundrums. Is the act of killing moral if it is in self-defense? Through these moments of ambiguous morality, this chapter directly relates an individual's agency to his/her morality. Katniss' morality is both relational and care-based although both Peeta and Gale influence her consideration of morality. Furthermore, this chapter takes a close look at the "love triangle" between Katniss, Gale, and Peeta which relates more to systems of morality than romance. Indeed, Collins incorporates Peeta's and Gale's contrasting belief systems to prompt consideration from both Katniss and readers. While Peeta immediately connects morality to identity and agency, Gale often forces aside the importance of morality when focusing on survival. During this investigation, I argue that a lack of morality results in unsuccessful agency. Indeed, within the last novel, *Mockingjay*, Collins' bright, heroic protagonist falls from her position as protector and engages in immoral actions. As her morality fades, so too does her sense of agency. This chapter illustrates how the loss of morality accompanies an individual's diminished capacity to exercise and maintain agency. Therefore, the strength of one's moral codes, at least in part, determines the success of individual agency.

Chapter Three analyzes the overwhelming presence of trauma within the trilogy, particularly within *Mockingjay*. Katniss' trauma, caused by her broken ethical foundation, negatively affects her ability to act at all, let alone to exercise agency. Scarring and muteness most clearly display the effects of trauma on Katniss' physicality and mentality. The outer appearance of a "fire mutt," an image that Katniss shares with Peeta, adequately depicts Katniss' inner turmoil as her mind cracks due to the horrors of her past and Prim's gruesome death.[15] In order to regain agency, Katniss must overcome trauma through vocalization and narration. Katniss' situation begs the question, must agency be vocalized? Indeed, this chapter highlights the importance of music and narrative through which many trauma victims, Katniss included, find healing. Surprising for a dystopian novel, the conclusion of the trilogy manages to offer hope in the form of a new life where Katniss' children can play safely in the meadow at last. Collins' insertion of "Katniss' book" places importance on remembering past experiences and using them to form one's ethical convictions. This chapter argues that Collins' portrayal of agency as continuously obtainable rejects traditional themes of dystopian literature.

The end of Chapter Three marks the shift for the remainder of the book as we explore characters whose thoughts we do not have access to as we are only able to witness their actions through Katniss—who would most likely admit to being a biased narrator. Even so, we can still examine additional characters from what we are given within the narrative as we learn to read past Katniss' biases.

Chapter Four focuses on Peeta Mellark, the Boy with the Bread, the ally, friend, lover, Victor, traitor, prisoner, and mutt. With so many different titles and identifiers, readers may find it difficult to understand who Peeta Mellark truly is. Modern readers may question their own identity and, therefore, their own agency. Throughout the narrative, Peeta undergoes various new personas as his insights adapt to his changing environments. However, with every new persona, Peeta maintains a singular core identity. At his center, Peeta demonstrates the Messianic archetype throughout each of the sub-roles mentioned above. His position as Savior, combined with his innately strong moral stance, makes his hijacking in *Mockingjay* exceptionally tragic as he loses all previous sense of morality and identity. Having based his agency on those two constructs, Peeta struggles to act based on any authentic desire. Collins' presentation of Peeta's brutal and traumatic journey of regaining his identity further highlights the necessary relation between identity and agency. Only in knowing oneself can the individual know how to act based on genuine desire and intention.

Chapter Five, using the metaphor of an avalanche, explores personal power struggles within Panem, specifically through the character of Gale Hawthorne—a nobody coal miner from District 12 who rises through the ranks of District 13 gaining influence, authority, and power. Although Collins initially presents Gale as a strong, kind, and sympathetic protagonist, protecting his family and Katniss, by the end of the trilogy, Gale loses his position within the major three (Katniss, Peeta, and Gale). Metaphorically, Collins banishes Gale to District 2 while Katniss and Peeta return home to District 12. Upon closer inspection, Gale's desire for power and revenge is evident even within the first novel. As Gale allows the rebellion to bring out his darkest desires in exchange for power and authority, his agency abates. According to Sir John Dalberg-Acton,[16] "Power tends to corrupt and absolute power corrupts absolutely."[17] Likewise, through his quest for power, Gale loses sight of his previously important relationships and friendships. Ultimately, Gales serves not as an example, but as a dystopian warning to twenty-first century readers, to be wary of the consequences of the excessive desire for power which can corrupt personal agency.

Chapter Six revisits the discussion concerning the body and explores the application of shared agency within society by analyzing the relationship between Katniss Everdeen and the moderately modified, Capitol-stylist Cinna. This chapter directly asks, is shared agency more powerful than individual agency or is there always an imbalance of power and knowledge? Although not much is known about Cinna's past, indeed readers are not privy to even his last name, Cinna has captivated audiences across the globe as thoroughly as his creations amazed the Capitol citizens. In enacting agency, Cinna refuses to conform to social standards physically or morally. This chapter expands on how Cinna's character carefully, but intentionally, confronts Capitol expectations through his physicality and his relationship with Katniss. Additionally, this chapter directly rebuts the assertions that Cinna manipulates Katniss during her time in the Capitol. Only through working together and in full commitment to each other's action can Cinna and Katniss rebel against the

Capitol's authority. The relationship between Katniss and Cinna, even after Cinna's death, demonstrates the strength and power accessible to all those who enact shared agency when based on mutual obligation and loyalty.

Chapter Seven approaches the character of Haymitch Abernathy, the Mentor for the tributes of District 12, with the intention of peeling back the drunken layers of supposed callousness and indifference to understand the contrasts between perception and reality. While the chapter concedes that Haymitch is indeed a qualified drunkard, it argues that Haymitch is much more than a drunk even within his inebriation. Haymitch, the Victor of the 2nd Quarter Quell in which double the number of children died in the arena, fell into drunkenness after surviving his Games—as he reminds readers there are no winners, only survivors. The Capitol encourages his public persona as "drunkard" to serve as a warning to the rest of the Victors. Much like many reality television stars today who exaggerate their worst qualities on television to improve ratings, Haymitch hyperbolizes his drunkenness when it best suits his rebellious desires. Therefore, his real drunkenness becomes a fake mask through which he can hide his hidden agendas. Again, we must question the effect that visibility has on agency. Must agency be tangible to be existent? In exploring Haymitch as a Drunk, a Rebel, and a Man we can understand how reality and faked perception affect and influence individual agency.

Chapter Eight devotes itself to investigating the short life of Primrose Everdeen, named for the flower that represents womanhood and, more importantly, hope. Prim stands as the crux of the entire series as Katniss would never have entered the Games, never have become the Mockingjay, and never have led a rebellion if not for her desire to protect Prim and her belief that she could. Throughout the trilogy, Prim most clearly represents the theme of hope as she offers encouragement to her mother, her sister, and even to the people of Panem. Like Rue, Prim becomes a motivational force behind the Mockingjay. However, Prim's death in *Mockingjay* proves to be inevitable for the sake of the narrative and Katniss' personal growth. Through Prim, Collins reiterates the necessity of hope and forces readers to ask "What was the point?" as Katniss loses the very one she strove to protect. Ultimately, Prim's death causes readers to question agency after death and the ability to hold on to hope when it is all that remains.

Chapter Nine briefly focuses on minor characters such as Finnick Odair, Mags, Johanna Mason, and Beetee Latier. Although there is not enough information on these characters to warrant each a full chapter, it is worth exploring them in relation to the themes previously discussed. Indeed, these four characters compare and contrast against the major three (Katniss, Peeta, and Gale), representing the complex intricacies of agency. For instance, Finnick Odair, the sex symbol of Panem who is the sex slave of Panem, is the perfect counterpart to Katniss when discussing the relationship between agency and the body. Like Katniss, Finnick attempts to enact limited agency over his body even within his restraints. Mags, the eighty-year-old Victor who volunteers in order to save Annie Cresta's life in the Quarter Quell, exhibits the same sacrificial nature as Peeta Mellark. Like Peeta, Mags' agency practically ignores personal well-being. On the other hand, Johanna Mason contrasts against both Peeta and Mags.

Furthermore, Beetee Latier displays both similarities and differences to Gale Hawthorne. Like Gale, Beetee focuses on the ability to act instead of focusing on whether he should. Beetee's desire for technological advancement, much like Gale's obsession with power, often negatively impacts his ability to later enact agency. Unlike Gale, Beetee sees past his own intelligence and regains morality, learning to consider the consequences of actions before acting. While there is less material to work with, these characters provide excellent avenues through which to explore how repetitious themes such as body, sacrifice, morality, and death interact with personal agency.

Chapter Ten questions the lack of parental and surrogate figures within dystopian young adult literature and how their absence creates a vacuum that young protagonists must fill, a situation that many twenty-first century readers are all too familiar with. Through analyzing Suzanne Collins' *The Hunger Games* trilogy, this chapter emphasizes how individuals foster agency due to the lack of parental guidance. Indeed, in *The Hunger Games*, parental and surrogate figures such as Mr. and Mrs. Everdeen, Mr. and Mrs. Hawthorne, Mr. and Mrs. Mellark, Cinna, Haymitch, and Effie ultimately fail the young adolescents, forcing them into early adulthood. Within the series it becomes clear that the lack of parental figures is intentional on the author's part. Katniss, Peeta, and Gale have only one choice—to refrain from depending on parental support and learn to rely only on themselves or each other.

Chapter Eleven brings together the individual discussions of agency and directly applies them to you, the fellow *Hunger Games* fan, with a yearning to understand more about the series and more about your own desire to act. As is typical with dystopian authors, Collins, like her predecessors Orwell, Huxley, and Atwood, creates a society that resembles our own. Indeed, many of today's aspects, from reality television programs to news coverage to a state of constant anxiety, seem pulled from the very nation of Panem. However, Collins does differ from her predecessors in one crucial way: her hopeful ending. Through each character, Collins offers her readers an image of agency that is constantly achievable through hope and perseverance. Indeed, it is this conclusion that ultimately connects the individual chapters and argues the importance and appeal of Collins' trilogy, which works to encourage young adolescents and even the adult reader who find themselves beaten down by a terror-filled society.

Ultimately, this book provides readable scholarship for those who are interested in a comprehensive and thorough discussion of human agency within *The Hunger Games, Catching Fire,* and *Mockingjay.* This book will enlighten fans with the numerous character analyses presented in these chapters and perhaps even encourage readers to begin their own research. Collins' series is far more than mere entertainment; it is a reflection on the attitudes of current society and is an encouragement for its readers to reclaim their own lost agency. This book does not claim to be all-inclusive on the multitude of topics concerning the series. It only intends to add to the discussion, to inspire young readers to dig deeper into their texts, and to emphasize the literary, academic nature of young adult dystopian literature. As you continue forward, be sure to listen closely for the harmonious sounds of mockingjays, even if the music is only in your head.

ONE

"I'm not naked"[1]

Agency and the Body

Once Katniss is whisked away to the Capitol, her initial torture begins not in the arena, but at the hands of her prep team as they rip, pluck, and otherwise attack her body, although, of course, they would never see it that way. They are only whittling her down to Beauty Base Zero in their attempt to make her more "human" and appealing to the Capitol audience. According to Katniss herself, the Games may not be a beauty pageant, but physical appearances matter; indeed "the best-looking tributes always seem to pull more sponsors" because within the Capitol beauty is associated with success.[2] Like Katniss, many readers have found their own bodies attacked, analyzed, and groomed by social media, magazines, and their surrounding communities. Girls, in particular, around Katniss' age are told how they should dress, how they should act, and what constitutes as femininity. Boys too are expected, like Peeta or even Cato, to be well-groomed even within their masculinity. Often, in the battle of agency, the ability to act as the individual desires, the first scrimmage takes place over possession of one's body.

Is it any surprise then that a twenty-first century dystopian novel, such as *The Hunger Games*, would place such significance on the motif of the body? Whether Collins is discussing the former beauty of Mrs. Everdeen, the fresh loveliness of Prim, or the ever-changing appearance of Katniss Everdeen while within the Capitol, the importance of physicality permeates throughout the narrative. This focus on the body is not new to dystopian literature. In previous years, novels such as George Orwell's *Nineteen Eighty-Four* and Margaret Atwood's *The Handmaid's Tale* paved the way for stories such as *The Hunger Games* with their depictions of totalitarian governments that appropriate the bodies of their citizens for the benefit of those in charge.

Scholars have widely noted the power that surrounds the body. Naomi Jacobs, author of "Dissent, Assent, and the Body in *Nineteen-Eighty-Four*," argues that "the body itself must be the locus of utopian or dystopian transformation, whether that transformation is to be brought about by liberating the body or by more effectively subduing it."[3] Indeed, this liberation or suppression of the individual body remains a subject undergoing intense exploration and investigation to this day. While the presence of physicality within *The Hunger Games* comes as no surprise, it does warrant further examination. According to Pamela Cooper, author of "'A Body Story with a Vengeance,'" "the problems of agency, identity, and power … are rout-ed [sic] irrevocably through the body."[4] In other words, the powers of another, particularly the ruling authority, over an individual's body directly affect that individual's successful enaction of agency. Katniss Everdeen, the girl on fire, physically outshines her competition in the Capitol, but it is her atypical responses to the Capitol's typical exertion of dystopian power that truly demonstrates how agency is first and foremost established through an individual's physicality and continuously shaped by the presentation and reclamation of one's body. In order to understand how Katniss enacts agency, it is first important to recognize how dystopian governments often attempt to control personal freedom.

Dystopian Control and "docile bodies"

In *The Hunger Games*, Collins opens her series with the presentation of the nation of Panem, controlled by an assuredly corrupt and oppressive government that exercises power of its citizens primarily through their bodies. While the institution known as the Hunger Games is the most obvious representation of the Capitol's power and the district's weaknesses, there are others to consider such as the Capitol's use of starvation, the tesserae system, and reproductive freedoms. Gregory Claeys, a frequent scholar of dystopia, states, "Control over common resources [such as food] … is often key to maintaining power in most dystopian societies."[5] The Capitol practically follows standard protocol of the dystopian government in suppressing its citizens by exercising its power directly in relation to weakening the body. However, this is not the extent to which the Capitol attacks the body. Through the tesserae system—only made necessary because of starvation—the Capitol dismantles family loyalties.

Historically, the term "tesserae" comes from Greek and Roman times, as does much of *The Hunger Games* symbology, and can mean "'a die, cube, square tablet with writing on it' used as a token or ticket."[6] The tesserae is indeed used as a "ticket" by children between the ages of twelve and eighteen who can submit their names an additional time to the reaping pool for an extra month's supply of grain. However, this system only further disempowers the individual and destroys the family unit in creating a society through which children must worsen their odds of survival for the sake of their siblings or parents. Susan S.M. Tan,[7] author of "'Burn with us,'" describes the tesserae procedure as "constructed to turn children into agents of their family's survival: adults cannot provide, but children can."[8] Through starvation and the necessity of the tesserae, the Capitol manipulates the bodies of the districts' children which serves to produce family dysfunction—a common theme of dystopian literature in which the natural bonds between family members are practically non-existent.

At the Reapings, Katniss acknowledges that it is "standard" for children to not volunteer to take the place of their siblings as "family devotion only goes so far for most people."[9] In dismantling the family unit, the Capitol intentionally weakens the districts' ability to unite and fight against their oppressors. After all, if a single family cannot remain united, how can an entire district combine against the Capitol?

Additionally, it is not only through starvation that the Capitol works to control the districts; indeed, the Capitol uses supposed reproductive "freedoms" to cause its citizens to exercise control over themselves. Unlike the governments of other traditional dystopian texts, such as *Nineteen Eighty-Four* and *A Handmaid's Tale*, the Capitol seems to allow more reproductive freedom to its districts. After all, the Capitol allows its citizens, Capitol or District-born, to marry or to not marry and reproduce as they see fit. However, underneath this seemingly benevolent allowance, the Capitol still exerts its power over marriage and reproduction by claiming the bodies created by these unions and subjecting them to the reapings between the ages of twelve and eighteen.

The fear that the Capitol may chose one's child as a tribute is a major deterrent for many citizens. In particular, we see this fear in Katniss' conversation with Gale, her hunting partner and best friend. Directly before the reaping of the 74th Hunger Games, Katniss rejects Gale's suggestion of fleeing into the woods, knowing that their "kids"—Prim, Gale's siblings, and even their mothers—could never survive in the wilderness. Gale's very usage of the term "kids" causes Katniss to declare, "I never want to have kids."[10] Although Gale attempts to negate this fear by discussing the possibility of having children outside of the Capitol's reach, Katniss quickly ends the conversation by returning to reality: "But you do [live here]."[11]

Katniss' concerns with the current and tangible restrictions of her society forbade her from even considering the prospect of entering into a romantic relationship with anyone as she fears the control the Capitol wields over her future hypothetical children. Repulsed by the possibility of bearing and raising children for slaughter, Katniss denies fulfilling any physical desires for companionship or family to negate the Capitol's control. In either case, whether Katniss would have children, but then risk them in the reapings or would not have children for the sake of avoiding that possibility, Katniss still forfeits an amount of agency, or individual freedom, to the Capitol which influences and restrains her actions.

The tesserae system, made necessary by intentional starvation and im-plemented by the authority as a way to "assist" its citizens, is truly a technique to destroy unity. Likewise, the supposed freedom of marriage and reproduc-tion is a farce and just as much a strategic restriction put in place to negate individual agency. After all, in causing wide-spread fear that the districts' children might be reaped, the Capitol ensures population control. As more citizens, such as Katniss, avoid having children to avoid the pain of losing them, the Capitol safeguards the balance of power. Each of these strategies, combined with the most powerful of all, the Hunger Games themselves, are used by the Capitol to mold the district citizens into nameless masses of "doc-ile bodies."

The tactics employed in the series find their basis in reality. Historicist Michel Foucault coined the term "docile bodies" in his 1977 book *Discipline and Punish*[12] and intends for the phrase to depict bodies that lack personal agency. Additionally, Foucault expands on how powerful figures within so-ciety manipulate and abuse such bodies for their own purposes. In Panem, docile bodies fill the districts that Foucault would describe as "subjected, used, transformed and improved" in such ways that "dissociate power from the body."[13] Consider the ways in which the Capitol separates the individual districts based on production: coal from District 12, agriculture from District 11, seafood from District 4, luxury items from District 1, etc. Each district garners importance not from whom resides there, but by what the residents of such districts can generate for those in the Capitol. Separately, the districts represent various limbs of a singular entity—a disciplined machine meant to provide both entertainment and sustenance to those within the Capitol.

Intentionally, Collins names her post-apocalyptic nation Panem and, as Plutarch mentions in *Mockingjay*, this name refers to the Roman culture and the Latin phrase *panem et circenses* which means "bread and circuses."[14] Just as the Roman emperors distracted their citizens with the abundance of food and gladiator games, so too does the Capitol divert the attention of its own citizens. The bread and entertainment come directly from the districts who provide both food and tributes. Without the districts, there is no *panem et circenses*, and so the Capitol must constantly work to retain absolute con-trol over their slave labor through forcing them to adopt the docile body. The most powerful way the Capitol does this is through the "spectacle" of the Hunger Games. According to Foucault, throughout history (particularly when it comes to power), the term "spectacle" refers to an atmosphere created by the authority in which privacy does not exist and the public depiction of pain ensures oppressive, all-consuming control. This is most often accom-plished through surveillance and public punishment.

The formation of the Hunger Games by the Capitol is what Foucault would define as "an exercise of terror ... [meant] to make everyone aware, through the body of the criminal, of the unrestrained presence of the sovereign. The public execution did not re-establish justice; it reactivated power."[15] As Katniss, and most readers, are well aware, the Games are not merely entertainment for the Capitol or punishment for past transgressions, but constant reminders of the district's lack of power or agency. Katniss thinks, "This is the Capitol's way of reminding us how totally we are at their mercy … the real message is clear. 'Look how we take your children and sacrifice them and there's nothing you can do.'"[16] By law, the Capitol requires the residents of the districts to participate in the annual reaping furthering commandeering their bodies for Capitol consumption. After all, the condemned man is only compelling when displayed.

Through the restrictions and degradations brought on by the Hunger Games, Collins succeeds in creating a society in which personal agency seems all but extinct. Before the televised Games begin, the Gamemakers continually monitor the tributes, parallel to how the Capitol surveys the districts themselves. Collins' integration of surveillance in the days leading up to the Games, and later within the Games, echoes Foucault's system of surveillance in which "power, even when faced with ruling a multiplicity of men, could be as efficacious as if it were being exercised over a single one."[17] In other words, surveillance and even self-surveillance prove just as effective over many as it would one individual.

For instance, the presence of the Avoxes serve as constant reminders to the tributes of the Capitol's vigilance and swift retribution to any perceived act of dissent. The Capitol considers Avoxes criminals and as such punishes them by removing their tongues and forcing them into silent servitude. The Avoxes' presence in the Training Center reminds tributes like Katniss of their own helplessness, their inability to defy the Capitol, and their upcoming brutalization, all without the Avoxes speaking a word. Just as the Capitol silenced the voices of the Avoxes, they will also silence the tributes' voices within the Games. Through the punishment and public display of an Avox servant, the Capitol exercises control over all twenty-four tributes without ever lifting a hand. This tactic works on a larger scale as well revealed through the televised murder of twenty-three children that serves as a warning to the district themselves.

Through surveillance, within and outside of the Games, the Capitol follow Foucault's examination of power and has "no need for arms, physical violence, [or] material constraints. Just a gaze. An inspecting gaze which each individual under its weight will end by interiorising to the point that he is his own overseer, each individual thus exercising this surveillance over, and against, himself."[18] For instance, on the rooftop of the Training Center, just nights before the 74th Hunger Games take place, Peeta informs Katniss of the force field that surrounds the roof preventing tributes from committing

suicide. "Always worried about our safety," Katniss mutters sarcastically before immediately worrying that the Capitol may have overheard her.[19] Instantly and instinctively, Katniss has been taught to exercise surveillance over
herself since she was a young child who learned to keep her thoughts to herself. Based on past experience, she anticipates the presence of the Capitol that
she feels is omnipresent. This prevalent fear of surveillance immobilizes all
tributes from even considering escape or suicide even though they are often
left to their own devices in their own rooms at night. The Capitol does not
need to have absolute control, it only needs to put forth the image that it does.

While the Capitol forces those in the districts to watch the Games, the
citizens of the Capitol happily look forward to the annual televised event.
However, both groups are "summoned as spectators."[20] Foucault contends
that there are two primary reasons why public punishment requires spectators. First, they must "be made to be afraid; but also, because they must
be made to be the witnesses ... to a certain extent take part in it."[21] Those in
the Capitol primarily fulfill the second role as they receive pleasure in taking
part of the Games. Those who sponsor a tribute within the Games do so not
because they care about that tribute's life, but rather because sponsoring a
tribute reflects the sponsor's social standing. Sponsoring a tribute displays the
sponsor's wealth and intelligence in picking the "correct" player. The tribute's
victory becomes the victory of the sponsor. As such, through sponsorship, a
Capitol citizen can participate within the Games without any personal risk as
they assume possession of the tribute's body. Consequently, even those without power in the Capitol demote individual tributes to docile bodies they can
use as puppets to engage with in the Games.

The Capitol forms a traditional dystopian government like those found
in *Nineteen-Eighty-Four*, *Brave New World*, and *A Handmaid's Tale*, all of
which that echo and exaggerate past and current societies described by Foucault. While Collins' Panem is hyperbole, it is eerily familiar to readers who
fight for personal freedoms against their own governments. In part, this is
why Katniss' response to typical governmental oppression differentiates her
from the heroes or heroines from previous traditional dystopian literature.
Katniss Everdeen does not lose agency due to the power the government exerts of her body, but rather she first establishes agency through the power she
exerts through her own body.

The Girl in the Woods

Long before the Games, Katniss rejects conforming to the role of docile
body. Within the opening pages, Collins demonstrates the power and personal freedom that Katniss achieves in the woods beyond District 12. Indeed,

Katniss confesses to the readers, "I never smile except in the woods."[22] In *The Hunger Games* series, the Capitol surrounds the individual districts with electrified fences or stone walls, claiming that the fences insure safety for the residents.[23] However, for Katniss, the spaces outside of these fences are what represent personal freedom and safety from the Capitol itself. After her father's death, Katniss rediscovers her sense of identity and agency through her trips into the woods. For instance, while searching for food after her father's death, Katniss remembers a time shared with her father in which they spent two hours by the lake gathering "katniss" roots. In venturing into the woods once again and stumbling upon this potato-like edible plant after which Mr. Everdeen named her, Katniss remembers that if she can find herself, she will never starve.[24] Already, Katniss responds to one of three primary ways through which the Capitol exerts its control over its citizens. While Katniss does take out extra tesserae, she also supplements her family's food supply by hunting and gathering. In physically unearthing these roots to provide for her mother and sister, Katniss metaphorically excavates her own identity as head of the household—a role that she assumes in place of her father—and denies the Capitol's control over that aspect of her life.

Through the woods, Katniss comes alive as a hunter, defying the Capitol's laws in supporting herself and her family. Regularly, Katniss abandons the confines of the Capitol-approved "safety" of District 12 in favor of exercising her agency literally beyond the boundaries set by the Capitol. Unlike Katniss, many in the district fear the natural world and "are not bold enough to venture out with just a knife."[25] Indeed, the majority of those in District 12 would rather starve to death in safety than to leave the confines of the fence. The fence is simply an additional tactic used by the Capitol to mold its citizens into docile bodies that are "subjected, used, transformed, and improved"[26] in such a way to benefit the ruling power instead of the individual to whom the body belongs.

Contrary to the majority of citizens from District 12, Collins portrays Katniss as resisting both artificiality and categorization of becoming a "docile body" through Katniss' escapades outside the legal perimeter and her lack of fear concerning the natural world. Katniss' illegal foraging, hunting, and trading activities mark the initiation of Katniss' rebellious spirit and her desire for agency. Physically, the woods are set apart due to the boundaries set by the Capitol, and likewise, Katniss sets herself apart from those without agency. Metaphorically, nature becomes the place where Katniss exercises the ability to control the movements of her own body, apart from Capitol control. Indeed, due to the circumstances of the Games, Katniss never has to enter the coal mines like her father and Gale. Instead, she continues to venture into and thrive within the forest. Collins contrasts the man-made, coal mines of District 12 that bring about death with the surrounding forest that grants life-sustaining provisions. Such juxtapositions of artificiality and authenticity set the background for Katniss' discovery of agency and emphasis the importance of Katniss' control over her body—where it goes and what it does.

However, Katniss' illegal actions are only moments of limited agency that seem inadequate in comparison to the supremacy the Capitol wields over her life. Every day, Katniss must depart from nature and return to District 12, where the Capitol's reach affects every area of her life. Due to the Capitol's power, Katniss must hunt in secret, must trade carefully, be aware of surveillance, and most importantly, attend annual reapings in which either she or Prim or Gale might be drafted into the Games. Indeed, Katniss' agency found in hunting seems worthless once Prim is chosen to participate in the Games—foreshadowing her immediate death.

Therefore, at the reaping, Katniss exercises the only type of limited agency that appears to remain—the right to die to save her sister. Limited agency is a sub-type of agency that an individual enacts within a situation controlled by forces other than the agent in which the agent's options to act are limited. This limited agency can be expanded upon through Peeta's words, spoken on the roof of the Training Center: "Within the Games. There's still you, there's still me."[27] While Peeta never desires to take part in the Games, he has no choice; however, he still has the ability to enact limited agency through the actions he takes within the arena.

Likewise, while Katniss does not desire to participate in the Games, under the circumstances of Prim's reaping, Katniss enacts limited agency by taking her sister's place. If Katniss had been free to choose, neither Prim nor herself would ever have been chosen in the reaping. However, within a situation that she cannot control, Katniss is still able to act, unlike Mrs. Everdeen who has no options available to her—too old to volunteer. In acting on her desire to save her sister's life, Katniss defies the Capitol's expectations of sibling loyalty that they work so hard to erase through their systems of power and control. However, this small act of rebellion would have had little to no effect on the nation of Panem had Katniss not supported it with additional acts of agency.

Before the Games, Katniss demonstrates the ability to act against governmental control in small, but meaningful ways. Throughout the trilogy, Collins devises trials that require her characters to either strive forward or fail. Although Katniss' volunteering is a key event in her journey for agency, a singular moment or action is not enough to defy the Capitol. Instead, every action that Katniss undertakes as she engages in the battle for the right to exercise agency through her body initiates the dismantling of a corrupt government. Therefore, agency, as depicted by Collins in her dystopian narrative, requires repetitious, rebellious actions against an unjust oppressor.

The Girl on Fire

Public perception is a concern of all within both fiction and reality. The ways in which others view each other can often result in an individual adjusting their physicality for the sake of acceptance. This forced "adjustment" can result in the negation of agency if an individual's actions are being compelled by another. However, during Katniss' time as a tribute, Collins' narrative demonstrates the ways in which adjusting is not conforming, and "playing along" does not mean forfeiting agency.

Following the reaping in which Katniss volunteers as tribute—her first public act of defiance against the Capitol—Katniss must substantiate her actions immediately to control how the nation of Panem views her within the Games. Katniss, hyper-aware of the media and the significance behind Panem's sponsors, forces herself to refrain from crying, and thinks, "Everyone will make note of my tears.... I'll be marked as an easy target. A weakling. I will give no one that satisfaction."[28] Not only would tears lessen her chances of gaining sponsorship and label her as a "crybaby," but they would also signal Katniss' surrender within the situation and the forfeiture of her own body to the Games. Anne Canavan and Sarah Petrovic, authors of "Tipping the Odds," discuss Katniss' ability to control her own narrative, or the public's perception, through her acceptance of specific roles. Indeed, they claim that Katniss' ability to act within a specific narrative, in this case as "tribute," is a "powerful tool that help[s] Katniss survive."[29] By refusing to cry and focusing instead of her family's survival—reminding Prim to use Lady's (her goat's) milk to earn money—Katniss further circumvents the Capitol's expectations of how a tribute should feel only fear for themselves instead of concern for another.

However, once Katniss enters the Capitol, she struggles to maintain this narrative. Surrounded by an artificial society, Katniss finds herself quite literally out of her natural element and often at a loss on how to function within a society that views her body as docile or public property—a commodity to be used and consumed. Subsequently, the gaze of the audience often severely affects Katniss' previous sense of agency, obtained through hunting and nurtured in the wild, which is "gobbled up" by greedy Capitol citizens and even her own prep team who pluck Katniss as if she were "a bird ready for roasting."[30]

Collins' repeated and intentional incorporations of such terminology depicts to readers how the Capitol views the tribute's body as an object. While we could, and many do, argue that the members of Katniss' prep team later come to recognize and value Katniss' individuality and humanity, they too initially see her as sub-human and primitive. The prep team considers Katniss "almost" human only after hours of scrubbing, plucking, waxing, massaging, and transforming her body. In this way, the Capitol exerts "biopower," a term coined by Foucault, by focusing on the "subjugation of bodies and the control of populations."[31] For instance, the Capitol requires the tributes and so forces them to enter the productivity of the economy as commodities for those in the Capitol.

Due to her understanding of what the Capitol expects from tributes, Katniss assumes that her stylist will transform her body into a consumable image, regardless of the indignity it might cause her. Truly, during her time at the Capitol, Katniss has little room to act according to her desire. Katniss can only hope for a stylist who will make her memorable to the audience, demonstrating how an individual's appearance appears to inherently connect to personal agency both in Panem and often in real life. Katniss desires to win the Games and return home, but she can only do that if she can garner sponsorship to aid her while in the arena, and she can only gather sponsorship by appealing to public perception. Many scholars of the series note that Katniss' makeovers are problematic as they erase who she is and put forth an image of who she is not. However, in understanding the necessity of image, Katniss allows herself to be molded into this specific narrative of tribute. The important phrase here is "allows."

Katniss allows the manipulation of her body, not only for public approval, but for the sake of accomplishing her own end goals of survival. Again, Collins' narrative demonstrates the presence of limited agency when it seems that there is none to be found. Within every circumstance, an individual still maintains some ability to act, even if it is on a limited scale. It is this refusal to back down and the determination to maintain any part of her agency that separates Katniss as a modern heroine. In transforming her own body in a way that supports her desires, Katniss rejects the Capitol's mold of docile body. Through accepting the necessity of public perception, but then manipulating it for her own advantage, with the help of some friends, Katniss exerts her own agency over the situation.

However, just as within her district, the Capitol continues to constrain Katniss' freedom. After all, regardless of the impressions Katniss makes, the Capitol still holds her captive, still sends her to compete in the Games, injures her with fire, attacks her with fellow tributes and "muttations," and sentences her to fight for her life—no amount of costuming can change that. So Katniss' reclamation of agency continues into the Games themselves.

Site of Punishment to Site of Redemption

As previously touched upon, Collins depicts the ways in which the Capitol claims the tribute bodies as public property, and as such, the Capitol subjects them to use, abuse, manipulation, and death. They are commodities through which the Capitol citizens obtain entertainment and alleviation from their day-to-day boredom. When tributes die within the arena, the Capitol glorifies their deaths and replays them repeatedly, most likely in slow motion, over the course of days and weeks. Assuredly, Caesar Flickerman and Claudius Templesmith—main commentators of the Games—make note of the exact moment when a tribute's heart stops beating and when their brain ceases to function. In gory up-close camera angels, these gruesome deaths are celebrated by Capitol citizens as the grand finale draws closer. These citizens are unable, or unwilling, to see the humanity of the tributes who are dying.

However, for those watching within the districts, the bodies of the fallen tributes are not images of entertainment, but rather these bodies are sites of punishment, used especially in their deaths to convey a message: The Capitol is all-powerful and unwilling to spare the lives of even innocents; in fact, the Capitol celebrates such deaths. The Capitol forces those within the districts to watch and relive each death repeatedly until the message is clearly seared within their thoughts. "This is the Capitol's way of reminding us how totally we are at their mercy," Katniss explains to the readers, "how little chance we would stand of surviving another rebellion."[32]

On the other hand, Collins' protagonists are not a part of the misguided Capitol citizens or the docile masses within the districts. Rather, characters such as Katniss Everdeen fully understand every implication behind the Capitol's actions. The Games rob these tributes, who clearly represent their respective districts in the Games, of agency and individuality even in death. Their deaths no longer belong to them, just as the districts' lives and livelihood do not belong to them either. Instead, the tributes belong to the Capitol, which displays their broken, bruised, bloodied bodies as flags of victory against district rebellion.

It is Katniss' response to this knowledge that further proves agency's initiation begins with the body. Upon Rue's sudden and graphic death, Collins re-instigates the power struggle between body and agency for both Katniss and readers. As Rue lays dying in Katniss' arms, a bloodied spear shaft buried deep in her organs, Katniss sings a lullaby at her request. In this moment, Katniss makes a conscious connection between Rue and her sister, Prim, thinking, "If this is Prim's, I mean, Rue's last request.... I have to try."[33] While it is true that both Rue and Prim are young, innocent, and named after flowers, there are far greater similarities between Rue and Katniss than there are between Rue and Prim. While adventures are terrifying for Prim, Rue is excited by the possibility of tag teaming with Katniss to destroy the Career's stockpile of food.

Both Katniss and Rue are elder sisters, fiercely protective of their family members, willing to break the rules to support their families, and both are manipulated and slotted to die by the Capitol's designs. Therefore, Rue becomes a reflection not of Prim in this moment, but of Katniss. In mirroring Katniss in this way, Rue forces Katniss to become aware of the sharp reality of the Games: the bodies of the tributes—both Rue's and her own—do not belong to themselves, not even in death in which their bodies are sent home in wooden caskets to display the Capitol's power. Clearly, it is through the body that the ruling dystopian authority first confronts agency and it is through the destruction of the body that it attempts to negate all agency.

Therefore, it is only natural that it is through the body that agency can be established and it is through confronting unjust deaths that agency is reaffirmed. Choosing to challenge this powerlessness, not only within the Games but also within her own existence, Katniss seizes this moment to exercise her own agency over the situation. Rue's lifeless body, made defenseless in death and worthless by the Capitol's propaganda, pointedly reminds Katniss of her desire to exercise agency, forcing her to "confront [her] own fury against the Capitol" and to recognize her own "impotence."[34] Just as Katniss manipulates public perception contrary to the Capitol's design, Katniss negates Rue's body as a site of punishment. Katniss decides "to shame them, to make them accountable, to show the Capitol that whatever they do ... there is a part of every tribute they can't own. That Rue was more than a piece in their Games. And so am I."[35] In these last sentences, Katniss recognizes the importance of ownership of one's body and one's actions along with the connection between Rue's body and her own, understanding how easily it could have been her body pierced by Marvel's spear.

To the Capitol, all tributes are similarly worthless outside of their intended use as spectacles to strike fear into the heart of the districts. Opposed to this idealism, Katniss does not abandon Rue's body after death. Instead, near enough so that the Capitol cannot send in a hovercraft to steal Rue's body, Katniss picks violet, yellow, and white flowers which respectively symbolize royalty, light, and innocence. By wreathing Rue's hair and body with these flowers and masking the wound, Katniss transforms the Capitol's intended site of punishment into a site of redemption. No longer is Rue a small, insignificant casualty of the Hunger Games who the Capitol citizens will forget within a week. Carefully decorated by Katniss, Rue's wounds no longer promote fear and violence, but rather display beauty, innocence, and peaceful tranquility. This proper burial honors Rue as an individual and grants her safety in a realm untouched by the violence of Panem. Finally, in death, Rue gains freedom from the Capitol, and with Katniss' help, even her body seems beyond the Capitol's manipulation.

Collins uses Rue's death as a significant turning point in Katniss' journey and following participation in the rebellion. Until that point, Katniss' main objective is to simply survive the Games, go home, and live as she had—silently and carefully confronting the Capitol in small but limited ways. However, after Rue's death, Katniss admits that something happened inside of her. This "something" ultimately provides the basis for Katniss' involvement within the rebellion. This "something" is what she cannot allow to happen again—the robbing of an individual's agency. Katniss' desires for rebellion clearly begins after Rue's death. For after her death, Katniss becomes "determined to do something to avenge [Rue], to make her loss unforgettable."[36] In challenging the Capitol's site of punishment, she challenges their claim on another's agency. When Katniss reclaims Rue's bodily power, she demands the right to reclaim her own. This scene is among the top examples within the trilogy that so clearly demonstrates the power struggles that surround the body; another is the finale.

Human Eyes and Poisonous Berries

In the finale of the 74th Hunger Games, the Capitol crowds expect a showdown between the bloody, brutal, sadistic male tribute from District 2 and the star-crossed lovers from District 12 who stole their hearts. No one expected one tribute from District 12 to make it to the finale, let alone both tributes. Crowds wait with bated breath as the final evening of the Games comes to a close. The Gamemakers set the sun and bring out the moon, the darkened lighting draws the viewers in close as they do not want to miss a single detail. Sponsors attach themselves to their screens, wondering what the Gamemakers might have in store and mentally planning their post–Games celebrations. Who, they wonder, will the odds favor tonight?

Of course, tributes know what the Capitol citizens do not. The odds are never in the tributes' favor and the game is rigged. Commenting on reality television that often pushes against accepted standards of behavior, Collins presents a graphic and horrifying finale that entertained audiences in theaters across the nation in 2012. The drawn-out climax practically mocks the entertainment industry as it compares Cato's ghastly death to the "final word in entertainment."[37] Not only is Cato devoured mercilessly, slowly gnawed away at until he is nothing but a "raw hunk of meat,"[38] but he is also mutilated by representations of the dead tributes. While Katniss reclaimed Rue's body, transforming it from a site of punishment to a site of redemption, the Capitol retaliates against her actions in the form of "muttations," genetically engineered creations also referred to as "mutts."

During the climax of the Games, the Capitol sends in a pack of wolf mutts, who genetically represent every fallen tribute, complete with human eyes that Katniss believes the Capitol stole from the human bodies of the tributes. These wolf-muttations further mock the tributes' deaths and, in using their eyes, return their bodies to sites of punishment by reducing every tribute to a mere animal. Among the pack, Katniss sees even tiny Rue, recognizable by her brown eyes and the number 11 inlaid in the collar. The muttations serve as a reminder of the Capitol's power of the bodies of the tributes and, through the tributes, over the districts themselves. The dead tributes are depicted as mindless animals that eagerly devour other tributes at the Capitol's command. The collars themselves portray servitude and enslavement. Even in death, the tributes are used as a spectacle by the Capitol to minimize and reject any hint of agency that might have been shown within the Games.

In doing so, the Capitol works to reposition the tributes back in their proper submissive place as docile bodies. Therefore, the showdown ultimately takes place not between Katniss and Cato and the Mutts, but rather between Katniss and the Capitol. Who ultimately holds the power over Katniss body and, through her body, her agency? Even after Cato's death, Katniss' agency is still at risk. By changing the rules of the Games at the last minute, the Capitol intends for either Katniss or Peeta to become a senseless weapon (much like the former mutts) aimed at the other resulting in one Victor and one victim. Should either die at the hands of the other, both would lose their agency and revert to docile bodies as their actions and fates become predetermined by the Capitol's design. Enlightened by the time spent in the Capitol, Katniss realizes, "They have to have a victor. Without a victor … [the Gamemakers will] have failed the Capitol."[39] Unlike the Gamemakers who are focused on the entertainment value of the show, Katniss is more than willing to disappoint the Capitol citizens in order to enact personal agency.

By pulling out the berries and offering Peeta the same choice, Katniss refuses to become a docile body—to accept either predestined status as Victor or victim—or to allow the Capitol to further manipulate them. Instead, by threatening suicide and fully devoting themselves to the idea—going so far as to taste the berries on their tongues—Katniss and Peeta employ the only agency available to them. While the achievement of agency through suicide is widely debated in academic scholarship, in this case, Katniss clearly utilizes agency. Katniss' threat of suicide is not born out of unstable emotions, instead it is through reasoning and logic that Katniss calls the Capitol's bluff. Her threat of suicide is not to escape the situation, but to exert dominance and ownership over her own body. With this action, Katniss rejects the supremacy of the Capitol, denying it the ability to control her destiny.

The first book of *The Hunger Games* trilogy ultimately depicts not only the importance of the body, but how it is the primary vessel through which an oppressive government seeks to rule and through which an individual first learns to utilize personal agency. However, if the first book is a proponent of agency enacted through the body, the sequel, *Catching Fire*, is a warning against the problematic implementation of limited agency within an oppressive regime.

Once home, Katniss tries to continue exercising agency through returning to nature and acting outside of the Capitol's confines. However, due to her actions within the Games, even nature is no longer safe as the Capitol extends its surveillance and catches Gale kissing Katniss when coming back from hunting. Indeed, President Snow's subsequent presence demands that Katniss chooses between self-preservation and agency. If Katniss can convince the districts that she acted out of desperation born from love with the berries, rather than out of defiance, President Snow will allow her and her family to live.

With this threat, the Capitol moves once again to regain control of Katniss' body, this time outside of the Games, in demanding that she behave as a mouthpiece to quell the dissent within the districts. Coerced by the reminder of constant surveillance and the threat of public punishment, Katniss resigns herself to the role of docile body. It is noteworthy that Katniss does not respond to a threat against herself, but rather to a threat made against those she cares for most as her moral code will be discussed in the following chapter. While Katniss may find her own suicide a suitable option—as seen in the Games—she cannot accept harm to befall her family and friends. Interestingly, Katniss views President Snow as having "no right, but ultimately every right" to occupy space in her family home, demonstrating Katniss' internal struggle with agency.[40] The part of Katniss that believes President Snow has no right in her home is the same part of her that would defy the Capitol with a handful of berries in order to control her own body and decide her own destiny. However, the other part of Katniss that concedes to President Snow's privileges in her home displays the Katniss who is willing to put on an act and surrender agency in order to appease the Capitol's fury.

Puppet-like during the Victory Tour, Katniss propels herself through an "indistinguishable round of dinners, ceremonies, and train rides … always linked together [with Peeta], by our hands, our arms … we kiss, we dance, we get caught trying to sneak away to be alone. On the train, we are quietly miserable."[41] Accustomed to at least a limited amount of agency, Katniss' misery grows as she knowingly allows herself to be manipulated by the Capitol to the point of even surrendering her marital rights by offering to become Peeta's wife and possibly bear his children. As long as President Snow dangles the possibility of safety for her family, Katniss is willing to sacrifice her agency and concede to any of Snow's demands. Through this backward slide, readers can view the downfalls of enacting limited agency and question whether such agency is worth the consequences.

Becoming the Mockingjay

While Katniss' predicament may lead readers to question the instability of personal agency, Collins' narrative also offers insights on the vulnerability of a ruling authority that relies on only threats and punishments against those who exercise agency. Within Panem, power is an unstable thing. Anthony Pavlik, author of "Absolute Power Games," comments that the Capitol's "dependence on the districts for resources makes it position somewhat precarious."[42] Indeed, according to Katniss, "it must be very fragile, if a handful of berries can bring it down."[43] As eventually seen, a handful of berries does prove powerful enough to dismantle the Capitol's power over all Panem.

Philosopher Michel Foucault states that "power would be a fragile thing if its only function were to repress, if it worked out through the mode of censorship, exclusion, blockage, and repression ... exercising itself only in a negative way."[44] This atrocious application of power is exactly how the Capitol operates: repressing its citizens, censoring information between districts, excluding the districts from the luxurious lifestyle of the Capitol, and repeatedly suppressing rebellious inclinations through the cruel spectacle of the Hunger Games. In these ways, the world of Panem directly relates to the Roman culture and its colosseum—Collins' inspiration for the Games. Just as the Roman empire used its strength to frighten its enemies, the Capitol exerts its power to suppress the districts.

Power, when used only negatively, balances on a precarious edge. President Snow is only able to control Katniss' actions during the Victory Tour because he offers her the hope of securing her family's safety. As long as Katniss remains fixated by this hope that the Capitol will exercise its power positively through forgiveness and leniency, she is unable to act as she desires and can only do as she is told. However, once Katniss realizes that all of her acting has been for nothing and that President Snow never intended to grant her or her family mercy, she immediately begins to act on her rebellious desires. Katniss discovers that forfeiting agency does not result in positive rewards; instead, it only leaves her lacking and empty.

Consequently, the Capitol's negative assertion of power prompts Katniss to rebel where positive power would have encouraged her submission. Elated by the idea that her actions cannot make the situation any worse, Katniss thinks, "If desperate times call for desperate measures, then I am free to act as desperately as I wish."[45] Ironically, in admitting the fragility of the government and refusing to show mercy, President Snow creates his greatest adversary and proves that he does not truly understand just how fragile his system is. When the ruling power is never used positively, then rebellious individuals have no reason to try and appease the government. While corrupt power may deprive an individual of agency, it often also provides the incentive for the repressed individual to revolt against such a system.

Just as Rue's death instigates Katniss' reclamation of bodily agency in the 74th Hunger Games, the death sentence pronounced over her loved ones by the slight shake of President Snow's head prompts Katniss' rebellious desires. Katniss regains previously sacrificed agency through her rebellious actions even before the announcement of the 3rd Quarter Quell as she makes the conscious decision to fight within the confines of the Capitol. Although she considers fleeing back into the woods, as she previously does to escape the Capitol's reach, Katniss remains in District 12 as she comes to realize that it is not only her own agency, but also the agency of others, at stake. The fact that Katniss mentally prepares herself for a "new life [of] fighting the Capitol" and accepts the assurance of "swift retaliation"[46] against herself and her loves ones directly demonstrates how Katniss craves the rebellion and even desires to be a part of it. While Katniss may not have been entirely aware of the rebel's plot, even concerning her own participation, that does not negate the fact that she exerts bodily control by following her own desires.

Even after the Capitol drafts Katniss into the 3rd Quarter Quell where chances for participating in a rebellion seem minimal, Katniss still exercises agency through her body despite the Capitol's intentions. Aware that all eyes are on her, Katniss understands that the rebels will either gain encouragement or lose hope based on her actions before and within the Quell. While the Capitol intends to display her body as a site of punishment, humiliating and torturing it as punishment for her actions, Katniss not only accepts but eagerly awaits the use of "her face on banners" by which the rebels can turn her "into some kind of martyr for the cause."[47] Long before Katniss dons the Mockingjay outfit, created by Cinna and held in high esteem by the rebels, Katniss already embraces the image of the Mockingjay. Indeed, the image of the Mockingjay, a creature whose body was never approved by the Capitol, is the perfect representation for Katniss, whose body the Capitol is never fully able to control regardless of its numerous attempts.

Repeatedly, what the Capitol intends as a negative display of power Katniss transforms into an image of personal agency. For instance, when ordering Katniss to wear her wedding gown during the pre–Game interviews, a gown chosen not by Katniss but voted on by the Capitol audiences, President Snow further attempts to rob Katniss of her dignity and mock her attempts to placate his revenge (by offering to marry Peeta). However, in one of the most iconic moments of the series, once on stage and encouraged by Cinna to twirl, Katniss finds herself "completely engulfed in strange flames. Then all at once, the fire is gone.... I'm not naked.... Cinna has turned me into a mockingjay."[48] The phrase "I'm not naked" echoes the fear of nudity that Katniss earlier experienced in the first novel. Internally, Katniss fears exposure and vulnerability before the crowds of the Capitol and just as before Cinna empowers Katniss rather than humiliates her. The gown will not only garner sponsorship in the arena, but more importantly, it also reminds Katniss of her own strength and resilience. This physical and fiery rebirth that burns away the Capitol's taint and claim on Katniss' body only symbolizes that which

Katniss had already become. Before ever entering the Quarter Quell or District 13, before the flames devour her gown, Katniss accepts her role as Mockingjay which symbolizes her pursuit of agency that is absolute.

Mockingjay: Image vs. Identity

Of course, even I admit that the Mockingjay persona becomes overly complicated in *Mockingjay* as Katniss exercises personal power and yet, at the same time, has power enacted over her. While Katniss accepts the role as Mockingjay early on, the image itself becomes morphed by rebel interference. Traumatized by her experiences, Katniss struggles in knowing her own desires. While District 13 may have only rescued Katniss because they intend to use her as a figurehead of their revolution, their actions do not entirely negate Katniss' agency.

After all, according to Katniss, though President Coin intends to use Katniss as only a symbol, Katniss proves to be a more resistive adversary than Coin expects. Katniss' awareness that President Coin intends to manipulate her allows Katniss to act contrary to what is expected of her, just as she did under the Capitol. Indeed, in the opening pages of the third installment, Katniss states that District 13 is dismayed to learn that their Mockingjay "might not want the wings."[49] This phrase seems problematic, especially considering that we have just spent several pages discussing that Katniss did indeed want and accept her Mockingjay wings which symbolize her desire for agency. However, in this passage, Katniss does not want the *artificial* wings that District 13 offers to her. When President Coin expects Katniss to perform as Mockingjay, Coin truly assumes that it will be a performance equipped with a sound stage, lights, cameras, smoke, and a surrounding green screen. When introduced to this fabricated setting, Katniss fails so tremendously that Haymitch insists her acting could kill the revolution in its tracks. Katniss' hesitance to become the Mockingjay for District 13 only represents her refusal to impersonate the Mockingjay in an artificial setting.

Rather, conducive footage of Katniss comes only once District 13 releases its grip on her body. Indeed, Katniss reclaims not only her body and identity as Mockingjay, but her sense of agency upon washing off a face full of garish Capitol-approved make up and stepping outside the walls of District 13 (walls that mimic barriers put in place around the districts by the Capitol). When visiting the wounded in District 8, Katniss is recognized not by her suit or by her pin, but by "the damage, the fatigue, the imperfections."[50] Katniss believes, "That's how they recognize me, why I belong to them."[51] Katniss adopts interesting phrasing in the idea of her belonging to someone else. Throughout the trilogy, Katniss has "belonged" to others, specifically the Capitol audience who attempted to claim her body as tribute and as Victor. Constantly, Katniss resists transferring ownership of her body to anyone apart from herself. On the contrary, Katniss thinks positively of these wounded, weak, disheartened survivors and sees herself belonging to them and among them. Like her, these people represent the true image of the Mockingjay—an abandoned creature strengthened by forced survival and resistance. Katniss succeeds in rallying the districts only when she portrays her genuine Mockingjay persona suggesting that agency evolves from authenticity.

Indeed, Katniss is the Mockingjay, but she is her own version of the Mockingjay and can never be an image promoted by another. Personal intentions and desires drive Katniss' actions such as her spontaneity in fighting back against the Capitol's hovercrafts when they attack the hospital in District 8 or in appealing to the man with the gun in District 2 after the bombing of the Nut. While District 13 demands that Katniss portray herself in certain ways, Katniss neglects their commands and denies their attempts to mold her into an acceptable rebel image. Constantly resisting commands, Katniss presents a threat to any authority that is threatened by personal agency. At the end of *Mockingjay*, even President Coin realizes that Katniss does not simply portray a Mockingjay, she is *the Mockingjay*—a creature who will exist on her own terms regardless of outside control—which is problematic for a new regime.

Through Katniss, readers can better understand the battle that takes place over the physical body between an individual and the government within dystopian literature which serves as an exaggerated reflection of their own societies. Indeed, agency is primarily established through the discovery of one's own body and the power that it holds. The individual gains bodily agency, particularly in dystopias, through exercising control over how others perceive his/her body. Furthermore, an understanding of oneself and acting on personal intent form the foundations of successful agency. Katniss' intimate connection to nature throughout the trilogy represents her overall desire for authenticity. Regardless of her situations, Katniss constantly works to transform the manipulations of others in order to control her own actions. Collins depicts the irrefutable affiliation of the body to person agency as Katniss first comes to wield private and public agency through the body.

In the twenty-first century, men and women around the world are transforming their bodies as they work to discover who they are and the power that they possess. Is it any surprise that Collins' protagonist, Katniss Everdeen, would spend so much time agonizing over the presentation, representation, and use of her body? Clearly not as this topic is one of current concern, especially among young adults who are attempting to grow into their own identities without outside contamination. Collins' presentation of agency as requiring continuous effort is represented by Katniss as she re-learns time and time again to adjust to new circumstances that affect her ability to act. *The Hunger Games* trilogy warns about the infinite nature of agency which the individual cannot maintain without constant vigilance and action. Just as Katniss continuously works to reclaim her agency through reconnecting with nature and reclaiming the agency of others, Collins' narrative reminds and encourages readers to do the same.

Two

"When the time comes, I'm sure I'll kill just like everybody else"

Agency and Morality

Morality is, ultimately, subjective. A person's actions, defined as good or bad, are based on society, on the individual, on religion, on culture, and on a number of different topics. While society attempts to define a standard for morality through laws and punishments, morality is primarily influenced by personal beliefs and ethics. In the twenty-first century, the issue of morality is, at times, ambiguous as society bounces between the ideas of "right" and "wrong." This uncertainty in their own societies is part of what makes Collins' trilogy so alluring to its readers. *The Hunger Games* trilogy deals with moral issues on a personal level instead of simply in abstracts. When discussing morality in dystopian texts, many scholars focus on the moral system of the entire community or on the government itself such as in George Orwell's *Nineteen Eighty-Four* and his illustration of Big Brother. However, in Collins' series, morality is not a discussion for only the community or government but a choice required for each individual. By placing the decision of morality on the individual, Collins inadvertently gives agency to her characters as they must decide for themselves what is right and what is wrong. Within Collins' narrative each person has the option to enact whichever morals seem best to him or herself and that these moral codes inevitably affect the success of exercised agency. Indeed, this issue of morality is so pronounced that it even determines the outcome of what some readers refer to as the "love triangle" between Katniss, Peeta, and Gale.

Initially, it is the Hunger Games themselves that form the most obvious source of moral friction within the books, causing a moral conundrum within the opening pages of the narrative. Within the world of Panem, the construct of the Hunger Games shines as a beacon of entertainment and dangerous luxury to those in the Capitol while it blares down like a spot-light on the children of the districts. During the reaping for the 74th Hun-ger Games, Katniss Everdeen defies social expectations by volunteering to take her sister's, Prim's, place as the female tribute for District 12. While Effie Trinket, the voice piece for the Capitol, is elated by the interesting turn of events and calls for applause, something unexpected occurs. Katniss depicts the scene as such: "To the everlasting credit of the people of District 12, not one person claps. Not even the ones holding betting slips, the ones who are usually beyond caring … they take part in the boldest form of dissent they can manage. Silence. Which says we do not agree. We do not condone. All of this is wrong."[1] Readers, and even viewers, of *The Hunger Games* series are sure to recognize this pivotal scene, but they may not understand its innate and moral importance upon first read.

Katniss' rescue of the young, beloved Prim arouses the crowd's sympa-thies although for years it had only watched in apathy as the Capitol con-tinuously slaughtered their children. Clearly, the lines of morality blur, not only in the Capitol where leaders claim innocent lives every year, but also in the districts where calloused indifference causes some members to bet on which children are most likely to be reaped. Morality, or the lack thereof, is a commonly explored theme within dystopian literature, both traditional and young adult. Benjamin Kunkel, a scholar of young adult literature, insists that, in speaking of dystopia, the difference between a literary novel and genre fiction is that "the literary novel illuminates moral problems … at the expense of sentimental consolation, while genre fiction typically offers consolation at the expense of illumination."[2] In adhering to this idea, Collins' trilogy is composed of literary novels as opposed to simply being genre fiction because of her exploration of moral problems while often negating consolation—spe-cifically in *Mockingjay*. This distinction is important as it sets the trilogy apart by jarring its readers' expectations in the traditional happy ending for the sake of mental and moral illumination.

To truly confront the complexity of morality, Collins' narrative includes and explores ideas such as brutal murder of children by children and the phys-ical, mental, and emotional consequences of decisions made during times of war. David A. Dreyer, author of "War, Peace, and Justice in Panem," asserts that "Collins is not neutral in her portrayal of war" and that she does indeed push "readers to consider peaceful alternatives to violent conflicts."[3] Another reading might suggest that Collins' inclusion of war forces readers into con-sidering their own moral codes and how their morals relate to agency. In her trilogy, Collins presents main protagonist Katniss Everdeen as repeatedly exercising agency through her sense of morality; however, as Katniss' strong sense of morality diminishes through the war effort, so too does her ability to successfully exert personal agency. Therefore, scholars and readers must

analyze how Katniss' morality presents itself through the Games and transforms over the course of the rebellion in order to identify how morality cor-
relates to agency. In presenting the complicated aspects of morality and its
relation to agency, Collins' trilogy warns readers of the adverse ramification
of actions based on immoral intentions.

Social Codes and Personal Conduct

Collins bases many aspects of the society of Panem on Greco-Roman
culture and mythology, which directly situates her audience in a world that
they can immediately recognize as sitting on the brink of destruction. Before
its fall to the Germanic leader Odoacer, who was considered a Barbarian of
the time, in 476 C.E., Rome was considered the undefeatable empire, one
that would last until the end of time. However, just as the Roman empire
fell, so too can any reader familiar with history assume that Panem must fall
eventually to its own barbarians—those residing in the districts. Even its
name, "Panem," is a direct reference to the breads and circuses the Roman
empire used to distract its citizens from its own corruption. Plutarch, head
Gamemaker-turned-rebel, acknowledges the connections and says, "In the
Capitol, all they've know is *Panem et Circenses*.... It's a saying from thousands
of years ago ... about a place called Rome.... The writer was saying that in
return for full bellies and entertainment, his people had given up their political responsibilities and therefore their power."[4] At its core, Panem is similar
to Rome, focused entirely on self-satisfaction and ultimately greedy, selfish,
gluttonous, and cruel.

Panem's greatest immorality, the institution known as the Games, is
inspired by Grecian myth of Theseus and the labyrinth. In this myth, King
Minos of Crete declared that the kingdom of Athens was required to send
seven females and seven males to the island of Crete to die in a labyrinth,
sacrificed to the monstrous minotaur who resided within. This chain of sacrifices continued until the hero Theseus volunteered as sacrifice—tribute—and
killed the minotaur himself. In the districts, twelve males and twelve females
are sent to fight and die in gladiatorial Games with only one emerging as
Victor and metaphorically taking the title of the monstrous minotaur. By centering the nation of Panem on Greco-Roman principles and mythology, Collins automatically associates her society with immorality, sacrifice, individual
action, and death while ushering in our discussion of moral agency.

As noted, the Games present the primary foundation of accepted societal morality throughout Panem through its spectacle. This type of spectacle
should not be confused with Foucault's spectacle as discussed in the previous
chapter, but rather read through the lens of Aristotle's philosophical perception

of spectacle which is the physical aspects of a performance. Aristotle, a Greek philosopher during the Classical period in Ancient Greece, and also considered the father of Western philosophy, considered many complexities such as physics, biology, zoology, metaphysics, logic, aesthetics, poetry, theater, music psychology, ethics, and more. In his writings called *Poetics*, Aristotle depicts the spectacle as the sixth element of a theatrical play—the physical aspects such as performance, staging, and costuming—and the "least artistic" of all the parts.[5] In fact, Aristotle argues, "those who employ spectacular means to create a sense not of the terrible but only of the monstrous, are strangers to the purpose of Tragedy."[6] In judging the use of spectacle, Aristotle considered entertainment the lowliest and least important part of any play when used incorrectly and without purpose. In other words, the purpose of Greek tragedy was not meant to simply entertain its audiences but rather to provoke the effect of catharsis. Catharsis itself means a release or purging of strong and repressed emotions.

Unlike the Grecian tragedies, the Games focused too heavily on the spectacle or entertainment value of the costumes of the tributes and the landscapes of the Games while neglecting the true purpose of any tragedy. The Games promote only non-productive feedback such as encouraged distraction and apathy in Capitol citizens. Neither those within the Capitol, nor those within the Districts, purge emotions; if anything, those in the districts learn to bury their emotions even deeper within. By displaying the brutal murder of innocents as pure entertainment, the Capitol obscures the lines of morality and encourages its citizens to do the same. By centering the trilogy around these Games, Collins exposes the controversy over morality, specifically in societies that promote violence and depravity without the purpose of catharsis as forms of entertainment.

In order to guide readers through such a society, Collins creates Katniss—a character with her own ethical battles. When considering her external circumstances, Katniss exercises a surprising amount of morality within both *The Hunger Games* and *Catching Fire*, especially when we remember that her survival depends upon the deaths of others. Within the series, Collins explores both the struggles between characters and, more importantly, Katniss' internal struggles as she attempts to exercise moral agency after determining what is moral. Having now used these terms several times, it is important to pause here and expand on morality, ethics, and moral agency.

According to Michel Foucault,[7] morality encompasses three primary aspects: moral code, moral agency, and ethics. In Volume 2 of *The History of Sexuality*, Foucault clearly distinguishes between what he calls "moral conduct" and "ethical conduct" in which ethical conduct is morals "perform[ed] on oneself, not only in order to bring one's conduct into compliance with a given rule, but to attempt to transform oneself into the ethical subject of one's behavior."⁸ Foucault's discussion concerning ethics, or ethical conduct, is most important when examining Katniss' morality. Unlike "moral code/conduct" which adheres to the rules set down by the ruling authority, moral ethics places "the emphasis on the forms of relations with the self, on the methods and techniques by which he works them out, on the exercises by which he makes himself an object to be known, and on the practices that enable him to transform his own mode of being."⁹ In a society that not only allows but also encourages the senseless murder of others, Katniss cannot act on the socially accepted code of moral conduct. Instead, she must act of her own "ethical-oriented moralities" by which she establishes her own ethical conduct, based not on what society promotes to be correct, but on what she knows to be morally right.

The Morality Triangle

Since the debut of the first movie in 2012, fans across the nations have passionately taken sides for either Team Peeta or Team Gale (although we all know Team Peeta is best) with matching merchandise. These fans give various reasons to support their claims, such as who was in Katniss' life first or who was with her in the end. This "love triangle" has been debated in scholarship as well. In her article "Katniss and Her Boys," Whitney Elaine Jones discusses how this triangle directly affects Katniss' sense of identity. In fact, Jones clearly argues, "Katniss' ambiguous and thus radical gender identity is manifested through the love triangle itself, creating for Katniss not a triangle of romantic choices, but a triangle of identity and gender choices."¹⁰ Jones' analysis of the love triangle offers an in-depth look at gender and identity revealed by the effects of Gale's hyper-masculinity and Peeta's passive femininity on Katniss' own construction of gender. However, I offer a new reading of this love triangle and argue that the characters of Gale and Peeta act on Katniss in the development not of her gender identity but of her own moral and ethical foundations. While the hyper-masculine Gale often pushes for more violent actions, the passive Peeta often encourages leniency, forcing Katniss to challenge her own moral obligations.

This "morality" triangle starts out as ambiguous as any love triangle. Like readers, Katniss herself often finds it difficult to distinguish what feelings she might have for either boy at any time within the novels as she is primarily focused on simply surviving. Toward the end of *Mockingjay*, Katniss even asserts, "I can survive just fine without either of them."¹¹ While Katniss might have more to be concerned with, the apparent love triangle appeals to readers who root for their favorite contender to end up with the girl. Perhaps this is because, as readers, we understand the importance that both young

men exercise over Katniss' life. Regardless of whether she romantically loves
them, Katniss relies on them throughout the trilogy. Rather than forming two
points of a love triangle, Peeta and Gale each represent opposing directional
points on Katniss' moral compass. Peeta and Gale hold differing views of morality, respectively political realism and pacifism. Consequently, both men act
as foils to Katniss' belief system, testing her ideas and attempting to impart
their own ideas onto her before Katniss ever enters the Games.

For instance, Gale's idealism is in accordance with classical political realism[12] that asserts humans are not entirely immoral in their decisions, rather
they are "skeptical about the relevance of morality to international politics."[13]
Gale himself is not without morals; however, he is continuously willing to set
aside his morals when it comes to either survival or the successful achievement of military power. In the Justice Building right after the reaping for the
74th Hunger Games, having come to say his goodbyes, Gale challenges Katniss view of her fellow tributes and competitors:

> "Katniss, it's just hunting. You're the best hunter I know," says Gale.
> "It's not just hunting. They're armed. They think," I say.
> "So do you. And you've had more practice. Real practice," he says. "You know how
> to kill."
> "Not people," I say.
> "How different can it be, really?" says Gale grimly.
> The awful thing is that if I can forget they're people, it will be no different at all.[14]

Based on the separation between districts and the restriction of relationships, the twelve districts act as differing communities bringing in the idea
of international relationships. By advising Katniss to view her fellow tributes
as animals, insisting that there is no difference when it comes to survival,
Gale attempts to impart his realist thinking onto Katniss' forming ethical
codes. By demoting the other tributes to animals, Gale strips them of their
humanity in a way that is eerily similar to how the Capitol rejects the Districts' humanity by depicting its residents as barbaric. While Collins portrays
Gale as acting with compassion and morals, specifically toward his own
family, she also demonstrates his inability to grasp the importance of acting
within ethical bounds for those outside of his immediate circle. At the end
of the day, it is not that Gale has no morals, it is simply that they are not his
top priority. As Katniss heads toward the Capitol and the arena, she must
consider her options—to kill or be killed—and seems primarily focused on
her survival instead of considering what consequences her actions might
have.

That is, until she reconnects with Peeta. In contrast to Gale's belief systems, Collins uses Peeta to provide a secondary opinion on morality, a voice
of reason and compassion. Although Katniss seems more concerned with her
survival than her moral obligations, Collins forces both Katniss and readers

to readdress the issue the night before the Games. On the rooftop of the Training Center, Peeta confesses to Katniss:

> "…My best hope is to not disgrace myself and…" He hesitates.
>
> "And what?" I say.
>
> "I don't know how to say it exactly. Only…. I want to die as myself. Does that make any sense?" he asks. I shake my head. How could he die as anyone but himself? "I don't want them to change me in there. Turn me into some kind of monster that I'm not."[15]

Unlike Katniss who focuses on the practicality of "the availability of trees," Peeta is concerned with "how to maintain his identity. His purity of self."[16] Peeta clearly expresses both his stance on ethical conduct and agency in these few sentences. Indeed, Peeta's actions are focused far more internally than Katniss' as he understands that the Games will test his moral identity and, by extension, his ability to act with intention. While Peeta's perspective is not entirely pacifistic, as he does admit that he cannot simply allow another to kill him without fighting back, Peeta often exhibits much more restraint within the Games than any other player, aligning him with a sub-form of pacifism.

In Western just-war tradition "pacifism is further defined through its dialectical relation to the idea of justified violence."[17] In this manner, Peeta does represent a form of pacifistic thinking as he never enacts violence willingly when another option presents itself. Even though he is opposed to violence, Peeta is not naïve about the situation and admits, "When the time comes, I'm sure I'll kill just like everybody else. I can't go down without a fight. Only I keep wishing I could think of a way to … to show the Capitol they don't own me. That I'm more than just a piece in their Games."[18] In *The Hunger Games*, the earliest and perhaps clearest demonstration of agency comes not from the main character, Katniss, but rather from Peeta, depicting the importance his character will ultimately have on Katniss and the story itself. Peeta's desires to act in accordance with his own desires and beliefs evidently illustrate agency even within external constraints. This iconic moment is particularly interesting when considering that Collins highlights the success of agency when enacted in accordance with a strong moral character. Peeta's internal focus reflects how not only the Games, but also the Capitol's authority, test the moral identities of the tributes and districts.

Consequently, Gale and Peeta significantly affect both Katniss and the overall narrative through their warring perspectives on morality and its necessity in making decisions. Once she becomes a competitor within the Games, Katniss mentally refers back to each of these conversations concerning morality. Gale's advice encourages Katniss to act offensively instead of defensively and to actively hunt down the other tributes as if they were only animals. On the other hand, Peeta's desire to be more than just a piece in the

Games reminds Katniss to retain her individual ethical conduct regardless of external influences. Although Collins initially portrays Katniss as a morally ambiguous character, after these conversation with Gale and Peeta, Katniss herself must scrutinize what she considers ethical and moral. Purposely, Collins inserts these three characters, Katniss, Peeta, and Gale, within the narrative; each possesses a particular view on morality. Through these characters, readers are able to physically connect the relationships and consequences that exist between morality and agency.

Perhaps at this point, you are asking yourself the same question that Katniss asked Peeta on the rooftop of the Training Center: Who cares? For Katniss, this interesting debate over morality is a non-physical reality and cannot take priority over the imminence of the Games. Such thoughts will not contribute to Katniss' survival; in fact, they may be detrimental to it. Why should we as readers care about these two passages, and how do they relate back to our discussion of agency or our understanding of the trilogy as a whole? An agent's moral center, which is often influenced by external constraints such as one's society, severely affects and corrupts an individual's actions. Katniss' social environment consists of those closest to her such as Gale and Peeta who can influence her decision-making processes. As such, the characters Gale and Peeta do form a triangle with Katniss, but not one focused on romance. Instead, the three form a triangle based on individual morality and how each other's character affects the other. Through the Games, it seems that when her morality is closer to Peeta's belief system than Gale's it positively affects Katniss' actions and her agency is more successful than not. However, this can only be determined through further scrutiny.

The 74th Hunger Games and Relational Morality

In light of these moral belief systems, Katniss enters into the Games and begins to exhibit her own code of morals/ethics that is highly relational, different from both Peeta and Gale. Surprisingly, Collins spends most of the Games placing Katniss in the role of caregiver as opposed to hunter-murderer. Although she is more than competent with a bow and less skilled in medicine, Katniss primarily cares for others. Indeed, Katniss' shining moments occur when giving Rue her food or caring for an injured Peeta. While some may argue that Katniss has ulterior motives for caring for Rue, such as Rue's similarities to Prim, Katniss is able to discern between the two and protects Rue because she sees her as an innocent. Likewise, Katniss' desire to protect Peeta stems from her understanding of his inner goodness. Throughout the series, other competitors admit that Peeta is the good one, the superior one, the accidental Victor, in regard to his morality. It is this goodness that draws

Katniss into her nurturing role. Through Katniss' care of others, Katniss finds her ethical code focuses on her moral responsibility to protect the innocent and good in others. Furthermore, with both Rue and Peeta, Katniss finds comfort in their close physical proximity. With Rue, Katniss realizes "how comforting the presence of another human being can be," and with Peeta, she thinks, "no one else's arms have made me feel this safe."[19] In the gladiatorial arena of death, where tributes slaughter one another left and right, Katniss inadvertently focuses not on death and killing, but on the importance of emotional and physical relationships. These relationships reveal how Katniss' actions are inherently based on moral obligations to another.

Of course, even as Katniss plays the roles of healer and nurturer, Collins cannot and does not allow her protagonist to escape the ultimate moral conundrum of kill or be killed. While Katniss principally represents a caregiver within the Games, she does still kill in response to and in defense of others. To examine Katniss' agency, we ought to look at those moments in which she does act—sometimes quite violently. Within the 74th Hunger Games, Katniss faces three primary moral dilemmas: while trapped in a tree by the Career Pack, when attempting to rescue Rue, and during the Grand Finale of the Games. In each of these moments, Collins presents an interesting and perhaps contradictory heroine who has tremendous capacity to kill and an overwhelming desire to protect. Burned and weak from the Gamemakers' fire-pods, Katniss finds herself maneuvered into the Career Pack's pathway and quickly scales a tree to escape certain death. Trapped, Katniss admits, "I'm going nowhere…. Even if I can last the night, what will the morning bring?"[20] In her moment of questioning, Katniss considers only the physical reality, but readers are gifted this moment to pause and think. What moral crises will morning bring once the Careers renew their attack? What actions on Katniss' part constitute justified violence? Here we touch again on Peeta's belief system which argues that violence should only ever be the response when there is no other option. In deciding to drop the Tracker Jacker nest, Katniss calls it "the sole option I have left."[21] While Katniss' actions result in two deaths, her actions are those of self-defense as opposed to military strategy. Thus, although her thoughts seem to again align themselves with Gale's belief in the irrelevance of morality, Katniss' actions actually correlate with Peeta's view of justified violence only when necessary.

Some may argue that Katniss' morality shifts upon acquiring the necessary tools needed to actively hunt down her competitors. So, we must ask, does obtaining the bow and arrow from Glimmer's corpse change Katniss' actions? Do they cause her agency to deviate from its current course set on the care for others? Had it been Gale in Katniss' place, we can assume that he would have begun trapping and hunting down the other tributes immediately—simply doing what needed to be done as efficiently as possible.

However, Katniss' first actions after her two-day blackout are not to pursue the Careers, but rather to form a friendship with Rue—the young and defenseless female tribute from District 11. No doubt, watching at home, Gale sighs in exasperation as Katniss teams up with this small tribute who diminishes Katniss' odds of survivals with her very presence. Although Rue may be detrimental to Katniss' victory, Katniss focuses her attentions on bonding and sharing food with Rue. Although Katniss finally possesses the appropriate tools to kill her competitors, she becomes interested in protecting Rue and working alongside her to blow up the Career's stockpile of supplies—making sure that Rue has the "safer" job away from the Career Camp. Even the plan to blow up the supplies is less aggressive than actively murdering the Careers one by one. Katniss' and Rue's friendship, once again, directs the reader's gaze toward Katniss' foundation for action, which lies in her relationships with others.

Katniss' second moral dilemma hits shortly after solidifying her relationship with Rue. Although Katniss had entered into an alliance, no one in the Capitol would have thought twice about Katniss abandoning Rue to her fate when she is trapped by Marvel's net. Rue's death would not have been Katniss' fault; the odds would simply have not been in Rue's favor. Even those in the districts who may have been disgusted by Katniss' actions would eventually come to feel the same apathy they felt for all that occurs within the Games should Katniss have abandoned Rue to her fate. However, regardless of her own safety, when Katniss hears Rue's cries, she thinks, "I'm running, knowing this may be a trap, knowing the three Careers may be poised to attack me, but I can't help myself.... I shout back ... so, *they* know I'm near, and hopefully the girl who has attacked them with tracker jackers ... will be enough to pull their attention away from [Rue]."[22] Although Rue's death is necessary in order for Katniss to survive the Games, Katniss' first thought and subsequent actions are to place herself in harm's way to protect Rue. Collins repeatedly depicts Katniss as primarily and instinctively protecting the innocent and helpless and pairs her care-based morality with her willingness to kill in defense.

Katniss' morality-based agency, in which her actions are formed by her moral concerns, results in her first intentional kill within the arena.[23] When Katniss finds Rue, she arrives in time to shoot an arrow through the neck of Marvel who has just thrown his spear into Rue's stomach. Katniss mourns Rue's death and realizes that "he [Marvel] was my first kill.... The boy from District 1 was the first person I knew would die because of my actions. A number of animals have lost their lives at my hands, but only one human. I hear Gale saying, 'How different can it be, really?' Amazingly similar in the execution.... Entirely different in the aftermath."[24] In this moment, Katniss remembers Gale's advice and immediately rejects it. In doing so she rejects any philosophical thinking that justifies the taking of another's life without admitting to the consequences. Katniss' own thought process reflects that of Collins, who also rejects realist thinking in the last book, *Mockingjay*. In both the attack with the Tracker Jacker nest and the killing of Marvel, Katniss does not rejoice at the violence or death, even though every death of her competitors brings her closer to winning and going home. Not only does Katniss take no pleasure in the killings, but she also suffers physically and emotionally for her actions.

Collins blatantly depicts the consequences that taking another's life can have on an individual. After dropping the Tracker Jackers, Katniss is physically wounded by their stingers and falls into a comatose state where she relives horrifying nightmares. After killing Marvel, even to save Rue, Katniss falls into a deep depression, forcing herself to eat, sleep, and hunt for food. Regardless of how just or necessary Katniss' actions were, Collins still demonstrates the inherent penalties associated with violence. While Collins does not condemn Katniss' necessary actions, she does not condone them either. Katniss is only able to heal and find motivation to act once the Gamemakers present her with the opportunity to ally herself with Peeta. In such a scene, Collins gives Katniss another opportunity to exercise agency that is specific to her relational-based morality. Through healing and working alongside Peeta, Katniss once again acts intentionally on her desire to return home.

Interestingly, Collins furthers this investigation of Katniss' moral agency through the climatic ending of the 74th Hunger Games in which Katniss must once again confront her own morality. Throughout the Games, Katniss often thinks negatively and even aggressively of Cato, the male tribute from District 2 who is particularly sadistic. Collins allows Katniss' hatred of the Careers and desire for revenge to build throughout the narrative, potentially corrupting her moral character that has previously been based on care and defense. When the showdown begins, even readers and viewers of the movie adaptations cheer for Cato's death—cheering almost like Capitol citizens themselves. Caught up in the Games, readers hope that either Katniss or Peeta will kill Cato and return home safe and sound. However, during the last scene, Collins twists the narrative and transforms Cato from a brutal and bloody barbarian into a defenseless and abused child. Cato, whom the wolf-muttations ravage and mutilate, begs and whimpers for death. Suddenly, like Katniss, readers no longer anticipate his death, they simply want it over with. It is "pity, not vengeance" that sends Katniss' arrow "flying into his skull."[25]

The important aspect here is that Katniss remains true to her own ethic-based, moral code. Katniss' decision to kill Cato does in fact adhere to her moral code in which she acts defensively instead of offensively. She does not kill Cato to save herself, she kills Cato to save him from the muttations.

Foucault argues, "A moral action tends toward its own accomplishment; but it also aims beyond the latter, to establishing of a moral conduct that commits an individual ... [to] a mode of being characteristic of the ethical subject ... this requires him to act upon himself, to monitor, test, improve, and transform himself."[26] Throughout the first novel, Katniss' own relational and care-based ethical conduct influences her agency. In this final death scene, compassion and mercy, instead of revenge and hate, guide Katniss' arrow. In having Katniss maintain her moral agency, Collins presents a stable, respectable protagonist for readers to emulate and challenges readers, who rooted for Cato's death, to scrutinize their own moral codes.

The Quarter Quell

"On the seventy-fifth anniversary, as a reminder to the rebels that even the strongest among them cannot overcome the power of the Capitol, the male and female tributes will be reaped from their existing pool of victors."[27] In response to Katniss' action, President Snow arranges for the Quarter Quell in which Katniss has no choice, as the only female Victor of District 12, but to re-enter the arena a second time. As the districts have come to view Katniss as their figurehead, she represents the possibility of obtaining agency and retaining personal moral codes even within the most challenge environment. The Quarter Quell arena, like the first Games, will test Katniss' ethical code of conduct. However, knowing that exercising agency is in direct opposition toward the Capitol's design, Katniss accepts that she will most likely die in the Quarter Quell as she intends to save Peeta's life in the process. It is Katniss' acceptance of her own death and her desires to save Peeta that again expose her moral codes.

Within her societal constraints, Katniss enacts limited moral agency, similar to that of the first Games. While she continues to kill, the intentions behind such actions are in defense of herself, Peeta, or others. Her relationship with and care for Peeta drives her actions within the Quarter Quell, and once again connects her morality to individual agency. Katniss' care-centered morality which once only included those closest to her begins to expand and encompass not only a few but many innocents within Panem who suffer in the same way. In this way, Katniss continues to separate from Gale's belief system in which protection is offered only to those in his immediate circle. Later, in accepting her probable death, Katniss hopes that her death will make it clear to the districts that she is "still defying the Capitol right up to the end, the Capitol will have killed me ... but not my spirit. What better way to give hope to the rebels?"[28] Subsequently, Katniss' moral responsibility grows exponentially in *Catching Fire* as she chooses to act in such ways that will benefit others—even individuals in other districts that she has never met.

The arena of the Quarter Quell, the environment itself and the Victor-tributes within it, test Katniss' ethical conduct which in turn influence her moral agency. Through the ending of the Games in particular, Collins stimulates the conversation of morality through Haymitch's continued reminder to Katniss to remember who her true enemy is. As the canons boom and Beetee's carefully thought-out plan evaporates into thin air, Collins forces Katniss and the readers into a state of panic and confusion. This state of anxiety disorients Katniss' briefly established code of moral conduct as she believes that previous alliances have been broken and that it has become a kill all (even friends) or be killed. Regardless, Katniss' agency remains dependent upon her desire to protect Peeta, and just as she attempted to draw the attention away from Rue in the first Games, she does so again in the Quarter Quell, crying out, "I'm here! I'm here" to attract the remaining Victors.[29] Consistent with her relational and care-based moral code, Katniss attempts to save Peeta at the cost of her own life, revealing the strength of her relational agency.

However, as Katniss approaches the lightening tree, still searching for Peeta, Collins advocates for a moral agency that encompasses more than just those closest to the individual. Relational moral agency demands a wider circumference. The decision to utilize the lightening tree represents this choice for Katniss: she can either choose Peeta and engage in a bloody battle to the end with the other Victor-tributes or she can choose Panem and blast apart the arena, directing her arrow at the Capitol's power. In her choice, Katniss displays how her moral agency has grown to embrace not only those she loves personally, but the unnamed, the unknown, because their lives also matter. Repeatedly, morality compels Katniss to act in specific ways often contrary to her own well-being.

Throughout the first two novels, Collins illustrates Katniss as a morally-orientated individual who successfully manages to exercise agency despite the oppressive and immoral government and society. Although she does not primarily hunt down the other competitors, she emerges from the first Games as Victor. In the Quarter Quell, although limited in her abilities, Katniss still acts out against the Capitol, demanding her own agency and displaying it for all of Panem to view. Katniss' rewarding agency is due in part to her strong relational and care-based ethical codes that are developed in these Games with Rue, Peeta, Finnick, and Mags. However, Collins' last installation of the trilogy does not sacrifice sentiment for illumination. Contrarily, in *Mockingjay*, readers explore the detrimental aspects of agency when based on immoral desires and intentions that push Katniss' agency past their limit.

Realist vs. Pacifist vs. Relational

As Collins explores, and often condemns, war ethics, she also compels her readers to address how morality and agency intertwine within such circumstances. Katniss' mental struggle to maintain her own fragile subconscious and the physical battle within a brutal and costly war distort and weaken Katniss' established moral code. Additionally, Peeta's absence and Gale's increased presence further obscure Katniss' ethical code which results in her loss of self and the inability to adequately exercise agency. For instance, just as Gale and Peeta influenced Katniss before the 74th Hunger Games, their belief systems once again affect Katniss' decisions in the final installment of the series as her relationships with others direct her ethical conduct. As noted, Gale represents a realistic belief system in which morality plays little to no role in survival or war tactics. In *Mockingjay*, Gale aggressively asserts, "If I could hit a button and kill every living soul working for the Capitol, I would do it. Without hesitation."[30] As seen in this quote, Gale's aggressive behavior often goes beyond simple survival, but for a sense of revenge and justification. In *Mockingjay*, Gale's moral code is in obvious and direct opposition to Katniss' relational ideology that encompasses more than just her immediate family.

Although Gale acts out of concern for his family, he neglects other innocent lives if they get in the way of accomplishing his goal. For instance, when the rebellion must face the problem of District 2's stronghold, the Nut, they consider causing an avalanche that will kill everyone inside, even the rebel spies. Gale, who thought of the plan, argues, "I would sacrifice a few, yes, to take out the rest."[31] Although Gale begins as a reasonable character, negative emotions such as hate and revenge corrupt his idealism. Indeed, he creates a trap that will set off a small bomb, killing innocents that will draw in first responders only to set off a second bomb to increase the casualty count. Interestingly, although scholars such as Tom Henthorne proclaim Collins' third book to be an anti-war novel, Collins portrays Gale, one of the most ruthless characters, as a sympathetic character to both Katniss and readers alike. No matter how far Gale's actions take him, readers often find themselves defending him. Collins initially presents Gale's ideology as understandable within *The Hunger Games*. However, as the narrative matures, Gale's actions become harder to defend which demonstrates to readers the quick dissent that morality can take if the individual leaves his/her motives of revenge and hatred unchecked.

On the other hand, Collins presents Peeta early on as a pacifistic character. However, throughout the novels, particularly *Catching Fire* and *Mockingjay*, Peeta too changes as he reacts violently at times, even taking the lives of others. Unlike Collins' presentation of Gale, who allows negative experiences to corrupt his sense of morality, Collins highlights Peeta's appeals for morality even while the Capitol tortures him. In an interview, Peeta tries to explain the cost of killing another individual, even when done in defense. He says, "It costs a lot more than your life. To murder innocent people.... It costs everything you are."[32] Although Peeta also suffers from uncontrollable circumstances like Gale, he clings to his personal code of morality. These two opposing views of realism and pacifism constantly surround and influence Katniss' own decisions.

Although Katniss desires the destruction of the Capitol, she finds herself disagreeing with both Gale's and Peeta's moral stances. Unlike Gale, Katniss' care-based morality encompasses all innocent lives even beyond her family and district. She refuses to concede to the necessity of sacrificing lives, even Capitol-lives, needlessly. Unlike Peeta, Katniss cannot accept a ceasefire that will only lead to more pain and suffering at the hands of the Capitol, although she understands the consequences that her actions might bring about. That the love triangle is clearly a morality triangle is nowhere near as clear than in the final book as Katniss is often left torn between these two separate idealisms.

Clearly, Collins' narrative argues that agency relates to morality in how it depicts Katniss' struggle to enact agency while unable to maintain a clear and moral stance within District 2. True to his established nature, Gale suggests complete annihilation of the District 2 workers in revenge of watching District 12's residents die—particularly the children. Katniss responds to the imagery that Gale paints and thinks, "The image [of dying children] rips through me. It has the desired effect. I want everyone in the mountain dead. Am about to say so. But then..."[33] Although Gale's words entice Katniss, at least in part, a significant portion of Katniss hesitates and cannot completely agree with the unbiased murder of innocents. It is this hesitation that reveals Katniss' own moral codes and her inability to support the plan. Although Katniss disagrees with the plan, she does not stop the rebellion from activating the avalanche either. Realistically, Katniss may not have been able to physically alter the rebel's plans; however, she does have a voice of influence that she might have used to persuade those in charge to show more leniency. Her hesitance to speak out in this moment reflects the weakening of not only her morality but, more importantly, her own agency as she wavers in her ability to act.

While the Katniss of the first or second novel may have spoken out in this moment, the Katniss of *Mockingjay* is lost without Peeta's constant guidance and relies on Gale's belief systems which corrupts her own. Without the strong moral foundation, all Katniss can do is watch in horror as the mountain crumbles and think, "We stand speechless, tiny and insignificant, as waves of stone thunder down the mountain.... I imagine the hell inside the mountain.... People slamming, shoving, scrambling like ants as the hill presses in.... *What did we just do?*"[34] Although Katniss disagreed with the plan, she accepts her accountability in the crime with the use of the term "we" in her exclamation. In refusing to speak up before, Katniss too becomes responsible for the actions of others and becomes speechless, representing her lack of agency. Here, Collins directly demonstrates the consequences of agency when enacted without a strong moral base. Although immoral individuals can have agency, in young adult dystopian literature, individuals with a strong moral code are more likely to successfully exercise agency overall. Meanwhile, those with unclear morals, such as Katniss, can only act as spectator, reducing their ability to act and their agency to almost nothing.

Through Katniss' dismay and questioning of such actions, Collins addresses the corruption of moral agency within times of war. In a war, a soldier's agency is automatically associated with that of the entire army (collective agency) and therefore the morality of his/her leader can obscure his/her individual moral conduct. While the rebellion initially began as a just war—with a just cause—the calloused actions taken in the name of a just cause can be unjust in their execution. While the rebels protest the Capitol's heinous acts, they also perform horrible deeds in the name of "peace." Intimately connected to the rebellion, Katniss must accept her own part in the destruction of the Nut. While she did not come up with the plan or initiate the bombing of the mountainside, her passive acceptance of the plan is enough to lay the guilt at her feet. Just as Katniss sacrifices her morality by refusing to argue against the plan, she forfeits her ability to enact her desired agency—or to act at all.

Throughout the first two novels, moral considerations spur on Katniss' agency such as volunteering for Prim and saving Peeta; however, within *Mockingjay* she struggles to act during crucial moments. After the fall of the Nut, Gale and others pass her by and eagerly prepare themselves for the following battle. Meanwhile, Katniss stays behind and thinks, "I wish Peeta was here ... he would be able to articulate why it is so wrong to be exchanging fire when people, any people, are trying to claw their way out of the mountain."[35] Continuously, Katniss compares Gale and Peeta when trying to re-establish her code of morality. It is their presence that determines not her romantic feelings but her moral inclinations. In the destruction of the Nut, the rebels set aside moral principles which formed the foundation of their cause so that they could achieve a strategic victory. Even though Katniss can acknowledge the immorality of such actions, she cannot act against them. This physical passivity demonstrates her overall lack of agency and her inability to act without a moral code. Indeed, Katniss is only propelled back into motion when Haymitch encourages her to give a speech, calling for a ceasefire to save the lives of those within the mountain. Just as her opportunity to save Peeta in the first Games reawakened Katniss from her stupor after Prim's death, the opportunity to save even one life propels her to act once again. It would seem that only through her relational and care-based moral code can Katniss possess agency.

Katniss' Descent

As Collins propels the narrative forward, she further displays Katniss' downward spiral caused by a lack of moral agency. After the events of the Nut, the rescued, yet hijacked version of Peeta rattles Katniss' sense of identity with his cruel remarks and causes her to think, "Finally, he can see me for who I really am. Violent. Distrustful. Manipulative. Deadly."[36] This image of herself, spurred by hijacked-Peeta's insults, ultimately influences the ways in which she exercises agency. Believing herself to be an immoral person, because of Peeta's words as he previously guided her morality, Katniss embraces her negative desires and acts on revenge and hate instead of love and protection. Scholar Brian McDonald notes, "We witness a very understandable but definitely dark and distressing change of Katniss' character in *Mockingjay* as the urge to kill Snow becomes her dominating drive ... she descends into a suicidal self-hatred."[37] This hatred, directed at herself and at others, contaminates her morality. Katniss admits to herself that she only wants to join the war effort in the Capitol to "carry out [her] own personal vendetta against Snow."[38] In other words, Katniss loses her desire to protect others as she switches and begins to act offensively instead of defensively. In this manner, Katniss' agency transforms from one based on a relational moral code to one like Gale's—based on revenge. This forgoing of a moral code threatens Katniss' autonomy; she fabricates a false mission to descend into the Capitol and kill President Snow herself. Multiple times, Katniss admits that the mission is most likely suicidal and happily accepts it, although she often ignores what pain her possible death would cause Prim. Katniss' actions, without strong moral foundation, are ill-conceived and disastrous not only to herself but also to those who trust in her.

Consequently, due to this lack of morality, Katniss' agency diminishes in both strength and successfulness. For instance, Katniss' plan to sneak into the Capitol through the sewers[39] and assassinate President Snow results in the deaths of several of her friends and comrades: Jackson, Homes, Castor, Leeg 1, Messalla, and even beloved Finnick who are all brutally killed—some torn to pieces by Capitol engineered lizard-mutts. Additionally, once having gained access to an apartment, Katniss sees an unarmed woman who "opens her mouth to call for help. Without hesitation, I [Katniss] shoot her through the heart."[40] Far from the girl who placed the protection of innocents—no matter their background—over her own survival, in *Mockingjay*, Katniss evolves into a cold, calloused murderer who shoots first and asks questions later. While Katniss' actions are still her own, her lack of ethical conduct weakens who she is as an individual. She transforms into a person that the Katniss of book one would be unable to recognize. While trauma plays a role in this metamorphosis as we will see in the next chapter, the lack of morality ultimately initiates Katniss' turn from her original character. Indeed, Katniss' agency only grows more disjointed and chaotic as she continues to ignore the moral implications of her actions.

To further condemn this lack of moral agency, Collins' narrative highlights the absolute worst consequences of improperly motivated agency, which is the lack of control over the self or anything else. Ultimately, Katniss and the remaining Star Squad members arrive outside of Snow's mansion, killing multiple innocents along the way: men, women, and even children. As rebels and Capitol Peacekeepers collide, there is only chaos. Katniss' mission fails as the bombs designed by Gale and Beetee explode over the barricade of children around Snow's mansion. As the first responders rush in, Katniss catches a quick glimpse of her sister Prim before the rest of the bombs explode, killing Prim and severely burning Katniss. Not only does the ineffectiveness of the entire plan negate Katniss' agency, but the use of Gale's bomb destroys any chance of accomplishing Katniss' goal. It is no accident that Gale's idea of a bomb is held responsible for Prim's death as Collins' narrative actively condemns the type of thinking that negates the importance of morality in times of war. While actions can be enacted without morality, within Collins' dystopian narrative, morality plays a significant role in the success of agency.

Through her descent into the Capitol, Katniss seems to exercise some amount of agency as she acts based on her desires and intentions. However, due to the way in which Collins has expertly intertwined morality within the story, it becomes clear that agency is more than just acting on animalistic desire. Although Katniss begins this trilogy as a self-sacrificing hero, she fails in the sewers of the Capitol having allowed her moral identity to be corrupted. For days after the events, Katniss exists in a type of limbo in which she imagines herself as a Mockingjay that drowns in the sea. Emerging from her nightmares, Katniss is rebirthed as a "fire mutt": a mute creature "with no wings. With no fire. And no sister."[41] The lack of a firm moral foundation causes Katniss' agency to become utterly ineffectual. This is painfully clear in the way in which she loses her sister, Prim, who originally instigated Katniss' battle for moral agency.

In a book that begins with the gladiator-style Games of children murdering children, it is impossible for readers not to recognize the presence or lack of morality within the text. Collins sets up her main protagonist, Katniss

Everdeen, as a young girl in an impossible situation who can exercise agency while acting primarily on a relational and care-based moral code. Within the last novel of the trilogy, Collins explores the relationship between morality and agency within the context of war. Those around Katniss, specifically Gale and Peeta, influence Katniss' moral/ethical code. Indeed, the Katniss-Gale-Peeta love triangle illustrates more about morality than romance or gender. Katniss develops her sense of morality based on the presence and actions of Gale and Peeta. Their existence in her life challenges her tendencies toward violence and causes her to re-evaluate the extent to which she cares of others.

Throughout the trilogy, Katniss' decisions are particularly successful when acting upon moral agency, and, contrarily, her agency diminishes as her moral foundation wanes due to negative emotions and the influence of others. Through Katniss, Gale, and Peeta, Collins presents a correlation between agency and morality, demonstrating when agency lacks a moral code, agency is corrupted and often results in trauma for the agent. When Katniss eventually chooses Peeta, she also chooses to establish a more passive and care-focused morality. While we often look at morality in dystopias in terms of the immoral government, Collins' trilogy illustrates that moral agency is far more important for the individual and their ability to enact agency within and despite any type of government. Within young adult literature, the protagonist must fight not only against external forces, but also against internal ethical conflictions as their actions affect the rise or fall of their societies.

THREE

"A mental Avox"

Agency and the Traumatized Mind

That *The Hunger Games* trilogy contains dark themes and extreme cases of violence is no secret, and because of such things many parents consider the trilogy's content to be unsuitable for adolescents (the target age group). Adults critique the novels' subject matter: children slaughtering children, monsters that tear humans apart limb from limb, and a sadistic society that cheers on such violence. Parents stormed social media asking, "Should my child read this book or watch this movie?" Overwhelmingly, the answer was no as the series was ranked in the top three of the top 10 censored books of 2011. *Mockingjay*, the third installment, further confirms the mature content of the series by presenting a very broken and very traumatized protagonist. Katniss Everdeen, having lost Peeta and undergone two rounds within the Games, struggles to maintain her hold on reality, much less to lead a rebellion.

Why, in a series created for young adults, would Collins present such a broken, immoral, and depressed protagonist? Katniss' traumatic experiences chip away at her sanity and strip her ability to exercise agency. Through examining this trauma it becomes clear that Collins highlights the prominence of mental and emotional wholeness as necessary for the individual to maintain and grow in agency. Trauma diminishes Katniss' agency by restricting her confidence in herself, separating her from others both physically and mentally, and reducing her sense of self. As we may remember, agency is the ability to exercise control over one's own intentional actions. As Katniss loses that sense of herself, she loses her ability to act. Consequently, Katniss can reclaim agency only through overcoming her own trauma.

Many critics and readers find the conclusion of *Mockingjay* as highly controversial due to the overwhelming presence of trauma that is too mature for younger audiences. Before its publication, a close advisor suggested to Collins that she rewrite the ending in a more positive tone and with less death. Collins argued, "This is not a fairy tale; it's a war, and in war, there are tragic losses that must be mourned."[1] According to Collins, the presence of trauma is not only prevalent, but also necessary. Despite Collins' defense of her work, one critic, Caroline Framke, elaborates on her frustration concerning the last novel. She writes, "*Mockingjay* is brimming with fascinating ideas and uncomfortable truths, but it ultimately collapses at the finish, with palpable exhaustion [due to being stuck inside Katniss' Everdeen's head]."[2] Framke insists that Collins should have written the war novel from a different character's perspective for the sake of storytelling. What Framke may not have considered is that the novel is not solely about war or story plot line, it is primarily about Katniss and her agency and the effects of trauma on her agency. The exhaustion that Framke notes may be intentional as it indicates the battle Katniss has undergone in her struggle to maintain agency. Collins has spoken out numerous times about her intention to teach and educate children about reality through her books, not only to entertain.

Along the same lines, even more academically-focused scholars debate the success of the outcome of the series. Bill Clemente states, "For Katniss, her world's future remains uncertain at the trilogy's conclusion, any happiness burdened always with painful scars both literal and figural."[3] While it is true that these scars remain and that the government itself is teetering on the edge of greatness or calamity, the conclusion of the trilogy directly and clearly points to Katniss' reclamation of agency after addressing and dealing with the trauma in her life. There is no ambiguity in that, at least, and it is agency that lies at the heart of *The Hunger Games*.

Trauma and the Everdeens

Regardless of how scholars tend to isolate *Mockingjay* as the most traumatic book in the series, it is important to note that it is not the only book within the series that addresses trauma. Indeed, within the very first novel, Collins introduces trauma to both Katniss Everdeen and her readers in a very real and brutal way. In *The Hunger Games*, Collins foreshadows the relevance of trauma in the overall trilogy through the Everdeen family. Katniss' pre-established strained relationship with her mother is more than just a means to create the familiar motif of the orphaned dystopian heroine.[4] Their relationship, or truly their lack of a relationship, caused by her father's sudden death is the foundation for all Katniss' traumatic experiences.

Perhaps displayed even better in the movies than in the books are the effects of Mr. Everdeen's death on Katniss' psyche. In the books, Katniss' trauma related to her father underlies all that she does, but the books do require readers to do their own in-between-the-lines reading at times. Taking inspiration directly from the book, the movie illustrates this trauma and its effect on Katniss' life. In one scene, Katniss remembers her father's death and as the mine shaft explodes, so too does her physical home. The explosion destroys the picture of her father and causes the house to collapse in on itself. Even after the damage to the house is reversed and put back together, Mrs. Everdeen sits silent in her chair, ignoring Katniss' pleas to respond to her. This carefully crafted scene is extremely beneficial in the visual depiction of how Mr. Everdeen's death annihilates not only Katniss' physical home but also the emotional bonds between herself and her remaining family members. After Mr. Everdeen's death, Mrs. Everdeen essentially orphans her two daughters, leaving Katniss to take on the role of head of household. It becomes Katniss' responsibility to care not only for herself and Prim, but also for her mother, while trying to hide their condition from others within the district.

This lack of parental support and the weight of becoming a parent while still a child stunts Katniss' ability to grow up unencumbered by trauma. Laurie Vickroy, a scholar of trauma, states, "Relationships—especially between mother and child—should provide both safety and independent recognition of the child ... trauma portrayed within the context of mother/child symbiosis demonstrates the devastation of isolation and helplessness, particularly in early, formative, and intimate contexts."[5] Due to Mrs. Everdeen's chronic state, anxiety and distrust inform Katniss' childhood development. Indeed, the mother's "orphaning" of her daughters causes Katniss to exhibit common traumatized behaviors such as isolating herself from others, having difficulty in forming relationships, reoccurring nightmares, and perceived helplessness long before the reaping of the 74th Hunger Games. Surprisingly, the trauma of losing her parents does not entirely crush Katniss' spirit, but instead it aids Katniss in realizing her own strength and autonomy in providing for her family. Early in the series, Collins foreshadows the presence and importance of trauma for the trilogy which only intensifies as readers progress through the narrative. Trauma, then, becomes a lens through which readers analyze Katniss' agency.

The Girl on Fire/Mutt

Throughout the series there is a plethora of traumatic events: Effie announcing Prim's name at the reaping, Rue's death, Cato's mutilation by wolf-muttations, Wiress' slit throat that resembles a bloody smile, Johanna's waterboarding and electrocution, Peeta's hijacking, and so on and so forth. However, the calamity that takes place toward the end of *Mockingjay*, in which Katniss watches most of her friends die before witnessing Prim being blown apart and catching fire herself, represents the critical trauma that completely shatters Katniss' identity, sanity, and agency. It is after these events that Katniss wakes, unable to speak even though doctors claim there is no medial reason for the loss of her voice. Traditional trauma theory holds that trauma is "an experience so intensely painful that the mind is unable to process it normally ... and if memories of the trauma return, they are often nonverbal, and the victim may be unable to describe them with words."[6] In the same way, the experiences that Katniss has undergone are too painful for Katniss to put into words. In speaking about Prim's death, she must accept it, which is something she cannot immediately do.

Indeed, the doctor concludes that Katniss is a "mental, rather than physical, Avox" and that her silence was "brought on by emotional trauma."[7] Here, Collins plays with the term "Avox" which originally referred to criminals of the Capitol whose tongues were removed or mutilated for their crimes, eliminating their ability to speak and stripping away part of their agency. While neither the Capitol nor District 13 physically removed Katniss' tongue, their actions and Katniss' "criminal" actions within the Capitol deprive her of her ability to use her tongue for quite some time, representing her inability to voice her individual needs and desires.

The juxtaposition that exists between voiced and voicelessness, or the ability to speak and the restriction of silence, is a strong and important one in trauma and in agency. Although agency often refers to physical action, an agent's ability to speak and, more importantly, to be heard is crucial. Through vocalization an agent conveys thoughts, feelings, desires, and intentions. By deeming Katniss Everdeen a Mockingjay—the songbird of the rebellion— Collins emphasizes the necessity of having and vocalizing one's own perspective and judgment. In previous books, Katniss has undeniably wielded her voice, both in speaking and singing, to condemn the powerful and encourage the weak. However, as a mental Avox, Katniss silences her own voice and stumbles around, literally and metaphorically, in her inability to vocalize either pain or desire. Unable to speak or act based on specific intention, trauma renders Katniss as without agency.

Collins uses the descriptive imagery of Katniss' physical wounds to reconnect readers to Katniss' previous foundation of agency. Within the first two novels, fire is a positive symbol that strengthens Katniss and displays her rebellious and contagious spirit. However, within *Mockingjay*, fire conveys the constant reminder of all the traumas Katniss has undergone, particularly the loss of her sister. Vickroy asserts, "Survivors' painful connection to past trauma is also displayed and replayed through the body, even branded into their flesh.... Characters' scars become both connecting points and obstacles to potentially intimate or sexual relations."[8] Likewise, Katniss' scars continuously replay her most significant trauma.

Branded by the bomb that killed her sister, Katniss describes herself as "forced to accept who I am. A badly burned girl with no wings. With no fire.

And no sister."[9] In this phrase, Collins inverts the journey through which Katniss has gained her agency, first through Prim, then through fire, and finally as the Mockingjay. Indeed, Katniss' first act of active dissent and of asserting her own agency over the oppressive regime in the entire series is through volunteering to take her sister's place in the reaping. She then became "the girl who was on fire" who stole the hearts of the Capitol citizens forcing Seneca Crane to spare her life.[10] Realizing that limited agency can only achieve so much, Katniss accepts the persona of the Mockingjay, vocalizing the inhumanity of the Capitol and its systems. However, trauma strips away such moments of agency and after losing her sister, the person for whom Katniss risked everything, Katniss believes her actions to be useless. In Katniss' words, the scars are reminders of "why I was in pain. And what happened just before the pain started. And how I watched my little sister become a human torch."[11] The physical scars are not only a reminder of the physical pain she endured, but also of the emotional trauma that she will never stop enduring. Until this point, the desire to protect Prim and then to protect other innocents such as Rue, Peeta, Bonnie, and the other helpless characters within the districts formed Katniss' individualized agency. However, losing this purpose, losing Prim, causes Katniss to neglect her hard-fought agency and her own self.

Additionally, these scars that decorate Katniss' body become both "connecting points and obstacles" with her remaining loved ones. The physical scars that represent her trauma and manifest through Katniss' silence cause a separation between Gale and Katniss, the first person that Katniss ever loved who was not a part of her blood family. A single conversation, ignited by Katniss' trauma and physical scars, destroy their relationship when Katniss asks Gale if he created the bomb that killed Prim. When Gale is unsure and claims that it does not matter as Katniss will never be able to stop doubting him, she thinks, "He waits for me to deny it; I want to deny it, but it's true. Even now I can see the flash that ignites her, feel the heat of the flames. And I will never be able to separate that moment from Gale. My silence is my answer."[12] Katniss' silence as she refuses to answer Gale, her inability to speak of her trauma, directly relates back to the origin of her scars and creates an unbreakable barrier between her once closest confidant and herself. At the conclusion of the series, Katniss' scars forever form an obstacle between her and Gale that can never be breached.

In contrast, these same physical scars that distance Katniss from Gale connect Katniss to Peeta. At the last meeting of the Victors, Katniss notices the burn marks that run along Peeta's skin, thinking, "We are both fire mutts now."[13] Through these same scars—Katniss' physical results of trauma—Katniss rejects Gale's continued presence in her life and accepts Peeta as alike to herself. Both Peeta and Katniss are fire mutts, changed and manipulated by the Capitol and the rebellion. This distinction from Gale and similarities that connect Katniss to Peeta further emphasize points made in the previous chapter on morality. Gale's agency, based on a foundation that rejects the necessity of morals in times of war and trauma, fails in achieving his desire to remain with Katniss. On the other hand, Peeta's agency, propelled by a strong sense of morality, connects him physically and emotionally to Katniss. Just as Peeta provides beneficial examples for moral agency, so too does he ensure that Katniss follows the proper methods for healing, such as planting flowers that symbolize rebirth. These physical scars of trauma become a clear indicator that Peeta, not Gale, understands Katniss' trauma and how to help her heal, perhaps solving the Team Peeta/Team Gale dilemma once and for all.

Suicidal Agency

Of course, healing for Katniss does not come quickly as she must first battle for survival against herself. Katniss' suicidal actions while in isolation have been interpreted in various ways. Can scholars consider actions of suicide, or even unsuccessful suicidal actions, as an individual exerting agency? It is a question that academics have asked and argued for years within different genres of literature. Can suicide represent an individual reclaiming agency? Many would argue that it depends on whether the suicide was a means of escape, or if it was brought about by psychosis, or if it was planned beforehand in minute detail. There are various reasons why an individual may commit suicide and every intention matters. This question concerning suicide and agency applies specifically to Katniss Everdeen whose intentions can be seen through the way she questions her own reality.

Katniss initially bases her agency on what she believes to be right and true, such as her desire to protect her family and overthrow the Capitol. In *Mockingjay*, having lost Prim and other such relationships, Katniss doubts her own beliefs and actions. Michelle Balaev, an additional scholar of trauma, asserts, "Trauma, in [any] novel, lurches the protagonist into a profound inquisitive state, in which the meaning of the experience and the process of conceptualizing the self and world are meticulously evaluated."[14] While the bombing of innocent children would still have been horrific, the bombs would not have had the same effect on either Katniss or readers if Prim had not been one of the casualties. Prim's death compels Katniss to discover the truth behind who set off the bombs and to question the motivations of all those around her. The trauma, not only the physical wounding, but specifically losing Prim, forces Katniss into what Balaev refers to as a "profound inquisitive state" in which she must discover the truth for herself. This questioning forces Katniss to rethink her own actions within the rebellion and to re-evaluate the actions of others.

At least in part, Katniss reclaims agency through her questioning; however, this questioning does not guarantee her emotional stability. In other words, the questions that Katniss ask bring her closer to a truth that she does not wish to know and prepares her for the last meeting of the Victors in which President Coin holds a vote to reinstate the Hunger Games, using the Capitol's children. Due to Katniss' previous inquisitive state of mind, she understands that by voting yes and appeasing Coin momentarily, she will suppress Coin's suspicions which allows Katniss to gain a clear shot later at the execution. Katniss' questioning of Gale, of President Coin, and even of the other Victors all work to warp Katniss' worldview. She believes, "Nothing has changed. Nothing will ever change now."[15] The questioning brought about by the trauma of losing Prim and the despair caused by Coin's attempted re-installation of the Games propels Katniss into a new consciousness where she views everyone, including herself, as toxic. For instance, just before the meeting of the Victors, Katniss confesses to herself that she cannot forgive Gale, because she would also have to "take into account my [her] own inexcusable crimes."[16] Unable to forgive others or herself, Katniss concludes that pain is all there is to life. Therefore, while Katniss gains the ability to act on her desire to punish President Coin she still lacks her pervious moral foundation as she believes that most of the world, herself included, is evil.

Collins' narrative repeatedly demonstrates the ways in which trauma negates Katniss' agency by blinding her to truths and contorting her worldview. Subsequently, Katniss desires not only to punish Coin, but also to escape from a world that she hates. These conflicting desires complicate the execution scene in which Katniss decides to kill President Coin instead of President Snow. True, it might seem as though Katniss has reacquired agency as she is acting on her own desires instead of according to someone else's plan. Tom Henthorne, a scholar of *The Hunger Games*, claims that Katniss is "performing as the Mockingjay … if only because playing a role enables her to distance herself from the trauma and become functional again, at least temporarily."[17] However, Katniss' performance is the problem. Although acting as the Mockingjay allows Katniss to become "functional," the intentions behind such functionality are corrupted. Indeed, Katniss is *performing*. As previously discussed in Chapter One, Katniss' role as Mockingjay is only successful when she is not pantomiming. Yet, in this scene, Katniss clearly acts in both her submission to Coin and her performance as Mockingjay with the intention of saving no one, only killing Coin and herself.

Additionally, Katniss lacks agency as her actions are not thought out or based on clear, unclouded, rational intentions; rather, emotional instability and self-hatred convolute her actions. In his book, Henthorne asserts that Katniss clearly plans out her suicide well in advance to the actual event and implies that Katniss is willing to commit this action for the greater good of

Panem. However, another reading might argue that Katniss' actions are spontaneous as seen by her last-minute change of aim when she first points her arrow at Snow only to shift upward and kill Coin. Watching Coin crumple, Katniss considers, "I think of what my brief future as the assassin of Panem's new president holds. The interrogation, probable torture, certain public execution. Having, yet again, to say my final goodbyes ... decides it ... [I] twist my neck down to rip off the pill on my sleeve."[18] Katniss never intended to face the law, but rather fully resolves herself to committing suicide not as an exercise of agency but as an act of escape from pain and from consequences, and she would have gone through with her plan if not for Peeta. The trauma of losing Prim, of not being able to trust Gale, and of a twisted worldview caused Katniss to desire not agency, but a lack of ever having to act again. Unlike Katniss' attempted suicide at the end of *The Hunger Games* in which she attempts to save herself and Peeta from the Capitol, or at least die trying, this suicide represents the complete surrender of self and autonomy because there seems to be nothing left worth fighting for. Collins uses trauma in the narrative to highlight how Katniss' agency diminishes over the course of the trilogy: beginning as a young, bright heroine who fights for her survival and the safety of others who later descends into a woman who is altogether sick of living.

Katniss' unsuccessful suicide attempt further demonstrates how she lacks agency toward the end of *Mockingjay* because she has lost her sense of self and purpose. While the new government physically separates Katniss from the rest of the world, trauma separates Katniss from herself. For days and then weeks, Katniss refuses to acknowledge her emotional suffering and even begins to deny her physical body by attempting to slowly starve herself to death. Interestingly, Katniss' refusal to eat does represent a semblance of agency even though her desire is still to commit suicide. Unlike before, in this scene Katniss acts in full consciousness of her actions and her desires. Furthermore, Katniss no longer bases her intentions on escaping from pain or self-hate, but rather to deny the new government any control over her body. Even if her captors were to offer her freedom, Katniss states, "they will never again brainwash me into the necessity of using them [weapons]. I no longer feel any allegiance to these monsters called human beings, despise being one myself."[19] This intention at least echoes Katniss' earlier desire to protect others even if, in this case, she is protecting others from herself. Therefore, in this small manner, Katniss exerts control over the use of her body, re-instigating her claim on agency.

Through Katniss, Collins rejects violence, even supposedly justified violence, when based on an immoral foundation. While Katniss previously built her agency on the idea of controlling her own destiny and creating a more just society for Prim to grow up in, these traumatic experiences smother her desire to act. Through these events, Collins displays the nullifying effects of trauma on an individual's agency. Trauma causes speechlessness that in turn demonstrates the individual's shattered belief in oneself and in others. According to Vickroy, individuals strongly affected by such trauma "do not feel the sense of agency characteristic of being in control of a narrative,"[20] most likely because they are candidly made of aware of their own limitations. Through invoking trauma within her narrative, Collins presents readers with an opportunity to examine how external circumstances negatively affect agency. More importantly, through Katniss, readers must maneuver through the complications that exist between agency and suicide, and how one might overcome trauma.

The Mockingjay's Song

In traditional twentieth century dystopian literature, it is common practice for authors to end their novel on an entirely negative moment: John the Savage's suicide in *Brave New World*, Offred's arrest in *The Handmaid's Tale*, and Winston's death in *Nineteen Eighty-Four*. Unlike such traditional authors, Collins does not leave her readers with this image of Katniss, crippled by trauma and robbed of agency. Instead, Collins allows Katniss to find healing through the vocalization of her pain in both music and narrative. In *The Hunger Games* when speaking to Rue, Katniss initially scoffs at music's usefulness, rating it "somewhere between hair ribbons and rainbows."[21] However, despite Katniss' seemingly negative opinion, music's prevalence is marked throughout the series as a significant motif. Whether it is Mr. Everdeen, Rue, or Katniss singing, Katniss whistling, or the mockingjays harmonizing, music courses through the narrative in crescendos. Music connects Katniss to those she loves, particularly to those whom she loves and has lost. Additionally, by attaching the icon of a songbird to her main protagonist, Collins implies that music is a medium through which Katniss can address the traumatic experiences of her past and her present. Therefore, by connecting Katniss to her past and forcing her to confront her emotional scars, music directly influences Katniss' first step in overcoming trauma and regaining her previous physical and moral agency.

Throughout *The Hunger Games*, *Catching Fire*, and even within the majority of *Mockingjay*, Katniss only sings reluctantly and under selective circumstances. The first is while Rue lay dying and requests a song to ease her pain. Katniss responds with the "Meadow Song," which depicts a kinder and safer world where Rue will finally be safe. Later she sings to Pollux, an Avox who is unable to speak or sing himself, unable to deny his request. Katniss sings "The Hanging Tree," a song her father taught her that ironically questions the idea of autonomy in suicide. While Katniss may seem reluctant to sing in the narrative, it is clear from Peeta's stories that she once loved to sing and often volunteered to do so as a child. The change from appreciation to disdain comes upon Mr. Everdeen's death and even Katniss admits, "It strikes me that my own reluctance to sing, my own dismissal of music might not really be that I think it's a waste of time. It might be because it reminds me too much of my father."[22] In essence, Katniss' first traumatic experience as a child, losing her father to the mines and her mother to depression, causes her to stop singing and silences her articulation of emotion.

Again, readers can realize that trauma has always been a part of the trilogy and diminishes Katniss' agency, portrayed here by her desire to sing silenced by the death of her father. Yet, at the same time, trauma compels Katniss' desire to sing, whether to comfort Rue as she dies or to offer joy to Pollux who has experienced so much pain. Without a doubt, there is this direct correlation between trauma and music. Unlike the scars that are born from trauma, music is not a result of trauma; instead, it is a method through which an individual can overcome suffering. Music shapes the individual and reveals their inner identities.

Therefore, it is unsurprising that after Katniss kills President Coin in retaliation for murdering Prim—while residing in the darkest moment of her life—the "unexpected happens. I [Katniss] begin to sing."[23] Weeks pass within her cell and Katniss fills this time by singing. This singing becomes a physical vocalization of her past traumas along with her present situation. As her song changes from something "rough and breaking" to "something splendid … that would make the mockingjays fall silent," Katniss finds serenity and peace.[24] The mention of mockingjays falling silent directly relates to how the birds would do the same for her father, Mr. Everdeen. In music, Katniss connects back to her original moment of trauma and finds a way to break through the silence by vocalizing the pain of her father's death and all the deaths that have followed. Still, this small breakthrough is not enough to regain her agency as Katniss resides in isolation and remains bent on the intent to slowly starve herself to death as an escape from reality. When Katniss realizes that her medication is shrinking and that she may be expected to perform violence once again on behalf of the new government, she vows, "If I can't kill myself in this room, I will take the first opportunity outside of it to finish the job … it benefits no one to live in a world where these things [violence against innocents] happen."[25] While freeing her voice in the cell partially restores Katniss' autonomy, she must continuously vocalize her pain. In the same way that her bodily agency required constant reclamation from others lest she become a docile body, so too does her mental and emotional agency necessitate constant affirmation.

It is only after the new government exiles her to District 12 when Katniss reconciles with Buttercup—Prim's cat and close companion—that music reaches its climax in reestablishing Katniss' voice and agency. Upon his return, Katniss screams at the cat, releasing the pent-up frustration she felt for months only to find that "a new sound, part crying, part singing, comes out of my [Katniss'] body, giving voice to my despair. Buttercup begins to wail as well."[26] Together Katniss and Buttercup sing, wail, and mourn the loss of Prim. Many scholars and fans have noted the resemblance between Katniss and Buttercup, two wild things tamed only by Prim. Just as Buttercup found his way home from District 13, banged up and covered in scrapes, so too does Katniss find her way home with her own assortment of scars. Not only is Buttercup a mirror of herself, but he is also a connection to Prim and a connection to Katniss' original home destroyed in the bombing on District 12 where Mr. Everdeen first taught Katniss to sing. It can be no coincidence that Katniss and Buttercup find healing with one another through music as Buttercup helps symbolize the connection to all of Katniss' past traumas. Although she does eventually move forward from such traumas, Katniss does not forget. Befriending Buttercup is just one way in which Katniss stays connected to painful past, refusing to let it go, and yet, through her vocalization, can enact agency through it.

Survivor Stories for a New Generation

In addition to music, Collins has Katniss construct her own narrative within the overarching story to strengthen her agency, once again proving the healing powers of vocalizing trauma—this time through writing. Joshua Pederson, a scholar of trauma theory, notes, "Speaking trauma pulls it from the realm of painful obscurity and hastens the process rehabilitation."[27] For instance, having been strengthened by music and constantly encouraged by Peeta's presence, Katniss slowly "come[s] back to life [and has an] idea about the book."[28] Katniss' idea is inspired by her family's book filled with herb and plant descriptions created by her father and mother. In her own book, Katniss plans to record the lives and stories of those she has loved and lost and all her memories concerning them. For Katniss to heal, she must first find an outlet for her trauma. In this manner, Katniss moves beyond using just music as an emotional release and writes down her experiences in order to confront the trauma and to honor those who are gone.

Furthermore, the success of Katniss' "survivor" book is due to the collaboration involved.[29] Katniss' survivor stories are not enough on their own because "trauma cannot be faced alone and recovery is possible only 'within the context of relationships.'"[30] Therefore, the book cannot only include Katniss' memories of trauma, but instead it must also include paintings from

Peeta and stories from Haymitch. As survivors of the Games, these three Victors share common traumas and assist each other in the healing process. Together, Katniss, Peeta, and Haymitch capture an array of the fallen including Prim, Finnick, Rue, Cinna, Boggs, and twenty-three years of tributes that Haymitch mentored and watched die. Together, they are able to record the nameless tributes of the past and their individual stories. Similar to how Katniss transformed Rue's body from a site of punishment to a site of redemption within the 74th Hunger Games and reclaimed her agency, through this book, Haymitch is able to reestablish agency for a multitude of forgotten children. In writing about their shared pasts, Katniss, Peeta, and Haymitch will never forget those who have died and they will not allow others to forget them either. This book, along with the arena sites, become ways to memorialize the fallen, just as we today erect Holocaust memorials so that we will never forget the horrors of the past. Through helping others, Katniss reinstates her moral agency based on the relation to and care for others. Though music may have initiated Katniss' revival, it is through narrative that not only is Katniss' voice fully restored, but also the voices of the dead, reclaiming agency for a multitude.

In this way, Collins' narrative works to demonstrate the possibilities for healing through the unexpected. Katniss once again circumvents what others expect of her and exercises agency based on her own intentions instead of other's expectations. As the hero of the rebellion, Katniss lives in exile in the destroyed village of District 12 working to rebuild her home instead of engaging any further with the revolution as Gale does. As the figurehead of the rebellion, Katniss lives in obscurity wherein she promotes the memories of others instead of her own renown. Additionally, Katniss focuses on restructuring her own identity apart from societal pressure. Indeed, through the survivor's book, Katniss records "all the details it would be a crime to forget."[31] The book that Katniss creates is not only significant in the ways it reclaims agency for the lost and for Katniss herself, but also for the ways in which it works to maintain current agency and encourage future agency.

This survivor's book records the past and also reminds Katniss and future generations of the necessity of bodily, moral, and mental agency. Indeed, Katniss and Peeta themselves intend to use the book to help their own children understand the past. The fact that Katniss has children at all is a direct correlation to her strong sense of agency at the end of the novel. As discussed in previous chapters, Katniss never intended to have children because of the possibility of the Capitol reaping them for the Games. However, by the end of Mockingjay, she has not only one, but two children with Peeta. Katniss says, "It took five, ten, fifteen years for me to agree. But Peeta wanted them so badly. When I first felt her stirring inside of me, I was consumed with a terror that felt as old as life itself. Only the joy of holding her in my arms could tame it. Carrying him was little easier, but not much."[32] Just because Katniss reclaims her agency by the end of the novel does not mean that the experiences of her past vanish. The trauma and the fears remain; however, through remembering and vocalizing, through the survivor book, Katniss can overcome them and encourage her children to do the same. Through this book, and truly through her children, Katniss constantly continues to exert and maintain agency by remembering the past and applying it to her future.

So are the dark themes present within Collins' concluding novel truly suitable for young adult readers? In short, yes. Collins presents Katniss Everdeen as brutally broken and purposefully scarred. Susan Tan, in discussing Katniss, states, "While the subject may be scarred … those traumas and scars are no longer passed down in silence, and the very fact of their articulation points to the potential for healing."[33] Katniss' own destruction and following rehabilitation illustrates the possibility for healing for readers broken by their own traumas.

Furthermore, Collins demonstrates the cyclical nature of agency within young adult dystopian literature specifically through Katniss' character. Agency that is discovered through the body, tested by morality, and shattered by trauma can only be regained through vocalization of pain and reclamation of past morality. By the end of the novel, Collins portrays a future in which Katniss must confess to her children the horrors of her past. She thinks, "I'll tell them how I survive it."[34] It is significant that Katniss uses the present tense "survive" as opposed to the past tense "survived." For Katniss, maintaining agency is a constant, day-to-day battle. A single action cannot accomplish total agency. Instead, maintaining agency requires repetitious actions based on intentional, moral desires. It is a lesson that every reader, even the young ones, can take to heart, to be strong and as enduring as Katniss, remembering the past and using it to safeguard the future.

FOUR

"More than just a piece in their games"

Agency and Identity

Identity, a defining feature of any individual, is constantly under attack from external forces, especially within dystopian societies that require and insist upon universal conformity. Within traditional dystopias, authority and governmental forces consistently threaten the individual's attempts at forming a personal identity. According to James A. Tyner, author of "Self and Space, Resistance and Discipline," totalitarian governments often "criminal-ize" any attempts at individuality and personality.[1] For example, in one tradi-tional dystopian novel entitled *Brave New World*, written by Aldous Huxley and published in 1932, a citizen's position in life is determined before birth. Due to medical manipulation, humans in Huxley's society are genetically pre-disposed to a certain hierarchical level in life, stripping away any chance at individuality. Likewise, in *The Hunger Games* trilogy, citizens are catego-rized by their districts and usefulness to the Capitol. They are born into their roles with no ability to alter their destinies apart from participation in the Hunger Games. In denying its citizens the ability to develop identities, the ruling authority or government works to constrict individual agency. After all, if individuals cannot form their own identity, then they cannot know themselves, and without that knowledge, they are unable to act intentionally.

Throughout the series, Collins' boy with the bread, Peeta Mellark, stands as the perfect character through which to examine identity and agency. It is Peeta who undergoes the most outward changes as he shifts from one persona to another. Through Peeta, Collins demonstrates the necessity of a solid es-tablishment of identity in the maintenance of one's own agency. When Peeta is confident of his identity, he acts solely based on his own intentions; how-ever, once Peeta loses his sense of self, he also loses his ability to exercise per-sonal agency. Most often, the individual reveals their identity through their relation to another person. Every day, we use lists of identifiers to categorize and understand those around us. Peeta does the same thing in *Mockingjay* as he tries to understand Katniss by attributing to her a list of identifiers: "Ally.... Friend. Lover. Victor. Enemy. Fiancée. Target. Mutt. Neighbor. Hunter. Tribute. Ally. I'll add it to the list of words I use to try to figure you out."[2] In the world of Panem, no one is who they seem to be or, perhaps, they seem to be too many different, conflicting identities all at once. Peeta himself uses the above identifiers to try and understand Katniss without even realizing that these same descriptions depict his own self as well.

Within *Mockingjay*, Peeta is both ally and enemy, friend and lover, tribute and Victor, target and mutt. With so many categories, Peeta's identity seems fluid at best and unstable at worst. When Peeta utters these words, he is in the middle of questioning his own reality with the game of "Real or Not Real." Simultaneously readers and scholars alike question if the real, true Peeta will ever return to Katniss or if he will forever remain this hijacked "mutt" version of his older self. Of course, this begs the question as to who is Peeta Mellark, what is his identity?

To answer the question "Who is Peeta Mellark?" we must first examine his sense of agency that is highly influenced by every persona he undergoes throughout the series: the boy with the bread, the tribute, the Victor, the tribute again, the prisoner/traitor, and the hijacked-mutt. While Peeta cycles through these personas, one important factor remains: his desire to sacrifice himself to save others. Peeta Mellark can be read as a Messianic-type character whose identity is constantly exposed to outside influences as he "dies" thrice throughout the trilogy. Scholars often characterize the Messianic archetype by its sacrificial nature physically, mentally, and emotionally. In fact, Peeta's cycle of life, death, and rebirth in each book within the trilogy further symbolizes his core Messianic identity.

The Boy with the Bread

Peeta Mellark first appears in the trilogy when Effie Trinket calls his name as the male tribute chosen for District 12. Immediately, Collins positions Peeta as a sacrificial character, in this case, a scapegoat to pay for the past rebellious crimes of District 12, crimes that he did not commit. Although Peeta has at least one older brother who could volunteer to take his place as Katniss does for Prim, no one volunteers. Instead, Peeta is sacrificed and abandoned by both his family and his district. Of course, so far this is not a unique identity within the series. Nearly every tribute within the Games is sacrificial at one point or another. The tributes from every district are metaphorical and literal sacrifices offered up to the Capitol who slaughter them for entertainment. However, Peeta's sacrifice is different from others, not in the sense that he chooses to be a tribute like Katniss, but in how he responds to his forced participation in the Games. Almost immediately, Peeta accepts the imminence of his death and focuses his intentions of saving Katniss' life along the way. The reaping does not initiate Peeta's sacrificial nature, it only represents his previously established identity as a Savior character.

This Messianic characteristic of Peeta is palpable long before the Games, most notably seen when Peeta, as a child, proves to be a savior to Katniss in her weakest moment. When only eleven years old, Katniss searches the empty bins of the bakery for food to feed her sister, mother, and herself, when the baker's wife, Mrs. Mellark, appears and screams at Katniss to leave. Unable to go far, Katniss slumps in the mud and rain, remaining there and willing herself to die. It is in that moment that Peeta emerges from the bakery with a large, angry welt forming on his face and two loaves of slightly burned bread in his hands. The image itself is extremely important as it literally paints a Messianic picture of a Savior character who willingly accepts the punishment of others in order to offer salvation. The presence of the bread is another connection to the Messiah, Jesus Christ, who is known for feeding his followers with loaves of bread. Through his bread, Peeta offers Katniss both physical sustenance and symbolic life for her and her family.

This scene, well-known to so many fans, is the purest example of Peeta's identity and the center of his agency. It also emphasizes that Peeta develops his identity as Savior at a very young age and focuses more on the salvation or safety of others than himself. Based on this particular identity, Peeta enacts his agency through helping others. Perhaps that is why the title "boy with the bread" is so revealing. The title strips Peeta of his name, calling him only a boy, and replaces the identifier with what Peeta has to offer: bread—which metaphorically symbolizes life. Usually when a title strips away the name of the individual, scholars consider it a negative action because the individual loses his/her name along with his/her identity. After all, through this title, Peeta becomes the background character, "the boy," who loses his name and is known simply for his abilities and actions, "with the bread." However, there is also power in such a title. The title itself strips away the various images and identifiers of "Peeta" that others construct and reveal that the source of his self-worth always lay in his ability to provide for another.

Now, some readers may view Peeta's actions with the bread as either completely selfish or selfless, or perhaps a mixture of the two. Some might argue that Peeta only helped Katniss because of his long-standing infatuation with her that dates back to the first day of school in which Katniss caught his attention with her rendition of the Valley song. However, as we read through the books, it becomes clear that Peeta aids and supports a multitude of characters including Katniss, but not limited to her. He also acts on behalf of Rue, the female morphling from District 6 in the Quarter Quell, Haymitch, even

Gale, and others. For the sake of the argument, though, let us focus on Peeta's actions with the bread. Perhaps he did throw Katniss the bread because of his crush. However, there still remains the element of sacrifice in his action. Peeta may have loved Katniss enough to throw the bread, but more importantly, he does not expect or demand reciprocation for his feelings or his actions. The day after the incident, Katniss says, "At school, I passed the boy in the hall, his cheek had swelled up and his eye had blackened.... Our eyes met for only a second, then he turned his head away. I dropped my gaze ... that's when I saw it. The first dandelion of the year."[3] Peeta's turn of his wounded head shows how he does not demand recognition from Katniss for his assistance. His actions were not intended to bring about thanks or returned affection, they were simply based on his identity as Savior who loves, gives, receives punishment for his actions, and expects nothing in return. At his center, Peeta cares for others regardless of the cost he pays. This initial establishment of Peeta's identity and agency later proves to be a contrasting point for all additional sub-identities that Peeta is forced to assume over the course of the trilogy which we will now pick apart identity by identity.

Tribute

As previously mentioned, Peeta undergoes a process, life, death, and re-birth in each novel, another attribute of the Messianic archetype, as he cycles through his various sub-identities. He begins as the boy with the bread who is willing to undergo a beating to offer salvation to Katniss. After Effie announces his name for 74th Hunger Games, Peeta must adapt to the new environment and transform into his new identity as "tribute." Collins explores and increases the complexity of Peeta's character through his sub-roles within tribute which include "Charmer," "Lover-boy," "Career," and "Savior." The most appropriate way to define Peeta during his time as tribute is as a chameleon who can change his appearance based on his surroundings. Consider the training center where readers can often find Peeta at the camouflage table "weaving disguises from vines and leaves."[4] Blatantly, Collins portrays Peeta as an artist, capable of manipulating paint to resemble reality.

Likewise, Peeta manipulates how the world of Panem views him, creating his own disguises through which he plays to his audience. In fact, he is so cunning and successful with his various portrayals that at times even Katniss, who is closest to him, does not understand who he truly is. Is he just a charming tribute, capable of waving to the Capitol crowd from the train and making them laugh during his interview? Is he a star-crossed lover, determined to rescue the love of his life? Or is he a Career tribute, a betrayer like Judas? He is all and yet none of the above identities. Again, Peeta's primary and focal identity is that of a Savior. However, Peeta cycles through these roles, or sub-identities, as each individual situation requires. Tribute, lover-boy, Career, these are only personas that Peeta "puts on," so to speak, to shield his true identity and desires while allowing him to act as he sees fit. Just as Peeta manipulates the paint in the Training Center, Peeta camouflages his identity in order to enact agency.

Ultimately, every persona that Peeta displays he uses to protect Katniss. Consider Peeta's actions before the Games: charming the crowds, gaining Haymitch's assistance, holding hands with Katniss during the chariot ride, and even his confession of love during the interview with Caesar. Peeta admits that he has no chance at winning, so why does he try so hard to earn every advantage? In every instance, Peeta is working to elevate Katniss' odds of survival, not his own. Understanding the importance of perception and knowing how to manipulate it far better than Katniss, Peeta knows that ultimately within the Games the crowd holds the power. Therefore, he appeals to the crowds of the Capitol and acts in whichever way that the crowds desire. He plays the strong, charming, star-struck tribute because it will enable him to succeed in saving Katniss. Already, we can see the direct correlation between Peeta's identities and actions. Even when pretending to be a part of the Career Pack, Peeta's desire to protect Katniss propels his every move which in turn determines which identity he displays. However, underneath every role he assumes, his identity as Savior forms his intentions to protect Katniss— creating a never-ending cycle between Peeta's sense of self and his agency.

Consequently, portraying so many differing forms of oneself can often lead to a crisis of the self. This is seen in Peeta's greatest fear, not dying within the Games, but rather, losing the ability to know and remain who he is. On the rooftop of the Training Center, Peeta says, "I want to die as myself.... Does that make any sense.... I don't want them to change me in there. Turn me into some kind of monster that I'm not."[5] Interestingly, Peeta knows all too well how good people can become corrupted by fear, anger, and hate. Peeta's awareness is most likely the result of his family home experiences. Peeta is often portrayed as distant from his family due to his mother's physical and verbal abuse and his father's inability to act on his son's behalf. No doubt, both Mr. and Mrs. Mellark's personalities were affected by their society and built by living in constant fear of the Capitol. The way in which they react to their environment and allow it to affect their identities provides first-hand cautionary experience for Peeta who fears how outside power can twist an individual's identity.

Aware of the inherent dangers that accompany the Games, not just the physical dangers, Peeta desires above all else to remain true to his previously established sense of self as Savior. Long before Katniss is aware of the connection between identity and agency, Peeta recognizes how easy it is for that connection to become corrupted. Consider Peeta's phrasing, "to show the Capitol they don't own me. That I'm more than just a piece in their Games."[6] In associating himself with a Game-piece, Peeta suggests the imagery of a board game such as chess in which the Capitol is the player who moves the pieces accordingly. Peeta understands that according to the Capitol, he is only a pawn, a tribute in their Games. While Peeta cannot decide whether to be in the game, he can decide how he is used. If he must be a piece, he would rather choose his own role and be the knight, willingly sacrificing himself to save his queen, Katniss.

Between Peeta's sly actions as a Career Tribute and his genuine portrayal of a boy in love, both Katniss and readers question the identity of Peeta Mellark. Nevertheless, there are obvious instances even within the brutal Games where Peeta demonstrates his Messianic characteristics. For instance, consider Peeta Mellark's weapon of choice. Although he carries a spear, a more defensive weapon when compared to Katniss' offensive bow and arrow that can kill her enemy from further distances, Peeta's strongest weapon is his ability to camouflage himself. He rarely takes the offensive and when he does, such as when fighting Cato, it is not on behalf of himself, but of another. Peeta is most violent when protecting Katniss, such as when fighting Cato once again on the top of the Cornucopia. In fact, when it comes to protecting himself over another, particularly one whom he loves, Peeta immediately accepts the necessity of violence and the reality of death.

After Cato's death at Katniss' hands, Peeta sheds his momentarily violent persona and returns to his initial identity as Savior. When told that only one tribute may survive, Peeta's first instinct directs him to toss his knife into the lake even as Katniss aims her bow at his heart. Again, Peeta displays his agency through sacrificial actions in which he easily forfeits his life for another. If readers still need convincing of Peeta's inherent identity, they would need to turn only a few pages more. True to his Messianic archetype, Peeta does indeed die for those he loves. At the end of the 74th Hunger Games, Peeta rips off the tourniquet that stops him from bleeding to death and quickly loses blood in his attempt to force Katniss to accept the title of Victor. Although the Capitol rescues both Katniss and Peeta from the arena, Peeta's actions cause enough damage that "his heart stops twice" while on the operating table.[7] Even though the doctors are able to resuscitate Peeta, the fact remains that his heart stops twice and he is, at least momentarily, dead.

This "death" is extremely important for multiple reasons. First, it firmly realigns Peeta with the Messianic archetype as his death and rebirth echoes Christ's willingness to die for another, having done no wrong himself, and rising from the grave after death. Second, Peeta's death affects his identity as he is "reborn" missing a limb—his leg, the blood flow cut off by the tourniquet that was left on for too long. This first death begins the dismantling of Peeta's physicality which later leads into the disassembly of his mentality. Lastly, the death marks a transition to yet another identifier. When Peeta dies, he dies as a tribute in the 74th Hunger Games. However, when he is reborn, he emerges into a new role as Victor of the 74th Hunger Games.

Disobedient Victor

Days after the events of the 74th Hunger Games, the Capitol patches up Peeta as best they can with a new prosthetic leg and re-introduce him to the nation of Panem no longer a tribute, no longer just a boy in love, but as a Victor with all the rights, fame, and wealth that accompanies the title. They dress him in the best clothing, give him the best food, and return him to District 12 to live a new life of luxury. In return for such generosity, the Capitol expects that Peeta will conform to societal rules, be thankful, and be obedient. However, Collins creates characters that are overwhelmingly disobedient, seen in this instance by Peeta who rejects conformity when it restricts his own identity as Savior. As a Victor, Peeta has the option to live a life of ease, but only if he keeps his head down and lives according to the Capitol's plans. However, Peeta repeatedly places himself in their crosshairs with his paintings, his words, and his actions.

Painting, an outpouring of emotions, often reflects the inner psyche of the artist and the artist's desires. Peeta plays the role of Victor well with his talent of painting—a hobby reserved only for the very rich. Indeed, on the Victory tour, Peeta has train cars brimming with canvases that reflect his talent and the amount of leisure time he now possesses. On the surface, Peeta portrays exactly what the Capitol expects from a Victor, someone with too much money and too much time. However, just as within the first novel, Collins' incorporates Peeta's artistic ability to demonstrate his versatility and an unexpected confrontational nature. Though a Victor's talent is meant to display the luxurious life of a Victor, Peeta uses his talent to focus on the inhumanity of the Games by forcing its viewers to relive the Games not through a screen, but through Peeta's own eyes. What the Capitol intends for one thing, Peeta uses for his own agenda.

In today's twenty-first century, hundreds of thousands of artists use their talents to protest anything and everything ranging from social unrest to political reform. In the same way, Peeta uses his art that is, in a sense, commissioned by the Capitol to shove the reality of the Games back into the public's face. In *Catching Fire*, Peeta paints "the Games. Some you wouldn't get right away, if you hadn't been with him in the arena yourself.... Others any viewer would recognize."[8] Katniss describes the paintings as "extraordinary," and yet she hates them and can hardly stand to look at them because of their authenticity in representing the reality of the Games.[9] Instead of using his talent to promote the goodness of the Capitol or to show his gratitude, Peeta paints the Games in excruciatingly realistic and brutal detail. As any good protest art should, Peeta's paintings hurt to look at. They confront the life and death aspects of the Games by forcing viewers to take another glance at the Games now that nearly all the children involved are dead. This initial grouping of paintings is only a sampling of how Peeta later uses his art to directly confront the Gamemakers with the image of Rue adorned in flowers. While Peeta is supposed to be displaying his skills to the Gamemakers, he chooses to paint a picture that will hold his captors accountable for one little innocent girl's death. Through art, Peeta continues to connect with the Messianic archetype as someone who is unafraid to confront the social norm so as to hold to a higher moral standard.

Peeta maintains his core identity not only through art, but also through words. During the Victory Tour, Peeta and Katniss make their first stop at District 11, the home of Rue and Thresh. There Peeta announces, "It can in no way replace your losses, but as a token of our thanks we'd like for each of the tributes' families from District Eleven to receive one month of our winnings every year for the duration of our lives."[10] Through his words, Peeta does what no other Victor has done before: he rejects the "generosity" of the Capitol by giving away his "winnings" to the losers' families, and unites two separate districts through this action. When Peeta speaks of the fallen tributes, he does not speak of them as insignificant playing pieces within the Capitol's game, but refers to them as human beings with families, worth, and importance of their own. Having never seen this done before, Katniss thinks, "There is no precedent for what Peeta has done. I don't even know if it's legal. He probably doesn't know either, so he didn't ask in case it isn't."[11] Once again, although the Capitol expects Peeta to act appropriately as their Victor, Peeta denies their classification and remains true to his identity as Savior by transforming the role of Victor. Just as he once appealed to the crowds of the Capitol, Peeta manipulates the social power given to him by the Capitol to circumvent their lines and hold them accountable for what he said while on air. In this case, he saves the families of his "enemies" by offerings his winnings that can provide for them every year. In enacting his own desires, Peeta maintains not only his own identity but also a strong sense of agency that exists contrary to what the ruling authority expects of him.

It is necessary to note that Peeta's identity as Savior shines through all his sub-identities and various roles during both times of peace and times of war. Peeta does not only speak out against injustice when he believes himself to be safe as a Victor, but also when he knows he is marked for death. After the Victory Tour, having dissatisfied President Snow with their performance, Peeta and Katniss return to District 12 to find the consequences of their failure. One of the most damaging responses of the Capitol is the installment of a new Peacekeeper, Thread, who breaks in his reign of terror with Gale's brutal whipping. At the sound of the whip, Peeta is the one who reacts first, "his face suddenly hard."[12] Unlike Katniss who cannot place the sound, Peeta immediately understands what it is. V. Arrow, author of *The Panem Companion*,[13] makes an interesting point in this moment, arguing that Peeta recognizes the sound due to his own abuse as a child in his own home.[14]

Assuming this to be true makes it both surprising and unsurprising that only a moment later, Peeta steps in front of both Katniss and Gale. If Mrs. Mellark used a similar tool on Peeta as a child, Peeta should fear the sound of a whip and strive to escape it. However, his identity as Savior propels his actions to protect others regardless of the consequences. With Haymitch, Peeta forms a barrier, willing to take the next swing of the whip. Like his childhood in which he took blows from his mother in order to give Katniss the bread, Peeta returns to his Messianic pose in front of Katniss and Gale with outstretched arms willing to take their punishment upon himself. Although Peeta is known throughout Panem as the Victor of the 74th Hunger Games, he rejects that identity in favor of his own. In every instance through which the Capitol demands obedience and submission, Peeta confidently exerts his own agency.

Tribute Again

Although Peeta is rebirthed from his first death during the Games as a Victor, he does not remain in that sub-identity for long. Due to the Quarter Quell, and some meddling on President Snow's part, no doubt, Peeta must return to the arena as a Victor-Tribute. The Games, whether the 74th Hunger Games or the Quarter Quell, continue to test Peeta in the most direct way by targeting his identity as Savior. After all, how can one person be both a Savior and a cold-blooded murderer?

Only days before the main events of the Quell, Peeta admits to Katniss that President Snow has most likely assured their deaths in the arena. However, even if he has, Peeta argues, "everyone will know we've gone out fighting."[15] While Katniss interprets this statement to mean that they will go out physically rebelling against the Capitol until death, there is another possible interpretation that Collins may have intended. Peeta plans to go out fighting in various forms: fighting to save Katniss, and more importantly, fighting to die as himself and planning to sacrifice his life along the way. Here, Peeta echoes his initial desire displayed before the 74th Hunger Games—the desire to be more than just a pawn in someone else's game. If he must play, he will play by his own rules. Readers see this in the way that Peeta forms allies instead of focusing on killing his enemies. While preparing for the Quarter Quell, Peeta is friendly with many of the other districts' tributes as he attempts to form alliances. Even within the arena itself, Katniss notes, "Peeta would at least have attempted negotiations first [before killing]. Seen if some wider alliance was possible."[16] While Katniss views Peeta's "friendliness" as problematic to their survival, Peeta distinctly separates himself from every other Victor, even Katniss, in his hesitation to kill. It is this hesitation that further connects Peeta to his identity as Messiah. Indeed, Collins portrays Peeta's fight not as a physical battle but rather as a mental struggle to remain true to his sense of self, unbroken by the Capitol's desires and devices.

Collins further demonstrates Peeta's sense of identity within the Games more particularly through his second "death." Having hit the electric force field that surrounds the arena, Peeta is electrocuted. Similar to what happened at the end of the 74th Hunger Games, Peeta's heart stops for several minutes. Collins crafts this scene for multiple narrative reasons: to expose the existence of the force field which will become important later on and to slow down Peeta's ability to run from the poisonous fog. However, this scene also has implications that are more important for our study of agency and identity. This scene returns Peeta to his sacrificial identity. Although he is not sacrificing himself for someone else in this scene, Peeta's death and rebirth allude to the Messianic figure. Additionally, Peeta figuratively "dies" on the very first day of the Quarter Quell as a Victor and is reborn back into his previous status as Tribute, highlighting the fact that the Capitol has stripped away his Victor status and protection.

In each of the arenas, Collins only attributes three possible deaths to Peeta's actions: the female tribute from District 8 and Foxface in the first arena, and Brutus in the Quarter Quell. In the 74th Hunger Games, readers are left to decide for themselves whether Peeta directly killed the unlucky female tribute from District 8 who lit a fire of the first night of the Games. Clearly, Cato wounded her badly enough that he thought she was dead. When Peeta supposedly went back to finish the job, there is no way of knowing whether the girl succumbed to Cato's wounds while Peeta stayed by her side, or if Peeta hurried her death along so that she would no longer be in pain. Either way, with what readers know of each boy, it is most likely that Cato's wound was fatal and Peeta was simply kind enough to stay with her as she died—just as he later does for the female morphling from District 6 in the Quarter Quell. As for Foxface, although her death is attributed to Peeta, Katniss and readers alike know that is was accidental coincidence that killed Foxface. During his time as both tribute and Victor, Peeta's hands are relatively clean of blood, supporting his Messianic character.

However, Collins forces Peeta to confront his relatively passive stance during the climax of the 3rd Quarter Quell. As all hell breaks loose within the arena, Peeta engages in a conflict between himself, his friend Chaff, and his enemy Brutus. Peeta later claims that "everything just went insane" as he watches Brutus kill Chaff before Peeta himself kills Brutus.[17] Out of the three tributes that the Capitol attributes to Peeta's kill list, Peeta only ever truly and intentionally kills one. As Katniss is the narrator of the story, readers do not see this scene first hand and can only take Peeta's word for what happened. However, this scene is crucial in the discussion of Peeta's identity and his agency as up until this point, Peeta pursued two primary objectives: to keep Katniss safe and to remain true to himself. Peeta's actions of killing Brutus, possibly in self-defense or in retaliation for Chaff's death, fracture his identity as Savior. Yet, does it negate his agency? Some might say yes. After all, it is during his time in the Capitol after the Quarter Quell while being held captive that many rebels call Peeta a traitor, perhaps even to himself.

Prisoner/Traitor

In *Mockingjay*, readers are privy to the intimate effects of war and trauma on Katniss' agency in excruciating detail. However, for the first half of the novel, readers only have access to Peeta through his appearances on live Capitol television. When he first appears, seemingly healthy enough, Peeta calls for a ceasefire, inciting hate from the rebels and ironically prompting Katniss to accept her role as Mockingjay. Previously, Peeta formed his identity and exercised his agency through his paintings and his words, by confronting social expectations and offering aid to the families of the tributes. However, during his imprisonment, Peeta seems to have turned against everything he once stood for and allows the Capitol to use him as a ventriloquist puppet through which they promote their own propaganda. When Peeta calls for a ceasefire, he seems to surrender the control of his own actions over to the Capitol for the sake of his survival.

However, it may well be Peeta's words that once again reveal the damaged spirit still fighting to reclaim his Messianic identity within. While Peeta concedes to putting forth the idea of a ceasefire in return for Katniss' immunity, he still weaves his own opinions into the narrative. Peeta confesses to his murder of Brutus to the entire nation of Panem, saying, "In the arena you only get one wish. And it's very costly…. It costs a lot more than your life. To murder innocent people…. It costs everything you are."[18] Against the Capitol's wishes no doubt, Peeta puts forth this incredibly important phrase: "innocent people." Even within his chains, Peeta holds the Capitol accountable for the part they play in the crimes committed in the arena by referring to the Victors, to killers, as innocent people.

Peeta does not view the other tributes as playing pieces, but instead he highlights their humanity and individuality. Peeta does indeed murder one of the most dislikable Career-Victors, Brutus, and yet, Peeta still refers to him as an innocent. Even though Brutus volunteered to go back into the Games, Peeta does not lay the blame at his feet entirely, but rather the system that created such a man. As the Messianic archetype, Peeta sees Brutus for what he is: a lost soul twisted by the Capitol's control. Instead of defending his actions, Peeta admits to the cost or the consequences of such actions. By murdering an "innocent," Peeta acknowledges the crack in his own identity as Savior as he took a life for his own survival. The connection between identity and agency demands constant vigilance and as the Capitol mentally breaks Peeta, his grasp on his identity wavers and his agency follows in the same downward pattern.

Regardless of Peeta's words, his third broadcast from the Capitol illustrates Peeta's losing battle with maintaining his identity as Savior as he struggles to act due to his instability in deciding how he desires to act. Readers later learn that beyond physical torture, Peeta also undergoes mental torture through hijacking—a process that directly targets his memories and his identity by twisting his experiences and distorting reality. In the last broadcast, Peeta physically struggles with finding the words to warn District 13 about the imminent bombing. While Peeta, the Savior, wants to warn District 13, Peeta, the hijacked Mutt, does not see the reason why he should threaten his own safety for others. The physical contortions of his face and body betray his inner conflict as Peeta struggles to maintain his hold of reality and his identity as Savior. During his last seconds on air, Peeta warns about the bombing, saving thousands of lives while endangering his own simultaneously. This is the last moment when readers see Peeta as his true self, hearing "the impact of the blow that's inseparable from Peeta's cry of pain. And his blood as it splatters the tiles."[19]

Beatings and blood are familiar occurrences for the Messianic archetype; therefore, it is no surprise that Peeta's blood should cover the floor much like a sacrificial lamb's blood is spilled over an altar one last time before readers witness fully-hijacked Peeta. This blow from President Snow echoes that of Peeta's first blow from his mother when he burned the bread to save Katniss' life. These blows and the subsequent presence of blood repeatedly demonstrate his willingness to accept pain to save another the same or worse agony. This quick moment connects the very first known instance of Peeta's sacrificial nature to his very last before President Snow corrupts his mind and, with it, his identity.

Hijacked

From the very onset of the trilogy, Peeta embodies the Messianic archetype as both sacrifice and Savior. In the first two books, he physically dies twice for several minutes and is then reborn, maintaining his primary identity while portraying a myriad of roles. However, the death that he undergoes in the third novel differs from the previous deaths in two ways: it is a metaphorical death rather than a literal one and Peeta is seemingly reborn lacking his primary identity as Savior. In *Mockingjay*, Peeta's sense of self dies at the hands of the Capitol during his hijacking. The torture strips him of his sense of self, and although the rebels later rescue Peeta, he is no longer the same boy who fed Katniss as children. Before the torture, Peeta had an appreciation for life that often shone through his paintings, his love for others (particularly Katniss), and an innate sacrificial, pacifistic, and kind spirit. However, upon waking in District 13, Peeta is extremely violent towards others (specifically Katniss) and unable to function at a base level. Indeed, from this point forward, Peeta exists in a type of limbo between two identities: his former identity as Savior and his mutated identity as hijacked-mutt.

Until this point, Peeta's identity remained consistent regardless of the roles or personas he adopted. Whether a boy with the bread, a lover boy, a tribute, a Victor, or any other identifier that others placed upon him, Peeta remained Peeta at his core. However, various scholars see Peeta's character in *Mockingjay* as more than challenging. In fact, Nicolas Michaud, a fellow fan and scholar of *The Hunger Games*, describes Peeta as "the problem of identity in Panem."[20] Michaud's discussion of Peeta and his identity spans pages through which Michaud proposes and analyzes various hypothetical situations as he tries to understand what determines Peeta's agency. Is it body, mind, memories, or DNA that determines a person's identity? With every hypothesis, Michaud's conclusions are vague and even he offers, "Maybe there never was an *I* in the first place, just a being who constantly passes away and is replaced by a new being, carrying with it recollections—some fairly accurate, others way off the mark—of what all the previous, now dead persons thought and felt."[21] In other words, according to this train of thought, as Peeta dies and is reborn into these varying roles, his identity continuously morphs and changes, holding on to small bits of his past while losing some at the same time. Aligned with Michaud's hypothesis, after his last metaphorical death to hijacking, Peeta is definitively different and set apart from the original Peeta in the first novel. However, this understanding that there is no solid identity is tested by the fact that throughout the trilogy, Peeta does indeed cling to and promote the consistent image of a Savior.

Although the Capitol-induced hijacking does corrupt Peeta's identity, his former self remains even if only minutely. Indeed, there are moments when his core self attempts to break through the haze of his hijacking displaying the importance that identity has on one's own actions. Only days after his rescue, District 13 sends in Delly Cartwright to hopefully appeal to the old Peeta. Although he cannot remember his past clearly, he vaguely remembers chalk drawings on pavement that included "pigs and cats and things."[22] Is it coincidental that Peeta remembers pigs and cats? Maybe. Or could it possibly be his inner consciousness attempting to reclaim one of his most important memories wherein he fed the burnt bread to Katniss instead of the pigs? Or even consider the frosted cake at Finnick and Annie's wedding, the cake that makes Haymitch think Peeta might become himself again. It is important that Peeta recollects and heals through his creative abilities. Whitney Jones, a fellow scholar of the series, considers Peeta the artist as a "role that links him with the more feminine act of creation."[23] However, another reading can connect Peeta's "creating role" to that of the ultimate Creator from the Christian faith. In other words, Peeta remembers himself as a Creator, linking his identity not only to his artistic abilities but to the Messianic archetype as well.

Of course, for every example of Peeta's goodness or his desire to reclaim memories, there are two more examples of his anger and his "un–Peeta-ness." However, underneath his cruel and biting words, the facts stay the same that Peeta, the true Peeta, remains somewhere inside underneath all the hate, confusion, and anger. If indeed the true Peeta endures the psychological torture, it is only further proof that while identity may appear to transform on the outside it stays consistent on the inside. The possible allusion to Katniss and the artistic expression of life and love gently remind readers that Peeta is still in there with Messianic tendencies: the desire to create instead of destroy. Peeta's "deaths" have constantly changed and challenged his identity as Michaud suggests, but they do not necessarily erase it.

While Peeta is manipulated by both President Snow and President Coin, it is his response to their hijacking that represents the lowest moment of his agency. In sending Peeta to the battlefield where he is likely to be overstimulated and enraged by the surrounding violence, President Coin hopes to rid herself of the Mockingjay problem. Both President Snow and President Coin, compared by other scholars as being two heads of one coin, attempt to use Peeta, opposite to his nature, by turning him into a weapon and they are both successful to some degree. After all, Peeta does strangle Katniss after being "rescued" by District 13 and while in the Capitol with the Star Squad, Peeta accidentally kills Mitchell after going temporarily insane. These scenes seem to represent the most non–Peeta moments within the series and while they are undeniably unlike Peeta, it is the scene that comes upon Peeta's awakening after killing Mitchell that represents rock bottom for Peeta's identity.

In a moment of pure clarity, watching himself killing Mitchell on the television screen, Peeta realizes that he has become the mutt programmed to hurt those around him. He understands that the change in the world around him was not caused by others but due to the changes within himself. Peeta sees that he has lost his identity and everything that made him Peeta, made him a Savior, and it breaks him. Before the very first Games, Peeta's one spoken wish was that the Capitol would not "turn [him] into some kind of monster that [he's] not."[24] His greatest fear, losing his identity, became his dreaded reality. Having lost this identity, Peeta forfeits his agency as displayed by his inability to control his own actions. Consequently, agency it would seem is only achievable when based on a strong sense of self. Afraid of his actions, due to his inability to establish his identity, Peeta wants nothing more than the desire to never act again and begs the others to kill him and to end his suffering caused by guilt.

While this seems like the sacrificial actions of a Messianic character, Peeta's intentions tarnish the offer. The problem lies in his words, "I don't care if I die…. Don't you see, I want to be out of this?"[25] It is not his love for others that prompts his suicidal desires, but rather it is his own self-hatred and his own need for escape. Like Katniss' own suicidal attempts later, intentions behind the act matter in determining agency. In this case, Peeta's request cannot be any further from his original identity. The Peeta pre-hijacking would have done anything, gone anywhere, to protect others. This desire for death—having already "died" three times and come back—demonstrates how far he falls from his position as Savior over the course of the narrative. If Katniss had allowed Peeta to die here, then perhaps Michaud would be right. Perhaps Peeta's identity would be nothing more than identifiers that change through the shifting winds.

Mutated Identity

And yet, Collins does not allow Peeta's hate-fueled sacrifice to occur. Instead, Katniss forces Peeta to continue and to keep fighting, much like Peeta later does for Katniss' sake. Due to Katniss' faith in Peeta, Peeta survives the war and has a chance to regain his lost identity. He even survives the bombing that kills Prim and wounds Katniss, along with himself. Scarred by the fire, Peeta becomes a fire mutt and remains a mutated version of himself for the remainder of the trilogy, never quite returning wholly to the boy with the bread. Nevertheless, this is not a negative thing. The scars reflect that Peeta's identity was tested by fire and that he has been reborn, once again, this time through flames.

After the bombing, Peeta seems more like his previous self, particularly in his actions. When asked by President Coin to the meeting of the last Victors in which every Victor must vote "yes" or "no" to holding a final Hunger Games using the children of the Capitol, Peeta responds, "I vote no, of course! We can't have another Hunger Games…. This is why we rebelled! Remember?"[26] Although some Victors see it as justice or revenge, Peeta sees it as murder. Additionally, Peeta's actions are once again clear, unclouded by outside influences. Peeta returns to his initial perspective of the killing of innocents, even though he has more than enough reasons to crave revenge. Instead, Peeta promotes peace and forgiveness.

Even Peeta's last actions within the Capitol validate his return to the Messianic archetype. Traumatized, dismayed, and aware of Coin's treachery, Katniss murders President Coin and then attempts suicide. However, when she turns her head to bite into the nightlock pill on her suit, Katniss' "teeth sink into flesh" and "blood runs from the teeth marks on [Peeta's] hand."[27] Is it any surprise at this point that Peeta's actions result in the shedding of his blood and his pain? The pages of this trilogy are painted in blood, specifically in Peeta's blood as his agency is born from his desire to help others.

Although Peeta Mellark eventually returns home to District 12 and marries Katniss Everdeen, even having the children he so desperately wanted, Peeta is never the same Peeta from the first book. He remains a mutated version of his old self who "clutches the back of a chair and hangs on until the flashbacks are over"[28] and who must sometimes question the reality of his surroundings with the game of "Real or Not Real?" After finishing the trilogy, readers must admit that, yes, Peeta is different than the boy who was reaped in District 12, but after everything, Peeta remains Peeta. By the end of the trilogy he reclaims his primary identity as Savior and provides "the dandelion in the spring. The bright yellow that means rebirth instead of destruction."[29]

Real or Not Real?

So who is Peeta Mellark really and why should we as readers care? Is he a tribute, an ally, an enemy, a lover, a mutt? All of the above and so much more. Peeta's character encompasses a range of identifiers that all lead back to his critical role as Savior. Whether that is through taking a blow to give Katniss bread, painting Rue's image to hold the Gamemakers accountable, or voting no in the last meeting of the Victors, Peeta's sacrificial identity shines through his words and actions. Indeed, through Peeta's character, Collins establishes a direct correlation between identity and agency. If Peeta had not identified as Savior, his actions would have reflected as such. Yet Peeta's actions are fueled by his desires constructed by his identity. As seen through this narrative, identity is something that can evolve, but never truly change. At the center, identity is the firm foundation on which agency is established.

While Peeta is not the main protagonist of this trilogy, he is an important character used by Collins to accompany and guide Katniss' own journey of agency. As is expected of the Messianic archetype, Peeta is meant to lead Katniss to some sort of salvation. Initially, Peeta does this physically by providing the bread that keeps her alive. Later, Peeta provides moral guidance and emotional support that eases her soul. However, it is Peeta's example of agency and his words that truly lead Katniss to a kind of salvation found in her ability to enact agency. Peeta is the first to bring up the connection between identity and agency to Katniss and he is the only one who provides a moral compass. Furthermore, Katniss finds healing through Peeta when they both return to District 12. His character is a constant source of encouragement and a reminder to Katniss, and readers, of how identity and agency intertwine.

More importantly, Peeta's character works to address our own questions about identity. Who are we? Is our identity based in our gender? Our occupation? Our location? Is it based on our birth? Or, is it based solely on our actions? From the above discussion, it would seem clear that identity is determined by action formed by choice and desire; in other words, identity is displayed through agency. To discover who we really are, we must take a hard look at our words and actions. In the end, if one's actions are to truly be one's own, the individual must have a strong understanding of who he/she is. Peeta Mellark's Messianic character should encourage readers to establish their own identity or perhaps to take a good look at their actions in order to determine who they truly are and what they really want. Then, when asked if their agency is real or not real, they will be able to answer, "Real."

FIVE

"Bring on the avalanches"

Agency and Power

In traditional dystopia, power struggles are a constant concern within scholarship. Who holds the power and what types of power does the ruling authority exercise over its citizens? Customarily, when scholars explore power in dystopia, they often apply their discussion to the whole of society. However, in this chapter, we will examine personal power struggles and witness how the overabundance of social power can actually negate personal agency as seen through our in-depth examination of Gale Hawthorne. Within *The Hunger Games* trilogy, power is constantly gained, transferred, and lost by individuals who strive for the ability to act despite the oppression of the ruling authority. While Capitol citizens struggle to maintain their relevance among their peers through fashion, those in the districts struggle to simply survive. Whether in the Capitol or in the Districts, most individuals lack true power to affect any sort of change over their own lives and even less so over their society. The only power inherent to all individuals is the power they have over their own actions and that too is limited.

Within the larger power struggle between the Capitol and the rebellion, the decisions made by the individual based on past desires and present intentions test personal agency, especially when those who were without power suddenly obtain it. Throughout the narrative, personal agencies tend to become corrupted when based solely on newfound chances for the individual to challenge the oppressive government. As characters gain such opportunities and grow in social power, they often forgo moral judgments as they work for the greater good. Gale Hawthorne—a nobody from District 12—is such a character who, when he finds himself with the ability to influence others, does not hesitate to think of the cost of such power most clearly seen through his actions in *Mockingjay*.

In the midst of a heated and seemingly pointless war strategy in which the rebels attempt to breach the Capitol stronghold known as "the Nut," Gale offers a suggestion that momentarily silences all other opinions: initiate an avalanche to kill thousands. When Katniss attempts to reason with him, reminding him of the rebel-spies within the mountain who would also die, Gale replies, "If I were a spy in there, I'd say 'Bring on the avalanches!'"[1] The avalanche, formulated by Gale and carried out by the rebels, leaving nothing but destruction and pain in its path is a clear metaphorical representation of the effect that power has on Gale's agency. At the beginning of an avalanche only a few rocks crumple, just pebbles really, alerting those nearby of the incoming danger. However, as the avalanche advances, it gains momentum and accelerates rapidly, obliterating every familiar path until it finally settles like concrete, often suffocating those caught unaware within the debris.

Gale, a Seam-born coal miner from the poorest District with little to no authority, is promoted through the ranks of District 13 until he is intimately connected to the inner workings of the rebellion. Throughout the concluding novel, Gale, with his new-found influence and power, quickly shoves aside all moral quandaries and focuses only on winning the war, regardless of the costs. Sir John Dalberg-Acton, an English Catholic historian, politician, and writer during the mid–1800s, penned the famous phrase "Power tends to corrupt and absolute power corrupts absolutely."[2] Indeed, as Gale grows in power, he strays from his original establishment of agency and allows negative emotions, supported by his desire for control, to blind his eyes and corrupt his actions. The power that Gale accumulates, like an avalanche, eventually grows in size and out of control until it destroys Gale's moral decision capabilities and, with it, his agency.

Crumbling Pebbles

Very few scholars who have written about *The Hunger Games* series ever discuss Gale Hawthorne in depth. Some may mention Gale in passing when discussing Katniss or they may dissect the Peeta-Katniss-Gale love triangle, but few academics analyze Gale's character apart from the others. Perhaps this is because he is the only character of the major three who fades into obscurity at the end of the trilogy, metaphorically banished to District 2. Why do scholars tend to skip over his existence except for how he relates to Katniss? Is it that there is nothing to say, or is it perhaps that we may not like what we discover? After all, Katniss practically charges Gale with Prim's murder at the end of the trilogy after his new-found power taints his actions and desires. Gale's character begs an analysis of the effect that power has on agency, especially when the individual pursues such power. To examine this effect, it is first necessary to look at how Gale's agency evolves over the course of the trilogy.

Gale primarily acts for others when they have something to offer in return, illustrating how his agency is based on a scale of personal power. Although Gale is only fourteen years old when his father dies, his immediate response is to find a way to provide for his family—his siblings become his children and his mother transforms into a co-parent. Gale's actions, risking punishment or even death by venturing into the woods and the black market known as the Hob, reflect his love for his family and his desire to protect them. The motivation behind Gale's actions is different than those displayed by Katniss and Peeta. Katniss extends her protection to encompass all the innocent and the helpless.[3] Peeta offers his friendship to nearly anyone due to his Christ-like, sacrificial nature.[4] Contrarily, Gale's protection comes at a cost. Gale shields and cares for his family because of their blood relation to him. They love him and in return he physically provides. Gale's love for Katniss, which develops years after their hunting partnership, originates from her hunting abilities. When Gale and Katniss first meet, Gale only offers to teach Katniss how to set snares if she gives him a bow in return. Once realizing that Katniss has something to offer, "he agree[s] something might be worked out … [and they] grudging began to share [their] knowledge, [their] weapons, [their] secret places."[5] Unlike Peeta's, Gale's relationship with Katniss begins not from generosity but from a reciprocal understanding of mutual benefit, based on an equal distribution of power.

This is not to say that Gale only acts when it benefits him. He later repeatedly protects Katniss at personal risk, particularly during the rebellion. However, Gale almost always initiates his relationships based on a reciprocal, transactional system. This could be due, in part, to the power that such a reciprocal relationship affords him. In these relationships, Gale's position is one of provider and/or teacher, giving him a sense of power and authority over others. Due to the joint nature of such relationships, power exists between both partners as Gale's siblings return his actions with love and adoration while Katniss shares her knowledge and weapons. In such relationships, based on the equal distribution of power, Gale's agency flourishes as his desires are played out through action.

However, even within the first novel, Collins hints at Gale's instability and anger concerning the power struggles within Panem, suggesting that Gale is not satisfied with the power he possesses. Gale's temper seethes beneath the surface, particularly concerning his own powerlessness, even between citizens within his own district. Only hours before the reaping of the 74th Hunger Games, Gale and Katniss sell strawberries to Madge, the mayor's daughter, who wears an expensive dress, an elaborate hair style, and a golden Mockingjay pin. Gale immediately fixates on Madge's extravagant appearance, specifically the pin which was "real gold. Beautifully crafted [and] could keep a family in bread for months."[6] When Madge suggests that she is dressed thus to prepare in case she is called as a tribute, Gale mocks her, "What can you have? Five entries? I had six when I was just twelve years old."[7] Even though Gale knows that the tesserae system is not Madge's fault, Madge's presence is an obvious reminder of Gale's own powerlessness as a Seam-born citizen.

Even within the poorest district of Panem, there is still the division of power between the upper and lower classes. Born into the Seam, the lowest class of the poorest district, Gale lacks any status or power in his society. The only power he has is in the woods. Due to his inherited position of poverty, Gale's options are limited. Regardless of how hard or how long he hunts, he still struggles to provide enough food for his family and must take out extra tesserae, furthering his odds that he will have to leave his family to compete in the Games. Meanwhile, people like Madge wear gold just for the sake of appearances. Furthermore, Gale's extra entries as a child show his forced surrender to the Capitol's system due to his own inability to provide for his family otherwise. While Gale does not hate Madge, he hates that she reflects his own impotence to stand against the Capitol's reign. The way in which Gale responds to those with more power than him demonstrates his own unhappiness and desire for social power—power that is exercised over and affects one's society.

In the same way that Madge reflects Gale's helplessness, so too does Peeta. While Gale is obviously jealous of Peeta after the Games, his attitude often borders on hate instead of dislike. This could be due to the fact that Peeta can protect Katniss in ways that Gale cannot. Even before they enter the arena, Peeta increases Katniss' odds of survival by manipulating the audience's emotions and gaining their favor for Katniss and himself. In the arena, Peeta physically protects Katniss, most notably from Cato when he returns to kill Katniss for dropping the tracker jacker nest. Meanwhile, too poor to even sponsor her, Gale can only watch Katniss on a screen and hope for her survival. Furthermore, after the arena, Peeta can connect with and emotionally provide for Katniss in ways that Gale cannot due to the shared trauma between Peeta and Katniss. It is Peeta who cares for Katniss during her nightmares while Gale encourages her to spark a revolution. Peeta's strength and ability to protect and provide unintentionally undermine Gale's value and place in Katniss' life. For this reason, and also due to jealousy, Gale is unable to accept or form a friendship with Peeta regardless of the fact that in a tit-for-tat system, Gale owes Peeta for saving Katniss' life.

Initially, Gale's desires to protect and provide for those in which he engages in a reciprocal relationship with motivate his every action. Gale exercises agency that is beneficial not only for himself, but for those around him. He forms his relationships based on reciprocal and equal exchanges of power between participants. However, even before the events of *Mockingjay* fall into place, Gale's inner hatred of his own powerlessness is evident through his anger at anyone who displaces his own supremacy. These moments of dissatisfaction reflect the small crumbling of pebbles and rocks that come before the avalanche signaling what is to come. Whitney Jones, one of the few scholars to truly analyze Gale's character, states, "Collins' depiction of Gale is hyper-masculine; he is the emotionally-hardened warrior, hunter, provider, and overall alpha male. He fits a traditional model of masculinity associated with power, aggression, and sexuality."[8] Although Gale's agency thrives in close, reciprocal relationships in which he fulfills his role as alpha male, he clearly yearns for more, particularly once his role as hunter/provider is displaced.

The Power Plays of Love

Undoubtedly, the greatest relationship for Gale is his friendship/romance with Katniss Everdeen. Fans online have spent years debating the complexities of the #TeamGale vs. #TeamPeeta argument. On one hand, Gale is the obvious choice—he is tall, dark, handsome, muscular, mysterious, and all the girls notice and like him. Then there is Peeta, of average height and looks, who works mainly in the kitchen and flirts subtly from a distance. Most devoted fans evolve beyond the surface argument of looks and of who was in Katniss' life first and turn to examining which character *loves* Katniss most. Is it Peeta, who harbored secret feelings for Katniss since they were children and will do anything for her without the need for reciprocation? Or is it Gale, who is constantly by Katniss' side as her best friend and closest confidant? Whose love is stronger? Between the two boys, readers are essentially arguing whether love is sacrificial or transactional.

Love, in any society, is a complex emotion shaped by personal beliefs and experiences. For Gale, love is not only about emotion, but more importantly, love is strategic. Love involves an exchange of power, and for the most effective love, that power is equal between the two partners. As previously mentioned, Gale forms his relationship with Katniss based on their mutual need for one another's survival expertise. Their shared usefulness to one another eventually develops into genuine enjoyment and affection: "He [Gale] turned into so much more than a hunting partner. He became my confidant."[9] For the most part, Katniss views Gale as a friend, a companion, not a lover. However, Gale's grudging admiration quickly turns into affection and then evolves into serious romantic interest. It is because of his love for Katniss that Gale continues to provide for Katniss' family even after she has left District 12 to fight as tribute in the 74th Hunger Games.

While Gale does display obvious love for Katniss, as the trilogy progresses, it becomes more evident that Gale understands love primarily through the exchange of power. In *Mockingjay*, while hiding in Tigris' clothing store, Katniss awakens to hear Gale and Peeta discussing who she loves more. Gale insists, "You won her over. Gave up everything for her. Maybe that's the only way to convince her you love her.... I should have volunteered to take your place in the first Games. Protected her then."[10] Essentially, Gale believes that Katniss loves Peeta more not because of who Peeta is but because of what he was able to offer. According to Gale, Peeta was willing to give up everything, to surrender all personal freedom and power, in order to remain with Katniss, and this is what gives Peeta an advantage over Gale. In Gale's mind, Peeta sacrifices power for a relationship whereas Gale sees the power that a relationship can offer.

Although Peeta argues against this reasoning, Gale asserts, "It's Katniss' problem. Who to choose.... Katniss will pick whoever she thinks she can't sur-vive without."[11] Katniss is, rightly so, insulted by Gale's evaluation of her char-acter in suggesting that she will make a cold, calculated decision based on who can best guarantee her survival. However, Gale's assessment, while incorrect, is not meant to be an insult but rather reveals his own personal understanding of love. For Gale, the choice of whom to love is dependent upon what his partner can offer. Gale believes that if Katniss chooses him, it is because he has the most to offer—the most power, authority, strength, abilities—to insure a long life. Likewise, if she were to choose Peeta, it would be because Katniss believed Peeta had more to offer. Love, for Gale, is founded on the bartering system prevalent throughout District 12 in which individuals exchange supplies in-stead of using money. Gale's fixation on such power structures, revealed by his personal relationships, further bleeds into his implementation of agency.

Power in Powerlessness

Ironically, Gale's greatest moments of uncorrupted agency occur when he is at his most powerless socially speaking. In both *The Hunger Games* and *Catching Fire*, Gale is most vulnerable as he watches the Capitol throw his best friend/romantic interest into an arena that spells inevitable death. Help-less to do anything but watch, Gale hopes for her survival but is devastated by her relationship, faked or not, with Peeta Mellark. Readers later learn that once Katniss and Peeta make it to the final eight of the 74th Hunger Games, camera crews came from the Capitol to interview close family members and friends of the individual tributes. Naturally everyone in District 12 pointed the Capitol crews to Gale who was "too handsome, too male, and not the least bit willing to smile and play nice for the cameras.... So, some genius made him my cousin."[12] While someone, most likely Haymitch, constructed the fabrication of Gale as Katniss' cousin to preserve the on-screen romance between Katniss and Peeta, Gale refuses to play along.

In response to this lie, Gale says nothing, and his silence demonstrates his inner power and agency. Although Gale never denies the constructed narrative because he cannot do so without hurting Katniss' odds in the arena, he still maintains a certain level of agency through his evasion of participating in the lie itself. After Katniss comes home from the arena, and she is no longer in immediate danger, Gale promptly breaks the façade and kisses Katniss, shattering the illusion of him as her cousin and disregarding the Capitol's power in constructing a narrative of his life. Although Gale was powerless to do anything against the Capitol itself, his refusal to play along with their game demonstrates his own personal power and agency. Additionally, after the announcement of the 3rd Quarter Quell in which Katniss will inevitably reenter the arena with either Peeta or Haymitch, Gale is seemingly powerless once again. He cannot stop Katniss from going into the arena, having missed their opportunity to run, and as this Hunger Games is for Victors only, he cannot even volunteer as the male tribute to protect Katniss. Although he cannot do anything to stop the Reaping, Gale still finds agency in his ability to help train Katniss, Peeta, and Haymitch by teaching them how to set snares. While he is powerless against the Capitol, he holds the power to influence, aid, and assist Katniss in her survival. These small actions seem insufficient when compared to the looming power of the Capitol, and yet Gale's best moments of uncorrupted agency come in times when he is seemingly powerless.

This contrast between social and personal power is best displayed by Gale as the narrative enters into full blow rebellion. After watching Katniss Everdeen destroy the force field surrounding the arena of the Quarter Quell, Gale knows immediately that something is wrong. In this moment, he is seemingly powerless as he is unaware of what is happening or being done to Katniss and can do nothing to help her. However, when the Capitol begins to rain down fire bombs, Gale acts, regaining his power and control by rescuing everyone that he can, including his and Katniss' family, by herding them toward the meadow. "The credit for the survivors' escape land[s] squarely on Gale's shoulders," and it is this credit, added to his proximity to Katniss, that places him within a position of influence and power in District 13.[13] Before entering District 13, Gale's actions are entirely his own, based on his own desires and formed by his own intentions, which strengthens his exercise of agency. However, upon entering District 13, Gale's character begins to transform and so too does his agency as he moves from personal power to social power that ultimately corrupts his agency.

"Obliterating any sign that human beings have ever set foot on the place"[14]

Although Gale can find power in his most vulnerable moments, it is clear through his rants in the woods that he is not content with the personal power he possesses and often desires to act in more physical and even violent ways. Within District 13, Gale becomes more preoccupied with the balance and imbalances of power than with maintaining his past relationships that once formed the backbone of his agency. Indeed, his drive for social power distances Gale from those closest to him. Within the rebellion, even after Katniss has agreed to become the Mockingjay, Gale and Katniss rarely see eye to eye over any issue concerning the leader of the revolution, President Coin. Unlike Katniss who is wary of President Coin, Gale admires her, at least in part, due to her recognition of Gale's importance and in granting him more authority and power than he ever previously possessed.

Focused on maintaining and implementing the power he now holds, Gale allows President Coin to manipulate his own way of thinking. For instance, when President Coin grudgingly agrees to Katniss' terms for becoming the Mockingjay, she announces to the entire population of District 13 that if Katniss is unsuccessful or deviates from her role as Mockingjay, she will revoke all the Victors' immunities. Katniss accepts the threat for what is it; however, Gale defends Coin's actions. He argues, "You put her in a bad position. Making her give Peeta and the others immunity when we don't even know what sort of damage they might cause."[15] While Katniss is more concerned with the lives of the Victors, Gale is more concerned over the imbalances of power that their actions and words might cause to their cause. If Peeta continues to speak out for a cease-fire, it might negate the rebellion's influence and thus diminish Gale's newly discovered power as well. Gale's faith in the rebellion, particularly in President Coin, continuously blinds him to moral and ethical considerations.

Moreover, as *Mockingjay* progresses, Gale moves further away from his initial relationships and the loyalties he attributed to them. At the beginning of the third novel, after Katniss runs from the war council, Gale blocks the path of a soldier who pursues Katniss. As a punishment, President Coin strips him of his communicuff—a digital wristband that allows high-ranking members to communicate with one another. Gale willingly accepts this "punishment" and afterward even mocks its absence with Katniss. However, only a few chapters later, President Coin restores Gale's communicuff, reconnecting Gale and his loyalties to her. The reappearance of the communicuff is symbolic of Gale's latest betrayal against Katniss as he hides his knowledge of the recently aired propo which displays a significantly damaged Peeta Mellark.

Although Gale attempts to defend his actions, claiming that he was concerned for her well-being, Katniss responds, "It did [make me sick]. But not quite as sick as you lying to me for Coin."[16] At this pivotal moment in which Gale must decide where his loyalties lie, with Katniss or with Coin (who can offer him more social power), his communicuff beeps, summoning him to Coin and "cold anger replaces [Gale's expression]. He turns on his heel and goes."[17] Much like before, Gale's anger over his powerlessness trumps his feelings for others. Gale's narrow focus on the strength and righteousness of the rebellion, along with his own position of power, causes him to neglect his relationship with Katniss as he believes his actions to be correct.

Not only does Gale distance himself from Katniss, but he also slowly separates himself from his family. Throughout both *The Hunger Games* and *Catching Fire*, Gale's family—Hazelle, Rory, Vick, and Posy Hawthorne—are present and actively influencing Gale's actions. However, upon their arrival in District 13, Gale no longer needs to provide for them in the same manner as before. His family is safe and fed daily; there is seemingly no need for Gale's abilities as hunter or protector. Physically, Gale is no longer necessary for his family's survival and as such, they are less present in the last novel than in the previous two. Indeed, the only scene in which we see Gale's family is in the dining hall after the prep team is released from their cell. Interestingly, in this scene, it is Gale's family who serve as examples to Gale after years of Gale leading the family. Only after Hazelle and Posy offer sympathetic and kind words to the battered prep team does Gale begin to see the prep team as humans. In this final role reversal, Gale is illustrated as no longer the leader of his family, stripping him from that former position of power. Subsequently, the fact that Gale's family no longer physically needs him creates a power vacuum for Gale who always found authority in his ability to care for his family. Instead of working toward filling an emotional need, Gale distances himself from his family and attempts to fill this vacuum by chasing social power through his position as soldier. Indeed, although Gale's family is presumed to be alive at the end of the series, readers never hear from or about them again, demonstrating Gale's complete disassociation from his family.

Of course, regardless of how Gale acts toward Katniss and his family, readers cannot deny the fact that Gale often accomplishes great and heroic actions. After all, he protects Katniss on multiple occasions, he volunteers to be a part of the team that rescues the Victors (including Peeta) from the Capitol, and he rescues Prim from the firebombing of District 12. This chapter is not arguing that Gale is a villain, but rather clarifying that even good men can commit villainous actions when they allow external influences to taint their personal agency. The fact remains that when in power "great men are almost always bad men, even when they exercise influence and not authority."[18] When Gale pursues social power, he inadvertently distances himself from loved ones as can be seen in the increasing amount of time that Gale spends in Special Defenses designing war weapons with Beetee.

Worth noting is that while in Special Defenses, Gale is in a place of power, but not authority. Instead, he is situated in a place of influence. If we were to attribute any power to the pair, as both Beetee and Gale technically work underneath President Coin, Beetee would most likely rank higher than

Gale due to his impressive intellect, Capitol insights, and technical capabilities. However, as an accomplished hunter, Gale can offer suggestions and influence Beetee's ideas and creations. Although Gale cannot physically create the trap due to his limited education, Gale is the idealist behind the creation of a two-timed bomb that will first cause an explosion, drawing in first responders, and then explode again to cause maximum casualties. When Katniss argues that they are "crossing some kind of line," Gale only stares "with hostility" and argues, "I have been following the same rule book President Snow used when he hijacked Peeta."[19] Although Gale only holds the power of influence instead of authority, he is still able to enact great, yet terrible ideas. As Gale gains the social power to finally act on his more vengeful thoughts as he always craved, he is unwilling to question whether he should put such thoughts into action.

When the time comes to trigger an avalanche that kills thousands, Gale does not consider the morality of the issue, but only if it is a physical possibility, once again reflecting his focus on the ability to act instead of the intention or consequences of such actions. Dalberg-Action insists, "Great men are almost always bad men ... still more when you superadd the tendency or the certainty of corruption by authority ... and the end learns to justify the means."[20] As such, Gale's actions negatively impact his original sense of agency in which he created relationships with an equal reciprocation of personal power. His attainment of social power and authority often interferes with his relationships with Katniss and his family. More importantly, Gale's new-found ability to act as violently as he wishes in retaliation for past crimes by the Capitol blinds him to any moral consequences. As the Nut crumbles underneath the rebel's attack, Katniss notices how the avalanche obliterates any signs of humanity. Likewise, as Gale's power continues to grow, it overshadows his own humanity.

As seen through the above discussion, when Gale is at his most vulnerable, he is able to enact kind deeds that reclaim individual agency by refusing to conform to the Capitol designs. Ironically, when Gale is at his most powerful socially and most influential, he allows power to corrupt his nature so much so that his final design, the two-timed bomb, is mistaken for that of a weapon created by those in the Capitol. In attempting to enact his revenge against the Capitol, Gale finds himself as a mirror of their own corruption, focused on the power of acting apart from careful contemplation.

"Stone conquers people every time"[21]

"Does it matter [whose bomb it was]? You'll always be thinking about it," Gale says to Katniss. Although he does not know if his bomb killed Prim, by the end of *Mockingjay* Gale finally grasps how far his desire for social power has corrupted his actions. It does not matter if he designed the bomb that killed Prim or if the Capitol did because Gale already consented to the practical and intellectual use of the bomb. Gale, in acknowledging that the bomb was fair game against the Capitol citizens, is unable to defend himself against Katniss' accusations. It does not matter if the bomb was his design because he already approved its hypothetical use in times of war. Jones clearly sums up that Gale's "aggressive masculinity makes him, ultimately, destructive and careless of innocent life, a sin for which, eventually, Katniss cannot forgive him."[22] Gale's desire for and application of power cannot coexist within Katniss' agency because of the consequences that such power—based on ends that justify the means—demands.

Although Gale begins the trilogy as a clear protagonist in support of Katniss Everdeen, the presence of social power swiftly corrupts Gale's sense of agency as his actions turn away from their initial desires. Originally, the transactional and reciprocal relationships between Gale and Katniss and his family motivate his actions. Through these relationships, Gale acts in small but strong ways even when he is at his most powerless. While underneath the Capitol's thumb, Gale enacts clear and pure agency. However, by the end of the trilogy, Gale ends up in "District Two [with] some fancy job there."[23] Gale, who loved the solitude and environment of the woods, finds himself in one of the largest industrialized districts with a fancy job that requires his frequent appearance on television. Gale, who loved Katniss and his family, finds himself separated from those who leave District 13 and return home to District 12 to rebuild. Although Katniss is the only character that the new government officially exiles, Katniss is allowed to go where she wishes: home. Meanwhile, Gale to whom the new government grants authority within the new regime, finds himself "exiled" from his home, his woods, and his past relationships due to his own desire to obtain social power.

Readers may argue that Gale's intentions evolved over the course of the novel and so too did his sense of agency. Perhaps they could argue that Gale's new position of power in District 2 fulfills this new agency. Although agency and intentions can evolve and change, ultimately, Gale's desire for power corrupts his agency because he comes to regret his actions as seen through his last conversation with Katniss. Just as "stone conquers people every time," so too does social power corrupt every time when the individual does not hold it in check.[24] As seen throughout the trilogy, personal power is necessary for agency in the sense that an individual must possess some level of freedom to enact their own actions. However, this power is different than the power that Gale chases after. For instance, while in the Games, Katniss is at her least powerful; she is nothing more than a tribute within the Capitol's design. However, Katniss is still able to enact agency through her personal decisions. Her power comes from her recognition and honor of Rue's body and her challenge against the Capitol. For Peeta, his power comes from his refusal to play the game according to the Capitol's plan. Both Katniss and Peeta hold less physical and official power and authority than Gale, and yet, they are still able to successfully and repeatedly enact agency. Power, as seen within the narrative, especially social power, when in excess, results in corruption.

Gale, a predominate character at the beginning of the trilogy, must fade into the background by the end of *Mockingjay* to serve as a warning to readers. Collins portrays Gale as a character who originally bases his agency off positive relationships in which power is distributed equally and who displays the quick decay of agency when corrupted by absolute power. In demonstrating how Gale is able to enact agency when at his least powerful, Collins' narrative shows how agency is accessible regardless of social power because every individual holds a measure of personal power. Collins intentionally presents Gale as a relatable character that readers root for, even when his actions are more than questionable. Even after Gale mentally conceives the idea of the bomb that kills Prim, readers still attempt to support and explain away his actions. By creating a character that is initially lovable, understandable, and defendable, Collins highlights the thin line that exists between justice and revenge, power and corruption.

Like an avalanche that begins small and grows until it is out of control destroying everything in its path, power can infect individual agency and grow until it obliterates the original intentions of the individual entirely. Consequently, Gale serves as a warning to readers, to exercise personal agency and personal power through their actions, to exercise authority, but to be wary of desiring excessive social power which, when left unchecked, corrupts the soul.

SIX

"Why don't you just be yourself"

*Shared Agency and Social Expectations
Within the Capitol*

Agency, in our simplified definition, states that individuals are able to act of their own accord based on their own intentions and desires although their actions may be influenced by internal and external constraints. As seen throughout these chapters, a multitude of topics affect personal agency, another being that of the connection between social expectations and physical modification. The standards of others continuously affect and influence individuals' abilities or desires to act one way versus another or even how they present themselves, depending on what is more socially acceptable at that time. The Capitol of Panem is understood to be a hyperbolic representation of the social standards that exist in today's so-called "developed world." In her book *Unbearable Weight*, Susan Bordo[1] describes the postmodern, Western body as focused on the "fantasies of re-arranging, transforming and correcting, limitless improvement and change, defying the historicity, the morality, and, indeed, the very materiality of the body. In place of that materiality, we now have cultural plastic."[2] While the nation of Panem takes place in the future, the society of the Capitol can be seen as a replication of the postmodern, Western culture described by Bordo in which the body is meant to be changed, re-arranged, and transformed based on current social standards and expectations.

One might argue that transforming one's own body *is* an act of agency because the action and desire originate within the individual. However, as always, we must consider the intentions behind the action. Are the individuals changing because they desire it? Or are they changing because they fear the repercussions of non-conformity? For the Capitol citizens at least, it is the second reason. Take, for instance, Octavia's dyed skin in *Catching Fire* which Katniss notes to no longer be "pea green … [now] It's more of a light evergreen."[3] No doubt, the change in skin tone is in response to Katniss Everdeen's (or evergreen's) victory in the 74th Hunger Games. This light evergreen color

98

displays Octavia's dedication to staying abreast of the latest social norms and it is through her appearance that she gains favor with others. However, on the other hand, when Octavia has a feather-themed birthday party that goes disastrously wrong, she bemoans her social faux pas as she loses the approval and social admiration she so desperately desires.

Although the slight change of color in her skin tone may initially seem as preposterous to the readers as it does to Katniss, is it truly such a foreign idea in our culture to dye the skin? One can find tattoo parlors around every corner in major cities while shows such as *Ink Master* promote the elaborate techniques of mastering how to dye each other's skin. Of course, not everyone in the twenty-first century is getting pierced or tattooed; however, the significance placed on and commonness of body modification and "improvement" only continues to grow. In 2016, *Huffpost* published an article on "geode lips," the latest cosmetic trend that seems to have stepped right off the streets of the Capitol in which the individual applies two-toned colors and gems to their lips. Abigail Williams, a writer for *Huffpost*, claims, "The world has gifted us with geode lip art, and frankly, it's giving us life."[4] Williams hyperbolic emphasis on the *life-giving* cosmetic trend is only one of the surprising parallels between *The Hunger Games* trilogy and real life in which both societies have members utterly obsessed and dependent upon appearances. After all, it was not long after the movies began to air that Nordstrom came out with their own *Hunger Games* themed cosmetic line. On their blog, *The Thread*, Nordstrom claims that *Catching Fire* is "inspirational beauty! Sure, the looks may be a little out of this world, but that's why we love them.... Take a cue from Effie Trinket. Makeup is a low-commitment way to show off your personality."[5] Now, while Nordstrom may be promoting individuality and self-expression, they might be missing the point of how Collins presents cosmetics in the world of Panem.

Bordo, a twentieth-century feminist philosopher, aptly asserts that the body is "a powerful symbolic form, a surface on which the central rules, hierarchies, and even metaphysical commitments of a culture are inscribed and thus reinforced through the concrete language of the body."[6] Indeed, this specifically reciprocal relationship between the body and its society demonstrates how social norms and expectations further perpetuate the cycle of what the community will and will not accept. Following a similar train of thought, Chad W. Timm, fellow scholar of *The Hunger Games*, discusses the "trick" prevalent throughout series in which the Capitol succeeds in getting "the people to control themselves, to fall into certain habits that perpetuate the existing social order."[7] This applies to both the Capitol citizens, who are more concerned with their own physical modification than any social injustices occurring around them, and, of course, those within the district.

Katniss herself falls prey to these social norms as seen on the opening page of the trilogy. Upon waking on reaping day, Katniss observes her small, coal-caked home and sleeping family which consists of her mother and sister. Katniss makes note of the fresh loveliness of her younger sister, Prim, and the spoiled nature of her once beautiful mother. A beauty, Katniss tells us, that she has never seen and only ever heard of. Collins begins her novel by pausing in this moment so that Katniss can inform the readers that Mrs. Everdeen was "very beautiful *once*."[8] This depiction of Mrs. Everdeen betrays Katniss' subconscious opinion of her mother whose usefulness in Katniss' life has faded away just like her wilted beauty. Unconsciously, Katniss draws this connection between outer appearance and inner worth which foreshadows the importance of body imagery for the remainder of the trilogy.

Within the Capitol of Panem, physical perception consumes the minds of the citizens as they constantly devote their attention to how they are viewed and in viewing others. Of course, the societies and worldviews of the Capitol versus the districts are often contradictory. District 12, being the furthest and most neglected district from the Capitol, is almost completely opposite of the Capitol as the residents do not fixate on their appearance, often leaving the coal dust in their homes and on their skin. Indeed, Katniss could not care less what she looks like, often braiding her hair not as a style choice but out of simple convenience. While it is true that those in the districts, Katniss specifically, show disregard for their appearance when compared to those in the Capitol, they cannot help but to allow the idealism of the ruling class to influence their views, even subconsciously. In fact, the Capitol's customs and social norms invade nearly every aspect of the lives of district residents, even as they rebel against them. Even though Katniss could never be as narcissistic as her prep team, she is still aware of the importance of appearance and perception. As seen in Katniss' initial, and perhaps unintended, reflection of her mother's appearance, the Capitol's obsession with the beauty of the body affects Katniss' own understanding of usefulness.

Combatting this idea of caving into social expectation is unexpectedly none other than the Capitol-born and raised stylist Cinna. While it seems natural for those in the districts to resist the Capitol idealism, it is astonishing that Cinna, who lives within the center of Capitol society and more particularly among the high stylists of the community, can clearly identify and understand the problematic issues of an overabundance of emphasis placed on cosmetic application. In this chapter, we will come to see that it is possible for an individual to exist successfully within a certain community without conforming to its idealism. Through the narrative, readers witness Cinna confronting social expectations both physically and symbolically. Through Cinna's character, agency is the ability to defy social and cultural standards in favor of acting based on intention, specifically through his cosmetic decisions and in exercising shared agency with another.

Cinna, the Stylist

Cinna, the stylist of District 12's tributes during the 74th Hunger Games and the 3rd Quarter Quell, is a man of mystery. He is one of the few characters to have only a first name and no last name, although perhaps we can attribute this to his occupation. Many stylists and prep team members only have a first name: Tigris, Flavius, Octavia, Venia, Portia, etc. Additionally, readers are completely unaware of Cinna's past as Katniss never bothers to ask. V. Arrow, author of *The Panem Companion*, has an entire chapter devoted to speculations concerning Cinna's character. In the chapter "Truly, My Name Is Cinna," Arrow discusses the possibility of Cinna the Capitol citizen, or Cinna, the citizen of District 4, District 1, District 8, or even District 12. Online, fans have gone so far as to speculate that Cinna is Mr. Everdeen after severe cosmetic surgery. While some theories have become far-fetched, these speculations only further demonstrate the fascination that surrounds Cinna's character.

Regardless of his origins, Cinna exercises agency in his ability to defy social constructions, expectations, and fan speculation. Perhaps that is why readers do not need to know his past, because he does not allow it to control his present. After all, the most logical explanation of his past is that Cinna is a Capitol-born citizen who grew up in a life of luxury and ease. As such, Cinna could have matured into adulthood just as shallow as every other Capitol citizen that admires worthless gestures. Instead, in keeping with his nature of non-conformity, Cinna does not allow his Capitol pedigree to inform his intentions, showing that while a society does impact an individual, it does not necessarily decide their choices for them.

The most obvious example of Cinna's deviation from accepted social standards is his own physicality. Many citizens within the Capitol spend most of their lives rushing off to the latest trend or fad out of the desire to keep up to date with social expectations. Two of the clearest examples of this are Effie Trinket with her ever-evolving hair or Octavia who dyes her entire body different colors. On the other hand, Cinna maintains his signature look throughout the narrative with natural hair, natural skin, simple clothes, and "the only concession to self-alteration seems to be metallic gold eyeliner that has been applied with a light hand."[9] As a stylist, Cinna stands out even more so due to the ways in which other stylists often disfigure their human appearances in the pursuit of beauty. In a society where the individual is *required* to constantly transform and evolve based on others' standards of beauty, the ability to withstand change displays personal agency. Physically, Cinna ignores what society demands when it comes to control over his own body. Note that this does not mean he altogether disregards cosmetic application; he still applies the golden eyeliner which differentiates himself from those within the districts.

Despite his differences from the other stylists, Cinna is a naturally talented stylist who understands and demonstrates how effective physical perception can be in exercising agency. Cinna may apply golden eyeliner; however, this is not a concession to outside demands, rather, it is a choice that represents his own desires. While many may think that Collins is portraying the evils of cosmetic application, the issue is far more complex. Collins is not arguing that all cosmetic application/alterations are evil, but she is highlighting the importance of intention behind the action. The fact that Cinna wears golden eyeliner throughout the trilogy, never changing colors to fit in with the popular trends, demonstrates that Cinna uses cosmetics because he desires it, not because he feels that he must keep up with societal standards. Using Cinna, Collins once again demonstrates the place and importance of intentionality within agency. While Katniss considers the other stylists to be freakish and villainous due to their appearances and how they treat the tributes, Cinna—a Capitol-born stylist for the brutal Hunger Games—is one of Katniss' closest friends and the trilogy's greatest heroes.

Cinna's prominence is also due in part to his clear perception of the society around him. Unlike most Capitol citizens who refuse to admit to their own depravity or the abuse that they inflict upon the districts, Cinna sees and confesses to it all. "How despicable we must seem to you," he tells Katniss during their first meeting.[10] Cinna not only refuses to conform to social standards because they are opposite to his own desires, but also because of the immorality that he accepts is prevalent throughout his community. It is Cinna's ability to recognize reality that both separates him from and endears him to the Capitol audience, although they may not be able to understand where their adoration stems from.

Indeed, although Cinna refrains from extreme cosmetic modification, the other Capitol citizens do not ostracize him. Instead, the citizens love and applaud not only his work, but him as well. Even though Cinna does not conform, the Capitol audience cannot help but to accept and love him because of his talent—talent that is born and created for the sole purpose of rejecting everything that the Capitol and its citizens stand for. In an ironic twist, the Capitol citizens often applaud Cinna's work that rejects their very society. Collins crafts Cinna, a character who shies away from personal modification and yet is capable of creating extravagant fashion designs, not to condemn artistic expression of the self, but to display how to maintain oneself within the elaborate constructions. Cinna does not need to conform to social standards for the Capitol society to accept him—perhaps it is his unique, consistent portrayal of himself that draws others to him.

This reveals that Capitol citizens, much like some of today's Western audiences, believe that they crave high fashion when in reality they crave authenticity. Individuality is not about the strangest fashion choices, but rather the choice to remain true to the self. Cinna the stylist uses his love of fashion not to fit in with society, but to confront its expectations. Additionally, Cinna demands that his audiences recognize and applaud his artwork regardless of his own plain physicality that shouts non-conformity. Indeed, Cinna's greatest creations, displayed through Katniss, are works of art that directly rebel against the social constructions set forth by the Capitol's government.

Cinna's Shared Agency

Cinna is particularly curious, not only in how he stands apart from his own society due to his physicality, but also in how his agency is based not primarily in the self but in working alongside others. Undeniably, Cinna's agency is strongest when enacted and shared with another individual, predominately with Katniss. When discussing agency, scholars usually refer to the individual's ability to demonstrate control over his/her own actions based on intention and desire. Indeed, it is the *individual* that many academics examine, analyze, and prod. However, agency is not only an individual matter but also a matter between pairs and even collectives.

Shared agency, occurring between pairs of individuals, takes place when the pair acts as one based on similar intentions and desires with the same goal in mind. However, this can be an oversimplified explanation. After all, surely many people in the Capitol race off to the hair salon at the same time with the same intention of showing off the latest fashion fads to their friends, but they are not enacting shared agency at all. What is missing from this scenario are two primary things: commitment to the specific activity and commitment between participants. According to Abraham Roth, a philosopher of agency, shared agency strictly involves these two types of commitments: to the act and to each other, and to the "need for an interpersonal conception of intentions."[11] In other words, intentionality matters in agency, particularly in matters of shared agency. In addition to intention, the obligations that one partner has toward the other solidify the shared actions and agency. These obligations require an honest rapport based on the needs and desires of each individual. Therefore, when speaking of shared agency, we can look not only at the actions accomplished, but also at the intentions behind the actions and if there is the sense of obligation between one individual and another.

Throughout the narrative, Cinna's actions revolve around both his desires and those of Katniss Everdeen, resulting in shared agency. In particular, Cinna and Katniss demonstrate shared agency through pre– and post–Game activities in which Cinna creates and Katniss dons stunning gowns that manipulate the crowd's perception of her character. While some scholars view Cinna's actions during the Games as those of a benevolent friend or guide, others argue that Cinna is problematic and just as manipulative, if not more so, than those in the Capitol or District 13. One scholar, Amy L. Montz, argues that Cinna molds Katniss' body into the figurehead of the rebellion, through the Mockingjay gown seen before the 3rd Quarter Quell, without Katniss' prior approval which ultimately "strips her agency and usurps her place within the rebellion."[12] A different reading of this text might dissect these two questions: (1) Is Cinna acting without regard to Katniss' desires or person? (2) Does Katniss herself not desire the rebellion? In this new reading, readers should focus on the fact that Cinna consistently places Katniss' needs above the desires of the rebellion or his own hopes to dismantle the Capitol. From the very beginning, when Katniss is no more than a tribute from District 12, Cinna does not work in opposition to Katniss, but rather he works alongside her to ensure her survival and concedes to her desire to participate in the rebellion regardless of the risk for her or him.

To truly understand the relationship between Cinna and Katniss during the interviews for the 3rd Quarter Quell when Cinna supposedly "strips" Katniss of her agency by turning her into a Mockingjay without her previous assent, we must return to the initiation of their relationship before the 74th Hunger Games. Having watched the Games for years, Katniss fully expects that her stylist will humiliate her during the chariot ride. In general, the stylists dress each pair of tributes to represent their districts, often reducing the tributes to nameless, faceless symbols of their district's productive values. Additionally, in attempting to appeal to the fashion-obsessed Capitol citizens, the stylists create over-the-top costumes that are often garish, obnoxious, sexual, crude, and unmistakably obvious. Throughout the history of the Games, tributes from District 12 have suffered from "skimpy outfits and hats with headlamps" to being "stark naked and covered in black powder to represent coal dust."[13] All for the sake of the spectacle, stylists literally strip their tributes until they are physical bodies and nothing more. Convinced that this will be her lot as well, Katniss "prepares for the worst" and thinks, "*I'll be naked for sure.*"[14] Katniss expects a stylist who will present her without dignity, without individuality, and without agency as she has no say in how they depict her body.

Contrary to this expectation is Cinna who differentiates from all other stylists in both his lack of flamboyant body modification and innate understanding of the injustice of the Games. During their first meeting, Cinna acknowledges Katniss' humanity and respects her individuality rather than seeing her as simply a moldable clay figure. Although Cinna may have considered how Katniss might ignite a nation during that first meeting, he consistently focuses first on Katniss the person instead of on Katniss the rebel. When Katniss enters the Capitol for the first time, the prep team grooms most of her body by scrubbing away layers of dirt, unnecessary body hair and skin. However, Cinna specifically orders the team to leave her hair, styled by Mrs. Everdeen before the reaping, untouched.

As readers, we understand that this hairstyle is extremely important for Katniss because her mother's hands crafted the design—the same mother that Katniss struggled for so long to accept any help from because of her anger and pain. The hairstyle not only represents Katniss' district heritage but also her fragile bond with Mrs. Everdeen. While Cinna may not understand the significance the hairstyle has, the fact that he preserves the design demonstrates how he both recognizes and appreciates Katniss' District 12 self. While any other stylist would have overlooked the beauty of the design because of its origin, Cinna does not immediately erase who Katniss is to transform her into a Capitol-approved tribute. Instead, Cinna sees the individual, Cinna sees *Katniss*. Even before diving into wardrobe choices, Cinna ensures that Katniss is clothed, seated, and fed, again preferring to meet her needs before seeing to the demands of the Capitol.

Of course, we cannot ignore that Cinna does still style Katniss for the Games and he does take a part in her eventual transformation for the rebellion; however, Cinna's intentions always match with Katniss' desires. Through their shared efforts, Katniss gains insights concerning her own appearance and power, particularly during the Chariot ride in which she thinks, "Cinna has given me a great advantage. No one will forget me. Not my look, not my name. Katniss. The girl who was on fire. For the first time, I feel a flicker of hope."[15] Katniss' acknowledgment of Cinna's beneficial actions not only suggest that she wanted Cinna to style her, but also that she appreciated his efforts which have given her the first inkling of hope for survival. Together, Katniss and Cinna exercise shared agency as they both strive to appeal to the Capitol citizens for the common goal of Katniss' victory in the Games.

Furthermore, although Cinna does indeed "remake" Katniss, he encourages her to be herself during the interview and to maintain her own identity even within the elaborate designs. Cinna intends, through his fashion choices, not to distract from the tribute within the flash and finery of the gown, but to focus on Katniss' strength and genuine identity through the gown. Dressed in shimmering fabric that mimics the movement of flames, Katniss refers to herself as a "creature [who has] come from another world."[16] Montz uses this language to suggest that Katniss distances herself from reflection in the mirror and that Katniss does not accept or desire to be a creature designed by Cinna.[17] However, another reading might look at the next line. "I am not pretty," Katniss thinks and then elaborates, "I am not beautiful. I am as radiant as the sun."[18] Not only does Katniss accept and reconcile her identity to this image through the use of the first-person pronoun, she also views herself as the sun—powerful, life sustaining, and magnificent.

Evidently, Katniss desires Cinna's intervention concerning her styling as

Katniss realizes how it might increase her odds of surviving within the Games. Both Cinna and Katniss' primary focus before the 74th Hunger Games is how her appearance will appeal to sponsors. While Cinna is the principal agent in this scene, by designing and then creating the gown, Katniss commits herself to Cinna's vision by twirling in front of the crowd. Truly, Katniss' twirl would have meant nothing without Cinna's design and Cinna's design could not have been fulfilled without Katniss' twirl that causes the dress to come alive in flickering flames. Together, Cinna and Katniss are committed to the same action and to each other. While Cinna, no doubt, desires the eventual revolution, and perhaps even at this point can already see Katniss' possible role in it, he consistently places the importance first on Katniss as an individual not as a tool for the rebellion.

Consider the events that take place after the completion of the 74th Hunger Games in which President Snow must announce that both Katniss Everdeen and Peeta Mellark are Victors having successfully fooled the Gamemakers with their bluff. Readers later learn that many in the districts, and President Snow himself, view Katniss' bluff with the berries as an act of rebellion. If Cinna's primarily motivations did indeed revolve around the rebellion with no concern for Katniss, he could have crafted gowns that highlighted Katniss as a Victor and a Rebel. Instead, in the post–Game interviews, Cinna designs a gown for Katniss that creates the image of "a girl. A young one. Fourteen at the most. Innocent. Harmless. Yes, it is shocking that Cinna has pulled this off when you remember I've [Katniss] just won the Games."[19] Instead of building on Katniss' actions and stirring up the rebellion by creating a strong figurehead to follow, Cinna masks Katniss as a young, innocent, harmless-looking girl—certainly not what you want as the face of the revolution. Cinna's actions here protect Katniss and reflect his desire not to promote Katniss' image for his own agenda, but to help her achieve her own goal of survival. These initial actions set forth the foundation for Cinna's later shared agency enacted not on but with Katniss.

"I always channel my emotions into my work"[20]

Cinna's rebellious motives are more prominent within the second half of the trilogy, beginning in *Catching Fire* as he engages in clear-cut propaganda art with Katniss' Mockingjay dress during the interviews before the 3rd Quarter Quell. Through the dress, Cinna channels his emotions, his anger at Panem, and his desire for a rebellion. Some scholars, like Montz, argue that Cinna uses Katniss as an image, a figurehead, a face of the rebellion without Katniss' consent.[21] However, another reading might consider Katniss' own agency and desires. Cinna only creates this rebellious gown after President

Snow orders that Katniss wear her wedding dress in the interviews to humiliate and mock her previous efforts to subdue the districts through promising to marry Peeta. Yes, Cinna's gown does display the rebel image, but more importantly, the Mockingjay dress physically burns away the Capitol's taint on Katniss' body. Cinna does not leave the Capitol audience with the image of Katniss as the Capitol's bride, but of Katniss the survivor, the Victor, and the Mockingjay—ultimately empowering Katniss. Montz claims that because "Katniss embodies someone else's definition of Mockingjay, she shifts from ownership of the persona to a more passive recipient of the designation."[22] However, Katniss herself insists, "he's [Cinna's] done it for me."[23] According to Katniss, what Cinna has done was for Katniss' benefit and it is an action she accepts and desires. We can read this scene as Cinna and Katniss enacting shared agency wherein they both act, not over the other, but with one another.

Furthermore, Cinna accepts and promotes Katniss' personal desires, unlike others such as Haymitch, Finnick, and Plutarch who hide the rebellion from her as they view Katniss too valuable an asset to risk. Regardless of the consequences that Katniss' desires might bring upon her or himself, Cinna encourages her decisions. Cinna may have been the one to physically design and create the Mockingjay gown, but it is Katniss who must twirl to ignite the flames that burn away the wedding dress and reveal what is underneath. Indeed, Katniss' own actions are required to bring about Cinna's vision. Only together can Katniss, in Cinna's hands, become the image of a Mockingjay, an illustration of non-conformity and rebellion. Both Katniss and Cinna must be committed to the action for it to have the intended consequences; separately the design and the gesture are empty. Cinna, understanding that Katniss desires the rebellion, offers her a way to put forth her own agency on national television, displaying to all Panem that the Capitol does not own her.

Furthermore, directly before the start of the 3rd Quarter Quell, Cinna displays once again how he places Katniss' needs, physical or emotional, above his own or the demands of the rebellion. For instance, after the interviews in which Cinna displays his rebellious tendencies, his job as stylist is finished. If Cinna was focused solely on himself or on the rebellion and how the rebellion could benefit from his efforts in the future, he would have sought safety far away from the Capitol after his actions the night of the interviews. From what we have seen and read, Cinna is no fool and extremely capable of reading the reactions of others. This is what makes him such a spectacular stylist—his ability to garner the desired response from his audience. While he woos the Capitol citizens with his Mockingjay dress, there is no doubt that Cinna also understood the immediate danger that he placed upon himself because of his actions. Even Katniss, who is not always the quickest at perceiving the meaning behind the actions of others, comments,

"I'm afraid he [Cinna] has hurt himself beyond repair. The significance of my fiery transformation will not be lost on President Snow."[24] Based on his character, Cinna must have known the reaction he would receive from Snow and the Gamemakers; he must have understood the direct threat against his life.

Additionally, Cinna, useful to the rebellion in more than just one way, unquestionably has friends in the Capitol, secret rebels, who could have snuck him out of harm's way and yet he stays for Katniss. He risks his life in remaining in order to see Katniss off into the arena, knowing that she needed his support in her last moments of freedom. Before she ascends into the arena, Cinna "walks [Katniss] over to the circular metal plate and zips up the neck of [her] jumpsuit securely.... He kisses [her] forehead and steps back."[25] Cinna's actions not only represent his care for Katniss, but his commitment in seeing her through this trial. He does not simply take a young tribute, transform her into a rebellious image, and then walk away leaving her to fend for herself. Instead, he remains, regardless of the personal risk which is realized when Peacekeepers beat and imprison Cinna for his actions. Through this analysis, readers can witness how Cinna never acts for or over Katniss, but always *with* to enact shared agency.

"I'm still betting on you"[26]

Cinna's agency, present through his confrontational actions during life, is still prevalent after his death through his connection with Katniss. In fact, Cinna is the only character within the trilogy who actively asserts his own agency, tied in with Katniss' actions, posthumously. Although hardly mentioned within *Mockingjay*, Cinna's presence is palpable in every single costume that Katniss adorns. In fact, Cinna's clothing, and his agency, can only come alive through Katniss' acceptance in wearing them. Cinna, although gone, is still existing in memory and exerting his own desires through his artwork which displays his intentions. Cinna's art, specifically the Mockingjay armor, clearly proclaims Cinna's deep involvement with the rebellion and yet, simultaneously, Cinna displays his continued loyalty to Katniss and her needs. Having already created the sketches for Katniss the rebels before his death, Cinna forces Plutarch to hide them from Katniss and to never use them as a bargaining tool. Although Cinna personally desires the rebellion and believes that Katniss will be instrumental in its success, he wants her to accept her position as Mockingjay of her own free will, not influenced by his or anyone else's opinions. Once more, Cinna bases his agency, in this case his futuristic, posthumous actions, on his relationship with and his commitment to Katniss' own desires.

In a similar vein as before, it is entirely up to Katniss to continue sharing agency with Cinna. Truly, Katniss' actions determine whether Cinna's agency will live on through her or die with his physical body. In *Mockingjay*, Katniss demonstrates her commitment to Cinna just as Cinna repeatedly displayed his commitment to her within the first two novels. Katniss proudly adorns the costume that "only one person could have designed.... Cinna."[27] Through her actions, Katniss allows Cinna's symbolic engagement in the rebellion, and as such, his presence accompanies her throughout the rebellion and into the Capitol. Both Cinna and Katniss, desiring a change, work to overthrow an unjust and cruel system. Their shared commitment to that action and to each other is what allows their agency to thrive. Cinna's desires for the rebellion never overshadow what he feels are his obligations to Katniss as an individual. Although dead, Cinna continues to rebel against the Capitol through Katniss as long as that is what Katniss also wants. Just as Cinna aided Katniss before the Games in helping her display her strength and agency through his gowns, Katniss gladly wears Cinna's costumes to remind the world of Cinna's contribution to the rebellion. Furthermore, their combined efforts reveal how Cinna's agency is built on the desire to act regardless and even contrary to social expectation while accomplishing personal and shared goals.

Collins' characters are constantly at odds with the ruling authority, attempting to exercise agency in a society that demands obedience, submission, and conformism. As we have seen, all types of constructs such as body, morality, trauma, identity, and power affect the personal application of agency. For Cinna, agency is a matter of standing apart from society's expectations and exhibiting the appearance you desire, not someone else's standards. Cinna the stylist is a man of simple taste when it comes to his personal design, and yet he creates exquisitely detailed gowns when promoting Katniss' agency. The difference between his own appearance and how he styles others further demonstrates how Cinna's agency is not only dependent on his own desires, but rather focused on the desires of those closest to him. Cinna's supportive agency focuses on the "other," specifically Katniss, and maintaining another's individuality and strength. Through such relationships, he fortifies his own individual agency in exchange for a stronger shared agency. Assuredly, the relationship between Cinna and Katniss demonstrates the correct implementation of shared agency. Repeatedly, Cinna acts to showcase Katniss' agency and through these actions, he enacts his own. Undoubtedly Cinna is a rebel; however, he never allows his rebellious motives to overpower his agency based on shared commitments and obligations. Alone, Cinna can withstand society's demands. Accompanied by Katniss, Cinna's agency can move a nation into a revolution.

SEVEN

"It's all a big show"[1]

Agency, Intentionality and Reality

The Hunger Games trilogy was conceived one night while Collins was "channel surfing between reality TV programs and actual war coverage … [and] the line between these stories started to blur in a very unsettling way."[2] It is the combination of the flippant carelessness of reality TV and the brutal violence of war that instigated the idea of the Games. The Games themselves drew inspiration from a mix of Greco-Roman mythology and modern-day reality television in which the Capitol audience holds the power. It is this connection between the Games and its audience that we will be investigating in this chapter. In today's twenty-first century, reality television pervades society and draws in audience members who have the ability to "vote off" contestants while rooting for their favorites to win, such as on *Survivor* or *America's Got Talent*. Audiences are drawn to watching shows even when they do not include participation whether it comes in the humorous packing of *Impractical Jokers*, the romance-flavored *Bachelor/Bachelorette* or the drama-induced, constantly-surveyed *Big Brother*. Whatever your taste, the odds are in your favor of finding at least one show that suits your fancy.

For the citizens of the Capitol, that show is, naturally, the Hunger Games in which twenty-four children are sent to a gladiator-type arena to compete against one another, brutally murdering each other until there is only one left. However, the Games not only involve the action that takes place within the arena, but also what happens before and after outside of the arena. Much like how cameras follow contestants behind-the-scenes, so too does the Capitol invade the lives of their tributes. The pre- and post–Game activities, such as the Chariot ride, the demonstration of a chosen talent, and interviews of the tributes before the Games, the interviews of the family members of the final eight surviving tributes along with the Victory Tour are all crucial elements to the Games. The Victory Tour, in which the Victor must parade through the districts and flaunt their survival in front of the dead tributes' families, demonstrates how the Games never truly end and the show must always go on. Consequently, the Victors are required to retain their status of "actor" or "actress" because they never know who might be watching.

Haymitch Abernathy, the Victor of the 2nd Quarter Quell and only surviving Mentor for District 12, knows the ins and outs of show business better than anyone else having lived within the performance of the Games for more than twenty-five years. As a "performer" of sorts, Haymitch's character questions the relationship between agency and reality as he cycles through his roles as Drunk, Rebel, and, finally, Man. Indeed, Haymitch's presence in the trilogy begs the question, if an individual must pretend to be someone else and must act in a certain way for the cameras, can he/she still maintain individual agency based on true desires and intentions or are they simply a puppet for the public? Through Haymitch's character, we will come to see that successful agency requires a certain amount of visibility in one's own actions in order to maintain the reality of their autonomy.

Haymitch, the Drunk: "It's how you're perceived"[3]

Speaking of our favorite, knife-wielding alcoholic, Haymitch Abernathy appears early on in the series as inconsequential and seemingly pointless as a mentor. Katniss describes him as "paunchy, middle-aged ... [and] drunk. Very."[4] Whether it is showing up late, staggering due to his inebriation, or falling off stages, Haymitch is best known to the audiences of Panem as the iconic, drunk mentor from District 12. This image of Haymitch the Drunk is well known to every District and Capitol citizen. However, as we pick apart the pages that concern Haymitch, readers can determine that this image is, at least in part, a fabrication or exaggeration of Haymitch's character. Yes, Haymitch does drink, and yes, technically, he is a certified alcoholic, but the idea that he is *just* a drunk only depicts the role expected from and within the Capitol. Much like reality TV stars in today's society who embellish their flaws or display reactions blown out of proportion for the sake of ratings, Haymitch is depicted by Collins as hyperbolizing his drunken nature for the audience's sake and to support Haymitch's own secret agendas.

After all, Haymitch was not always just the drunk mentor for District 12. When chosen as one of the male tributes for the 2nd Quarter Quell as a teenager, Haymitch is "young. Strong ... something of a looker. His hair dark and curly, those gray Seam eyes bright, and even then, dangerous."[5] Within the 2nd Quarter Quell, Haymitch is a primary contender for multiple reasons and none of them have to do with his compulsion to drink. Not only do his good looks and arrogant attitude garner sponsorship from the onset of the Games, but the extreme intelligence he displays while in the Games proves to be both his salvation and his undoing.

During his Games, having finally made his way to the edge of the arena, Haymitch discovers the force field that encompasses the entire landscape. Any item thrown off the cliff or at the force field will rebound back to its origin owner. This knowledge proves instrumental at the climax of the Games when Haymitch faces off against the female Career tribute from District 1 who throws her axe at his head in a last attempt to win the Games. Unknown to her, but obvious to Haymitch, they had reached the edge of the arena and when the axe flies over Haymitch and off the cliff, it rebounds and kills its owner, the girl from District 1. Her actions, and his trap, leave Haymitch to claim the title of Victor of the 2nd Quarter Quell. When reading about Haymitch's own Games, it seems difficult to understand how he deteriorates so quickly from the young, arrogant Victor of the 2nd Quarter Quell, capable of outsmarting forty-seven other contestants to the humiliated drunk who cannot walk across the stage of District 12 before the 74th Games. Collins' inclusion of Haymitch's backstory provides an excellent avenue through which we can explore the necessity of visibility in agency. As we move forward, we will see that Haymitch uses his drunken persona to his advantage as another means of survival.

Much like Katniss' own victory, Haymitch's relief of surviving the Games is short lived. He may have won the 2nd Quarter Quell, but his actions in using the Gamemakers' design for his own ends embarrassed the Capitol and as such required recompense. Later in *Mockingjay*, Haymitch admits to Katniss that he did indeed pay a price for his actions: "My mother and younger brother. My girl. They were all dead weeks after I was crowned victor. Because of that stunt I pulled with the force field…. I was the example. The person to hold up to the young Finnicks and Johannas and Cashmeres."[6] Before and during the 2nd Quarter Quell, Haymitch presents his agency as a badge of honor on his sleeve. He proudly displays his intentions and succeeds in achieving his survival, but at a cost. In using the Gamemakers' design, Haymitch demonstrate the intelligence and personal agency of a nobody-tribute from nowhere-District 12—granting himself too much power and autonomy.

Individual agency, as we have seen in our previous chapters, is problematic for the ruling authority of any dystopian society. Therefore, it is not enough to punish Haymitch for exerting such personal power by killing his family and loved ones, but they must also remove his dignity to weaken his sense of agency to set an example for any of the audience members, in the District or Capitol, who are watching and looking up to Haymitch. The Capitol accomplishes this by forcing Haymitch to play the role of Drunken Mentor, an example of what "could happen to a victor who caused problems."[7] The image of a cocky tribute who could survive the 2nd Quarter Quell when the odds were doubled against him has no place in the Capitol's design. As such, they strip away at Haymitch, taking his family and his loved ones, until he deteriorates into the drunken shell of a man consumed by loss who can hardly focus on reality without a bottle in his hand. The Capitol only allows Haymitch the Drunk to live because he became the perfect image for them to use of a broken Victor.

Or did he?

On the surface, Collins initially presents Haymitch solely as a drunk who seems to have given up on mentoring any incoming tributes or even in exerting his own agency, preferring instead to go where he is told and do what he is ordered. He stumbles through the formalities and often disregards his duties as Mentor. On the train before the 74th Hunger Games, Katniss thinks, "No wonder the District 12 tributes never stand a chance ... he's [Haymitch's] a big part of the reason why."[8] As many readers may note, Katniss' biases often flavor the narrative and are not always correct; as such, neither is this early hypothesis entirely accurate. At the end of the series, Haymitch retells the stories of tributes from twenty-five years of mentoring, revealing how every one of his tributes meant something to him and that their deaths stayed with him forever. While his tributes died, there is no proof that he did not try to save them. Indeed, from everything that readers learn as the narrative progresses, it becomes obvious that Haymitch never actually gives up on others or himself. He simply learns to hide his agency instead of displaying it as he did before. Helping manipulate the rebellion from behind the scenes, Haymitch is not nearly as defeated as he seems. So why then does Collins initially present Haymitch as nothing more than a worthless drunk?

In reality television it is well-documented that reality is anything but authentic. Eric Deggans, a media critic, observes, "Even the term 'reality TV' is highly misleading ... the goal for too many modern reality TV shows now is to push the envelope just enough to inspire a tut-tutting 'talker' segment on the 'Today' show, without shocking viewers so much that they reject the program itself in disgust."[9] Similarly, the Hunger Games is considered the reality TV show of Panem, and while it is actually far more authentic than many of our own reality TV shows in the sense that children really do fight to the death, there is still an enormous aura of false appearances and storylines throughout the Games. For instance, the Capitol promotes the idea of the Games being entertainment instead of executions, Katniss and Peeta pretend to be star-crossed lovers to ensure survival, the Careers over-embellish their vicious desire to participate for sponsorship, and Haymitch accepts and thrives in his role of drunk because that is what the show demands.

Through the previous characters examined in this book, it would seem that agency can only ever be accomplished by those who display it noticeably. Katniss reclaims Rue's body publicly, Peeta gives his winnings to the families of the District 11 tributes on live television, Gale refuses to play along with the Capitol's storyline on camera, and Cinna rejects conforming to Capitol society even as he performs in the Games. On the other hand, Collins initially and repeatedly illustrates Haymitch as playing along with the Capitol's narrative. The Capitol requires that Haymitch attends every function relating to the Games, so he does. While he may desire a rebellion, he cannot present his agency as he once did, but rather through clandestine actions in which he pulls the strings of others. Acting as a cocky and arrogant Victor who can manipulate the Capitol's arena will only bring about death, so instead, Haymitch personifies the drunken fool while hiding his agenda concerning the rebellion.

Let me again clarify, Haymitch *is* a drunk, there is no doubt about it. Readers see this through his various benders and the withdrawal symptoms he experiences when alcohol is no longer available. However, Haymitch is *not only* a drunk and his drunkenness does not detract from his mental fortitude. In the reality TV show known as the Hunger Games, Haymitch exaggerates the role that the Capitol assigns him as drunk and comic relief. Certainly, he becomes the shock value that Capitol commentators use to devalue District 12's salute to Katniss during the reaping: "one [commentator] says that District 12 has always been a bit backward but that local customs can be charming. As if on cue, Haymitch falls off the stage, and they groan comically."[10] These commentators use the drunk Victor to fill up what Deggans terms the "tut-tutting talk" on the Capitol's talk show. To them, Haymitch is merely a puppet to provide fodder for the gossip mill and to distract from a meaningful gesture in District 12 that demonstrates their defiant attitude toward the Games and their refusal to condone them.

However, if we examine this same scene from Haymitch's angle, we can see the possible agency that lurks behind his actions. During the reaping, Katniss volunteers for Prim and does her best to hide her emotions from the crowd as she does not wish to appear weak. At the very moment when Katniss is about to break and needs a distraction, Haymitch appears. He wobbles across the stage and attracts all attention onto himself as he directly issues a challenge to the audience, and possibly to the Capitol itself, before falling off stage. Are we really to read this moment as simple coincidence?

The Capitol views this moment as Haymitch the drunk presenting his iconic and worthless self. On the other hand, perhaps we can read this as Collins intending for Haymitch, who we all know can function quite well while inebriated, to act intentionally within his narrative as "drunk," but still for his own desires. Consider this: Haymitch has seen his fair share of tributes walk across that same stage. However, he has never, not once, seen a volunteer from his own district. Even drunk, Haymitch is bound to notice the presence of a volunteer. Also, he is a shrewd man with a careful eye, so it is more than possible that he sees the tears threatening to break Katniss' composure. In fact, it falls in line with Haymitch's character that he might plan his own humiliation in front of the cameras to give Katniss a moment to herself. Of course, this begs the question, why?

If we are reading this scene correctly, why does Collins create such a character? Why would Haymitch humiliate himself further in front of the crowd for a tribute he does not know? It is possible that he has seen Katniss before as they both traded illegally in the Hob: Katniss with her game and plants, and Haymitch with his drink. While their paths may never have crossed physically, it is logical to assume that Haymitch knew who Katniss was and her hunting abilities. Not only is Katniss a volunteer from District 12, which is unique in and of itself, but she actually stands a decent chance of winning the Games due to her physical abilities and activities outside of the fence. Having the possibility of knowing all of this, Haymitch most likely acts intentionally in this scene to shield Katniss from the cameras not because he cares for Katniss, but because he guessed at what she might accomplish within the Games and even for the rebellion which we know Haymitch has worked toward for years.

Through the dissected scene above, readers can view agency in a new way that we have not yet viewed it before. Indeed, Collins' portrayal of Haymitch requires further investigation. On one hand, Haymitch accepts the drunken "narrative" assigned to him by the Capitol, and yet within that designated space, he still displays agency that relates to his previous characteristics seen in the 2nd Quarter Quell. Within the Quell, Haymitch won because of his intelligence and his desire to push the boundaries of what the Capitol considered acceptable. When his actions resulted in punishment, Haymitch had two choices: to fight or to submit. Collins found a way for Haymitch to do both. Much like actors in today's reality TV, Haymitch became an actor and adopted a role that exaggerated his very worst qualities for the Capitol's satisfaction, submitting to their image of a broken Victor. However, beneath that exterior, Haymitch maintains his agency through working toward an ultimate rebellion. Indeed, he uses the Capitol-approved image of "drunk" to exert his own agency such as shielding Katniss momentarily without suffering any repercussions for his challenge against the Capitol. Similar to his actions in the arena, Haymitch manipulates the boundaries set by the Capitol, but learns to do so secretly. Having witnessed the way in which District 12 responds to Katniss' sacrifice, Haymitch sees the beginning of something, possibly the beginning of a rebellion.

Collins' presentation of Haymitch is necessary to the overall understanding of agency. We have discussed the importance of intentionality behind agency, but with Haymitch, we must examine its visibility as well. Through presenting Haymitch as being able to act according to the Capitol's design, but enacting his own desires beneath its façade, Collins' narrative suggest that how the world perceives an individual does not commandeer his/her agency.

It would seem that an individual can exist within a certain narrative, constructed by another, and still exert their own individuality and identity.

Haymitch, the Rebel: "The less you knew, the better"[11]

However, readers may simultaneously realize that there are problematic issues that arise due to Haymitch's clandestine implementation of agency. After all, as seen in previous chapters, agency is often made stronger through relationships, which Haymitch repeatedly does his best to avoid. Indeed, he consistently uses his public image as the worthless, cynical drunk to hide his true motives even from those closest to him. For instance, in *Catching Fire*, even after Haymitch forms a friendship with Katniss, he still refuses to let her see behind his pretense. While Katniss might realize that there is more to Haymitch than just his drunkenness, he still conceals his rebellious motives from Katniss and even directly rebuts her own rebellious desires. When Katniss believes that District 13 may have survived the Capitol bombing, Haymitch mocks her hopes and calls it "the kind of rumor desperate people cling to."[12] Re-readers of the novel, of course, know that at this point Haymitch is already aware that District 13 is not only alive and well but is also arming itself for the attack. Instead of letting Katniss in on the secret, Haymitch denies Katniss the ability to actively participate within the rebellion even though the Capitol has already forced her hand in accepting her desire for a revolution. In essence, he ignores her desire to enter into the same clandestine space that he inhabits, retreating back to solitude.

Although Haymitch encourages the Mockingjay persona and conspires with other rebels such as Cinna and Plutarch, he still hides his motives from Katniss—the person who is arguably closest to him. In doing so, Haymitch directly challenges Katniss' own agency. Unlike Cinna who works alongside Katniss, Haymitch enacts agency over Katniss and denies her the ability to act based on her own desires. It is this disconnect between their two agencies that separates Haymitch from any meaningful relationship. After the announcement of the 3rd Quarter Quell, Katniss begs Haymitch to help her save Peeta's life this time around. Before Haymitch agrees, "something flickers across his bloodshot eyes. Pain," because he knows that even as he promises, he is lying.[13] While Haymitch could have used his friendship with Katniss to strengthen both his and her agencies through working together as Cinna and Katniss do, Haymitch refrains even when his actions hurt those around him.

Perhaps Haymitch-supporters could argue that he lies to Katniss and Peeta to protect them. After failing to rescue Peeta from the arena, Haymitch insists that Peeta will be better off in the Capitol because he does not know anything about the rebel's plans. Of course, this is not true. The Capitol tortures

Peeta just as much, if not more, than the other prisoners. Like Johanna and Annie, Peeta is physically, mentally, and emotionally tortured. Even without knowledge of the rebel's plan, Peeta is punished simply because of his association to Haymitch and Katniss. Consequently, through his secrets, Haymitch intentionally drives a wedge between his agency and other's which inadvertently damages the success of his actions.

The truth may be that Haymitch has played his Capitol-approved role for too long and finds it nearly impossible to break old habits. For more than twenty-five years, Haymitch has played the part of a drunken and *solo* mentor. In the 2nd Quarter Quell when he teamed up with Maysilee Donnor, he had no choice but to watch her die a bloody and painful death. No doubt this first loss, followed by the deaths of his family and his girl, reinforced Haymitch's desire for isolation. More than likely, Haymitch refuses to share agency with anyone due to the danger it places on them and the pain it could cause himself. Truly, his individual agency is one of isolation and seclusion. While this type of clandestine agency is successful against the Capitol, it proves to be detrimental for the rebellion as it poisons his relationships with others. Through this exploration, Collins' narrative begins to demonstrate a need for visibility in one's actions and intentions for the success of individualized and collective agency.

Haymitch, the Man: *"This is the moment ... when we find out exactly just how much alike we are"*[14]

Within *Mockingjay*, the realism of reality TV comes in at full force as Collins strips away false personas right and left, and the Games evolve into a real war. Collins does not leave Haymitch untouched by the new status quo as he is literally forced to surrender his previous persona of Drunk Mentor or Secret Rebel. Possibly intentionally, Collins deprives Haymitch of all pretenses which leaves his agency bared for readers to scrutinize. Within District 13, Haymitch must enter "into sobriety ... in seclusion until he's dried out, as he's not deemed fit for public display."[15] No longer an actor underneath the Capitol's control, Haymitch must move beyond the mask of his drunkenness and reclaim the man that he once was. The war efforts have no need for a drunk, they do not wish to tut-tut his actions on live commentaries; District 13 needs the Victor of the 2nd Quarter Quell who arrogantly demanded the ability to enact his own intellectual agency regardless of the odds against him. In other words, Haymitch's agency can only regain its worth through his rejection of an outside narrative and the acceptance of his own authenticity.

Many reality TV stars, who have lived their roles for years, have a hard time coping after the cameras are gone and flounder to discover who they are without the constant surveillance. Likewise, without the Capitol's cameras, Haymitch too must discover who he is away from their prying eyes and the Capitol's design. It is no coincidence that District 13 never portrays Haymitch on live television, rather he is always the voice in an earpiece off screen. No longer having to portray his drunkenness on screen, and indeed, having no option to hide behind alcohol along with having his secret motives fully exposed, Haymitch has one option. He must learn to exercise agency through forming relationship based on authenticity.

Although Haymitch and Katniss struggle to renew their relationship in District 13, it is through this bond that he begins to emerge as a man enacting agency instead of hiding behind an assigned role. While Haymitch initially attempts to step right back into his role of Mentor, Katniss, due to Haymitch's previous actions of withholding information and honesty, refuses to listen to him. She even goes so far as to physically break the connection between them by ripping out her earpiece when in District 8 and disobeying his orders. When Haymitch attempts to enact agency as he did before, by enacting it over Katniss instead of with her, it fails. It is only after he shares about his own past and the fate of his family and learns to communicate with Katniss that the two begin to work in harmony, once again demonstrating the need for reciprocal loyalty and obligation between two partners when enacting shared agency.[16] Although Haymitch is not the same boy who won the 2nd Quarter Quell, his ability to work alongside Katniss as partners echoes Haymitch's earlier alliance with Maysilee. Connected by a genuine desire to rescue Peeta and end the Capitol's reign, Haymitch and Katniss work in sync, forcing Haymitch to emerge from his shell of isolation.

Furthermore, Haymitch's strengthening relationship with Katniss reveals the growth in his own agency. During the siege of the Nut, when Katniss goes out into the square to deliver a message before the cameras, a train that carries wounded Capitol soldiers and workers emerges from the destroyed Nut and Katniss finds herself at the mercy of a man from District 2. During this scene, the nation of Panem can only see two people on the screen: Katniss and the man from District 2 who holds a gun against Katniss. However, there is a third actor in the same scene. Through the earpiece (that Katniss now willingly wears), Haymitch prompts her, "Keep talking. Tell them about watching the mountain go down."[17] Through this, Haymitch reveals the depths to which he understands Katniss' emotions because they echo his own. He does not need to feed her line by line because for a moment, all barriers and pretenses are down and they understand each other perfectly. The calloused and unfeeling Drunk Mentor of District Twelve is gone and, in his place, stands Haymitch, the intelligent survivor and sympathetic mentor. Likewise, Katniss strips away her lofty position as Mockingjay and reduces herself to a mere girl from District 12 who has no business killing a man from District 2. "Who is the enemy?"[18] Haymitch asks as Katniss echoes, returning readers to the crucial question. The enemy of the rebellion is the Capitol while the enemy of agency is deception. Through Collins' presentation of Haymitch, it is clear that agency cannot be a performance, it must be based on the legitimate and genuine intentions of the individual. Haymitch can no longer be substantiated by the limited agency found in hidden motives and performances, he must pursue full agency in authentic relationships and actions.

By the time the war ends and the Victors come together for one final meeting to decide the fate of the future, Haymitch is fully willing to move past his isolation and enact shared agency with Katniss. President Coin proposes one last, symbolic Hunger Games in which the tributes are the children and grandchildren of those who were in power in the Capitol—including President Snow's granddaughter. Haymitch, like Katniss, realizes then that President Coin is no better than President Snow. He also understands that when Katniss votes "yes," that she must have ulterior motives. In making his choice and voting one way or another, Haymitch must decide whether he will trust another individual and share his agency, something he refused to do since Maysilee's death. By voting "yes" alongside Katniss, Haymitch must allow himself to let go entirely of his role of drunken Mentor or isolated Rebel by placing his trust in someone else and allowing Katniss to call the shots. Consider his choice of words, Haymitch does not vote "yes," but instead he declares, "I'm with the Mockingjay."[19] In this statement, Haymitch is not agreeing to a last symbolic Hunger Games, but rather, he is extending his agency to encompass another's, successfully moving past his inability to do so at the beginning of the trilogy.

The Reality of Agency

Suzanne Collins designs the character Haymitch Abernathy as a drunk, sullen, irritable man who challenges the ideas of action and reality within a society focused on perception and deception. Although Haymitch must exaggerate his worst qualities for most of the trilogy, he is not without agency even as he puts forth the image of having none. While Haymitch acts the part of a worthless drunk, he plays the role of an influential member of the revolution. Although he acts as a helpless mentor, Haymitch succeeds in bringing home two tributes instead of one. Haymitch's agency, within the first two novels, is a more personal limited agency, independent of others' desires and enacted through hidden gestures and clandestine motives. However, as we have discussed, this type of hidden agency results in isolation that causes a rift between himself and others, instigating a realization in readers that agency requires visibility within authentic relationships.

Although Haymitch returns to his drinking by the end of the final novel, he is no longer known as the drunk Mentor. When the liquor runs out, Haymitch "raises geese until the next train arrives" demonstrating the addition of a productive hobby instead of just a destructive habit.[20] Retiring from the reality TV known as the Hunger Games, Haymitch settles for living in reality. Haymitch's character clearly connects to twenty-first century readers in ways that many other characters cannot. While readers are not fighting for their lives in a gladiatorial style arena, most are struggling with presenting an authentic version of themselves instead of playing along with an assigned narrative. These narratives are often assigned by society in which labels persist, naming and categorizing who the individual is based on how society views them. Although Western society encourages the fabrication of reality, often twisting and corrupting what reality looks like on television, Collins' trilogy encourages her readers to strip off whatever role society assigns them. Instead, they, like Haymitch, must focus on finding authenticity in themselves and their actions for the sake of presenting visible autonomy that belongs solely to them.

EIGHT

"You will try, won't you? Really, really try"

Agency and Hope

"I reach her just as she is about to mount the steps. With one sweep of my arm, I push her behind me. 'I volunteer!' I gasp. 'I volunteer as tribute!'"[1] The entirety of *The Hunger Games* trilogy evolves from this one crucial scene and from Katniss' key desire: to protect Prim no matter the cost. Although the novels become increasingly complex as time moves on and readers find themselves captivated by the love story or entertained by the brutality of the Games, Katniss always focuses on Prim before all other concerns. Although Katniss may come to metaphorically ignite the rebellion and figuratively lead the revolution, she only accepts and desires this role on behalf of Prim for whom Katniss envisions a better and brighter future. Katniss, who keeps her head down during all of her adolescent life, blatantly and violently fights against the Capitol in *Mockingjay* in response to President Snow burning down her home. Of course, President Snow only obliterates District 12 with firebombs in retaliation of Katniss' actions in blowing out the arena of the 3rd Quarter Quell, and Katniss is only in the arena as punishment for her rebellious actions in and after the first Hunger Games. Furthermore, Katniss is only in the 74th Hunger Games, not because the Capitol chose her, but because she willingly volunteered to take the place of her sister, Prim. In the end, everything leads back to Prim.

The relationship between Katniss and Prim affects every action made not only by Katniss but by others. Every major event leads right back to this crucial scene in which Katniss' love for her sister and her desire to keep her safe sets an entire rebellion into motion. Regardless of Katniss' efforts to protect her sister, in the end Prim still dies a violent and gruesome death—blown apart by a two-timed bomb that leaves nothing but pieces. Katniss' actions only prolong Prim's life, but they cannot stop the inevitable, and Prim's demise truly is inescapable. In this chapter, we will see that as a vital component to the overall trilogy, Collins had to kill Prim and had to allow Katniss to fail in her protection of her sister. Prim, although physically representing the presence of hope throughout the rebellion, dies so that Katniss can learn that hope is more than just a physical entity. Through the curiously short life and death of Primrose Everdeen, along with additional characters such as Rue, we investigate the presence of hope within the trilogy. Readers see hope throughout the narrative as characters hope for survival, hope for love, and hope for a better future. Collins' thorough incorporation of hope demonstrates its necessity in the preservation of individual and collective agency, specifically within a dystopian society.

Hope Ignited

Named after the primrose flower—well-known for symbolizing both youth and womanhood in literature and history—Prim is the epitome of femininity. Indeed, according to Ellyn Lem and Holly Hassel, Prim serves as a foil to Katniss by highlighting Katniss' "male-identified strength against [Prim's] feminine weaknesses."[2] Collins often blurs and distorts gender lines with many of her characters: Katniss who hunts and provides for her family as the father figure, Peeta who stays in the kitchen and bakes, Finnick the male sex-slave, and even Johanna, the small female who proves to be a brutal killer. On the contrary, Collins aligns Prim perfectly with traditional feminine qualities. Initially depicted as "fresh as a raindrop, as lovely as the primrose," Prim proves to be quite the domesticated young lady.[3] For instance, when Katniss tries to find a suitable, feminine talent as a Victor, she fails at cooking, flower arranging, and playing the flute, while Prim apparently excels at all three. Of course, each of these "talents" represent traditional domestic qualities that highlight Prim's femininity. Even in her healing capabilities, Prim is often reduced to only a nurse or an assistant, regardless of her medical abilities due to her gender. Consequently, due to Prim's stereotypical appearance as the blonde-haired, blue-eyed, innocent young girl, many critics quickly glance over her importance in the narrative beyond her death as evident by the lack of scholarship concerning her character. This chapter works to rectify that lack by discussing how it is Prim's unyielding grasp on hope that affects not only her own agency but the agency of everyone around her.

From the onset of the trilogy, Prim is a metaphorical representation of hope incarnate. In the worst moment of Katniss' life—at least up until that point—when she volunteers to participate in the Games even believing that it will bring about her imminent death, Prim offers hope. Prim encourages her, "You're so fast and brave. Maybe you can win."[4] Perhaps readers and scholars could assume that Prim's hopefulness stems from her naïveté as a young child. After all, young children are more likely to hope for the impossible than adults. However, the Capitol does not make distinctions in maturity between the young and old when it comes to the Games. Forced by the Capitol into watching the Games every year since infancy, Prim is fully aware of the horrors in her surrounding society as she watches children just like her die every year. Prim's nightmares, referenced on the very first page of the series, demonstrate the depth to which Prim understands and anticipates the brutality and violence of the Games. These nightmares illustrate a constant reality for Prim of a society built upon fear that she can only combat with hope.

Therefore, Prim does not hope for Katniss' survival because she does not understand the odds against her sister, but rather, because Prim chooses to place her faith in Katniss' abilities. Prim hopes even when the odds are not in her favor. For instance, when Mrs. Everdeen falls into a catatonic depression, Prim hopes for her healing and is delighted when Mrs. Everdeen returns to reality. Unlike Katniss who waits and fears that Mrs. Everdeen will leave them again, Prim moves on completely, strengthened by her hope that her mother is back for good. Likewise, Prim hopes for Katniss' survival in the Games and because of that strong hope, Katniss knows that she will have to try harder than ever for Prim's sake. While the fruition of her desires encourages Prim's hopeful nature, Prim maintains the same hopefulness during times of loss, such as after her father's death and the destruction of her district. Collins' narrative clearly demonstrates that hope is not only relevant when an individual's desires are fulfilled, but more importantly, hope is essential when everything goes wrong. In the dystopian society, where the Capitol stacks the odds against the Districts, hope proves to be the only weapon available and often, the most powerful. Ultimately, Prim's hope establishes her personal agency, guides the first novel, and influences major events within the following two novels as her hope encourages Katniss' agency and in turn, Katniss' actions offer hope to an entire nation.

Hope Spreads

Intricately involved in the writing process for the first movie, Suzanne Collins includes more dialogue within movie scenes that helps develop characters and themes apart from Katniss. For instance, although the following scene is unique to the film adaption of *The Hunger Games*, its content is still relevant due to Collins' participation in the creating of the films. In the film, President Snow's conversation with Seneca Crane is extremely enlightening concerning the theme of hope. Played by Donald Sutherland, President Snow explains to Seneca and the audience that the Games are not only an exercise of fear but also of "hope. It is the only thing stronger than fear. A little hope is effective. A lot of hope is dangerous. A spark is fine as long as it's contained."[5] While this scholarly investigation intends to remain as closely to the written trilogy as possible, in this case, it is necessary to pull from the film in moments that do not directly conflict with the written narrative. Working as a screenwriter alongside Gary Ross, Collins has the liberty to play with characters such as President Snow and Seneca Crane, who readers rarely get to see since the narrative takes place from Katniss' point of view.

The above quote, approved by Collins, connects the well-known theme of fire to the lesser recognized theme of hope. While Katniss Everdeen may be the fire behind the rebellion, Primrose Everdeen is the hope behind the fire. Throughout the series, there are numerous references to the idea that "fire is catching" and how the revolution is sweeping through the nation of Panem. However, long before the nation had fire, they had hope. Characters such as Peeta represent the yellow dandelion, the hope for the end of winter. Even the most pessimistic of characters express hope early in the trilogy. Gale hopes for the prospect of having his own children in a society where they would be safe. Even Haymitch hopes for a "pair of fighters" who might not have to die bloody, gruesome deaths in the arena while he is unable to do anything besides watch.[6] While fear may restrict individual action, it is hope that encourages the individual to continue acting regardless of such fear.

It is worth noting in this chapter that while Prim is the primary symbol of hope throughout the novel, she is not the only exemplar. Rue, the young twelve-year-old female tribute from District 11, reflects and mirrors Prim in various ways that compel Katniss' actions in the arena. Rue represents everything that could have happened to Prim had Katniss not volunteered to take her place in the 74th Hunger Games. Rue, like Prim, is a young girl who fancies feminine things like singing and music. Rue, on her death bed, encourages Katniss and echoes Prim's earlier assertion, "You have to win."[7] It is through Rue, who Katniss buries and honors in wreathing her with flowers, that Katniss rebels against the Capitol by asserting not only her own agency but in reclaiming Rue's. Unsurprisingly, Rue's four-note whistle becomes the anthem of the rebellion. In District 11, the whistle alerted field hands that their workday was over, offering them the hope of relaxation and moderate safety in their own homes. In the Games, Rue offers the whistle to Katniss as a sign of hope, that they are both safe. In the rebellion, the whistle becomes a demand for change founded on the hope that they might overthrow the Capitol's unjust reign. Hope abounds throughout the trilogy, primarily because of the actions of two hopeful girls on the brink of adolescence. Together, Prim and Rue represent everything that Katniss is fighting for and illustrate the true faces of the rebellion—the hope behind the fire.

Indeed, without hope there would never have been a revolution. It is hope, represented first and most clearly by Prim, and then echoed by Rue, that ignites the spark known as Katniss Everdeen. When Katniss considers actively joining in the rebellion's cause during *Catching Fire*, her own thoughts confront her with the danger that such actions present to Prim's safety. Rather than allowing that fear to stop her, Katniss realizes, "Prim.... Rue ... aren't they the very reason I have to try to fight? It's too late to help Rue, but maybe not too late for those five little faces [Rue's siblings] that look up at me from the square in District 11. Not too late for Rory and Vick and Posy [Gale's siblings]. Not too late for Prim."[8] Katniss' hope to create a new society in which children are not expected to be sacrificed by the ruling authority is ultimately stronger than her fear of repercussion. Hope does indeed prove to be dangerous when left uncontained as hope is the initial spark that sets the fire of rebellion into motion. Worth remembering is the fact that Katniss' hope, demonstrated in the above quote, starts and ends with Prim. As always, agency encouraged by hope revolves around Primrose Everdeen.

Hope Manifested

Prim not only affects Katniss' actions, but also the actions of the entire nation of Panem. During the Quarter Quell, Johanna comforts Katniss after the jabberjays attack—muttations which mimic Prim's dying screams as a form of mental torture. Johanna states, "The whole country adores Katniss' little sister. If they really killed her like this, they'd probably have an uprising on their hands."[9] Of course, this statement overflows with irony as Johanna already knows that the nation is uprising. However, her statement also reveals just how far Prim's influence has spread. Prim, the young girl who was destined to die in the Games, was rescued by her sister who was also meant to die in the Games. However, the survival of both Prim and Katniss encouraged those in the districts to hope. If two unknown, Seam-born children from the poorest district could survive the Capitol's agenda, then perhaps they could as well. Every time the Capitol features Prim on screen, whether during the reaping, mid–Game interviews, etc., the districts see a bright icon of hope.

In *Mockingjay*, Prim often switches maternal roles with Katniss who previously assumed the role of father and mother. Although Katniss often refers to Mrs. Everdeen as a healer, it is Prim who nurses and cares for Katniss when injured physically or emotionally. For instance, after Peeta attempts to strangle Katniss, having been hijacked while in the Capitol, Prim asks, "You can reverse it, right?"[10] In this scene, Katniss is unable to speak due to her injuries and so Prim asks questions that Katniss cannot. Prim also continues to offer hope to those around her, specifically Katniss, insisting that they must at least try to reverse the effects of the hijacking. Such scenes, as those just mentioned, demonstrate how Prim matures quickly over the course of the trilogy, influenced by what she witnesses and experiences while still a child. In focusing solely on Katniss, some readers and even scholars, forget the trauma that Prim experiences in having been chosen to participate in the Game when only twelve years old and to then have her sister willingly take her death sentence. Then, after the Capitol returns her sister, they claim her yet again, and Prim must watch as Katniss struggles to survive a second time in an arena where the odds are even worse. Furthermore, Prim experiences the firebombs that rain down on District 12 firsthand as she runs for her life and watches her entire world burn around her. Surprisingly, Prim's traumatic experiences do not mentally damage her or diminish her ability to hope or to enact agency. If anything, as Prim matures, she also grows in hope.

Furthermore, Prim not only encourages Katniss' persona as Mockingjay, but she is also a physical representation of the hoped-for future. In the same way that Prim hoped for her mother's return and her sister's survival regardless of external circumstances, Prim continues in *Mockingjay* dreaming for a brighter future, offering that hope to everyone around her. Readers see this most clearly through Prim's deepest desire. In the concluding novel, Prim's greatest dream is not to be free from the Capitol's control as she is already free while living in District 13. Rather, Prim's greatest desire is to become a doctor, not a nurse or a healer, but a certified doctor. While Prim could never have received the proper medical training in District 12, District 13 grants Prim the possibility of obtaining her greatest wish. Additionally, Prim's choice of career is symbolic of her overall nature and sense of agency. Prim chooses a career that aligns her with Mrs. Everdeen just as Katniss hunts like Mr. Everdeen. Unlike Katniss, Prim easily forgives their mother's failures as a parent and follows in her footsteps to heal others. Through working as a doctor, Prim can continue to offer hope even after the war: hope for recovery or hope for easing pain. Prim bases her agency, her every desire and action, on the existence, prevalence, and necessity of hope. Prim seizes the opportunity to become a doctor not necessarily for personal satisfaction but because her agency requires nothing less than her helping others as she works toward building a better reality.

Such opportunities, social, political, or personal, that allow an individual to move beyond the existing standard often represent the heart of hope. Upon hearing that District 13 is training Prim to become a doctor, Katniss thinks, "Something small and quiet, like a match being struck, lights up the gloom inside of me."[11] Prim's ability to obtain her goal encourages Katniss to continue hoping and again, there is the connection between hope and fire. Hope, represented time and time again by Primrose Everdeen, is the motivating force beyond Katniss' actions after she has lost the will and focus to enact agency. The hope that Prim might be able to become a doctor motivates Katniss to keep moving forward. Ultimately, hope is the fire that burns when all else has gone out.

Hope Remains

Noted by various scholars, and confirmed by Suzanne Collins herself, Collins draws inspiration from Greco-Roman mythology for her trilogy, specifically from the story of the Minotaur and the Labyrinth. No doubt a scholar on such mythology, Collins is also familiar with Pandora and her mythical box. In Greco-Roman mythology, the gods created a young woman named Pandora and sent her to earth as punishment for men learning how to make and use fire (fire was supposedly only for the gods until Prometheus stole it and gave it to mankind). Zeus gave Pandora a box (originally translated as a jar) as a wedding gift that he instructed her never to open. However, as Zeus created her with an innately curious spirit, Pandora opened the box anyway. Out of the box, or jar, flew all of mankind's greatest miseries: greed, envy, hatred, pain, disease, hunger, jealousy, poverty, war, and death. When Pandora closed the lid the only thing that remained inside was hope. According to the original myth, throughout time, mankind must hold on to the hope that was left inside the jar to survive all the evils that Pandora released when she opened the lid.

Similarly, Katniss Everdeen defies the gods with her own fire as she ignites the rebellion first with the berries and then with an arrow that blows apart the arena of the 3rd Quarter Quell. In doing so, Katniss opens a metaphorical box that unleashes all types of evil from both the Capitol and District 13: violence, betrayal, mistrust, muttations, two-timed bombs, and death. Neither side is immune from the atrocities associated with war. With her home obliterated, Peeta imprisoned, and a rift forming between her and Gale, Katniss clings to the one positive thing left in her life: Prim, who we have already established is hope incarnate. Like mankind who clings to hope after Pandora opens the box, Katniss holds tightly to her sister believing that all the violence will be worth it only if Prim can survive and live to see and take part in a brighter future.

Of course, Prim does not live to see the future that Katniss envisions. Like a flower plucked before its full bloom, Prim is cut down just as she begins to blossom into womanhood. More than likely, the bomb that kills Prim is constructed and targeted on President Coin's orders to force Katniss into hysteria after her sister's death to mitigate Katniss' influence over the nation. As Katniss later notes, although Prim would have wanted to be on the battlefield, she was too young to be there without having authorization from high up. If we concede to this argument, that President Coin did indeed send Prim to the field with the intention of sacrificing her to damage Katniss' psyche, then it begs the question: What happens to Prim's agency? What becomes of hope?

No doubt, Prim enacts her own agency by rushing toward the victims within the Capitol, whether she volunteered or President Coin sent her. As seen by her chosen vocation, Prim bases her agency on providing hope for others, particularly for her patients. However, her death was not her decision and so removes choice, complicating the issue of free will. After all, it would seem that death ends Prim's agency as it successfully destroys the hope that she offers to others. After Prim's death Katniss is bereft of hope, the only thing she had left to keep her sane in the violent and gruesome world. Without Prim, Katniss sinks into despair and hopelessness and thinks, "*Let me die. Let me follow the others.*"[12] Prim's death completely robs Katniss of her hope and she is not the only character to feel Prim's absence. Gale too is affected by Prim's death as her survival was the only hope he had of maintaining his relationship with Katniss. After Prim's death, at the hands of Coin through Gale's design, Gale loses hope in ever winning Katniss over and exiles himself to District 2.

Perhaps ironically, in the Language of Flowers,[13] the primrose flower is associated with the phrase "I can't live without you."[14] Indeed, without Prim, Katniss does not desire to live and spends the days following Prim's death in a drug-induced haze. It would appear that Prim's death ends not only her own agency, but also the agency of those closest to her. However, Prim's presence within the trilogy does not end with her death. Months after Prim's death and Katniss' exile to District 12 as punishment for killing President Coin, Katniss is alone for days without Prim and lacking hope. When Peeta returns to District 12, he greets Katniss with a wheelbarrow filled with Evening Primrose that he plants alongside Katniss' house. The flowers trigger something inside of Katniss and after their appearance, she can fully grieve Prim's death with the reappearance of Buttercup. Prim's presence, represented here by the flowers, is the only thing that encourages Katniss to grieve and then move forward out of her catatonic state.

Although Prim is physically gone at the end of the trilogy, she remains a vital part of Katniss' life, just as Rue did after her death. Prim's death forces Katniss to learn to hope on her own through memory—memory encouraged by the Primrose plant for which Mr. Everdeen named Prim. In regaining her hope, as displayed by Katniss' eventual desire to have children, Katniss demonstrates that death does not steal Prim's agency. Indeed, through Prim, Collins' offers a new interpretation that is hardly ever found in dystopian literature. Death is not the end. Although murdered at another's hand, Prim's agency does not die with her as long as the memory of her presence continues to affect and give hope to her loved ones. Prim's agency, repeatedly based on the ability to hope and to instill that same hope in others, endures posthumously. The hope that fills Katniss after Peeta plants the Primrose in memory of her sister illustrates the enduring quality of hope. Therefore, Collins recognizes that Prim's death is necessary in such a dystopia for Katniss to learn how to hope on her own.

Readers too must learn to hone this type of individualized hope that endures regardless of what has been lost. Throughout the narrative, various characters lose and gain hope as they struggle to find happiness in a society that stacks the odds against them. Innocents like Rue are sacrificed in a meaningless game and women just approaching maturity, like Prim, are cut down before fully blossoming. And yet, regardless of the pain inflicted or borne, hope remains. Collins shows us that hope is not just a physical being or a destination. Hope is something that no one can steal, not even death. Hope is eternal and agency, when based on such hope, is enduring.

NINE

"You can't put everyone in here"

Agency and Those That Should Not Be Forgotten

Although I would love to, I cannot include all the diverse, amazing characters created by Collins in this analysis as Collins dictates the novels through Katniss' perspective. As such, there is simply not enough information to dedicate an entire chapter to minor characters individually. However, like Katniss who writes down the stories of those who it would be a crime to forget, I too intend to write about those characters who we cannot forget in our analysis of agency. After all, Collins adds as much depth to some of her minor characters as she does her major characters. By the end of the trilogy, readers know much more about Finnick's life, his Games, his loves, his lies, his pain, his ambitions, his soul, than they really know about Prim's. In traditional dystopian literature, minor characters typically remain on the side as one-dimensional and flat members of society. Contrarily, Collins fully develops her minor characters. In this chapter, we will analyze this development of minor character that compels an emotional response of "sonder" from the readers that forces us to consider "other" individuals as more than stock characters.

Colorful individuals, such as Finnick Odair, Johanna Mason, Mags, and Beetee abound throughout the trilogy. As Collins first introduces these characters as Victor-tributes for the 3rd Quarter Quell, readers are immediately set against them as they pose a threat to Katniss' and Peeta's survival. However, as the narrative continues, most readers cannot help but to appreciate each of these individuals, even coming to love them. Transforming from antagonists to protagonists, these minor characters reflect and conflict with the character qualities of the main three: Katniss Everdeen, Peeta Mellark, and Gale Hawthorne. Collins does not only demonstrate the journey of agency through her major characters, but she also investigates and reflects agency through a myriad of minor characters as well. Through a comparative and contrastive analysis of these minor characters alongside Collins' major characters, it becomes clear that agency is a varied and complex entity possessed by even minor players in the Game of life—a lesson that all readers should strive to remember.

Finnick Odair—Body, Perception and Reclamation

Finnick Odair, the darling of the Capitol, crowned Victor when only fourteen years old, the heartthrob and playboy of Panem, is truly a sex slave. Furthermore, he is a *child* sex-slave that the Capitol sells to the highest bidder for consumption while Finnick is still underage, most likely only fifteen or sixteen years old. Of course, as long as Katniss remains oblivious to the truth, so do readers. Finally, in *Mockingjay*, when Katniss becomes aware of Finnick's reality, she shares her shame with readers who may have previously judged Finnick for his seemingly promiscuous lifestyle. Undoubtedly, it is interesting that Collins portrays a *male* sex slave as opposed to a female sex slave, as it is women who are traditionally thought of when it comes to prostitution. While Collins insinuates that the Capitol allows its wealthy patrons to purchase many tributes of both genders for various reasons, Collins depicts Finnick—the strong, sexually charged, specifically *masculine* Victor—as the clearest example of a rape victim.[1] More importantly for our discussion, the significance placed on Finnick's body is paralleled to that of our discussion on how Katniss first discovers agency through her body.

Like Katniss, Finnick is inherently connected to the natural environment around him, representing his own desire for authenticity as it does for Katniss. As discussed in Chapter One, Katniss' connection with nature reflects her identity, her family, and her initial claim to agency through her rebellious actions within the woods. Likewise, Finnick is the only other Victor-tribute who Collins repeatedly illustrates in correlation to his district's environment.[2] Hailing from District 4, which oversees all distribution of seafood within Panem, Finnick is as familiar with the ocean as Katniss is with the forest. For Finnick, the water is a place of healing, enjoyment, and escape. Although we never see Finnick's home district, we do witness his reaction to the arena of the 3rd Quarter Quell which Katniss believes the Gamemakers designed specifically for Finnick due to the overabundance of water.

Finnick feels right at home within the waves which prove to have comforting and healing capabilities. After the Gamemakers trigger the poisonous fog, Finnick, Katniss, and Peeta find healing in the saltwater as it helps to draw out the poison. Afterwards, Katniss watches as Finnick plays in the water and she thinks, "If the seawater healed Peeta and me, it seems to be transforming Finnick altogether.... It's like watching some strange sea animal coming back to life."[3] In *The Hunger Games,* Katniss told readers that the woods transformed her, and within the 74th Hunger Games, Katniss drew safety from the familiar looking environment. Likewise, in the 3rd Quarter Quell, water plays the same role for Finnick, strengthening him and revealing his identity as someone who is more playful than promiscuous. His interactions with water in the arena no doubt echo its importance to Finnick outside of the arena as well. While the forest may represent Katniss' ability to exercise agency underneath the Capitol's reign, the water acts as a cleansing ceremony for Finnick. Water, often a symbol for baptism, rebirth, and cleansing, is repeatedly associated with Finnick's character as it is through water that Finnick metaphorically cleanses himself of the Capitol's control, specifically in relation to his sexual abuse.

Additionally, like Katniss' experiences, public perception greatly affects Finnick's enactment of agency. Collins first introduces readers to Finnick moments before the opening Chariot Ride that commences the beginning of the Games. Immediately, it is obvious that Finnick's stylist is one whom values nudity above all other design choices. Yes, Finnick has a "golden net that's strategically knotted at his groin so that he can't technically be called naked, but he's about as close as you can get ... [because] the more of Finnick the audiences see, the better."[4] In *The Hunger Games,* Katniss dreads the possibility of falling into the hands of a stylist who promotes the nudity of the tributes and readers feel her distress. However, when it is Finnick's body being displayed, Katniss does not show the same level of repulsion. Due to his sensual attitude, and yes, his gender, readers do not think of Finnick's body as being sexually exploited for the Capitol's sake as they would have had it been Katniss' body exposed for all to see. Just as the Capitol commandeered Katniss' body, it also claims Finnick's as they use his body to display the ideal physical image of a man, a Victor, and of a slave. While the Capitol holds Finnick's body captive, Finnick must go where they order and do as they command; however, even within his bonds, Finnick exercises limited agency through manipulating his public perception.

Just as Katniss uses her image of the "girl on fire" to persuade the Capitol's audiences to sponsor her in the arena, Finnick uses his image as "playboy" to achieve his own goals. Before the 3rd Quarter Quell, Finnick admits to Katniss that while he is engaging in various sexual relationships he does not deal in anything as trivial as money with his "patrons," but rather, he trades in secrets. Although Finnick has no control over which patron the Capitol sends him to or what they do to his body, Finnick refuses to surrender all control. As a slave, money from his patrons means very little to him. He has money and it cannot save him. However, in gathering secrets, Finnick uses the circumstances forced upon him to his own advantage and enacts limited agency. Through the years of his abuse, Finnick continuously rebels against his captivity by gathering secrets and intelligence on high-ranking members of the Capitol government, even President Snow, which he can and does later use against them.

However, much like Katniss, Finnick finds that his limited agency is indeed minimal compared to the Capitol's control. As long as Finnick cares for, and the Capitol threatens, Mags and Annie, Finnick can only bide his time and allow the misuse of his body to continue. It is only after Mag's death and a rescue mission for Annie is underway that Finnick reclaims full, unrestrained agency in publicly condemning those who used his body for their pleasure. Like many rape victims, Finnick's decision to speak out about his experiences empowers him, even if his abusers are not legally held accountable. In speaking out, Finnick not only sheds his false persona of a playboy revealing his true identity as a rebellious slave, but he forces accountability on his perpetrators by revealing not only their actions but in sharing the secrets they spoke of in confidence of his silence.

In this same scene as Finnick unloads the sexual exploitations of his past, Collins herself directly links together Katniss' and Finnick's characters. Katniss realizes, "Finnick's fate would have one day been mine. Why not? Snow could have gotten a really good price for the girl on fire."[5] The connections and implications between Katniss and Finnick, highlighted here by Collins, are apparent throughout the trilogy. Finnick, a physical and metaphorical slave of the Capitol, reflects everything that Katniss may have become without a revolution. Additionally, Finnick echoes Katniss' own journey with agency as he too is innately connected to nature and uses his public perception to his own advantage.

Following these same comparisons, Finnick, like Katniss, becomes a speaker for the dead and metaphorically reclaims their agency through his stories. When Fulvia, assistant to Plutarch, comes up with the idea of airing a series of "propos" dedicated to the murdered tributes, she asks Finnick to narrate their stories as "he knew so many of them personally ... [which] makes it so effective."[6] In highlighting these fallen tributes, such as Rue and Mags, Finnick displays how these tributes are worthy of remembrance. Although Finnick is a fleeting character, only appearing halfway through *Catching Fire* and perishing toward the end of *Mockingjay*, his importance to the narrative should not be underestimated. Like many other characters who die within the narrative, Finnick still retains his agency having accepted the possibility of his own death when he chose to follow Katniss into the sewers of the Capitol because he trusted in Katniss' ability to kill President Snow. Through both Katniss and Finnick, Collins' narrative teaches readers how to implement limited agency even within the most restrictive circumstances and the power of speaking out against one's abusers.

Mags—Sacrifice, Well-Being and Achievement

Furthermore, Collins reinforces the idea that a sacrificial nature can be beneficial toward an individual's sense of agency, although it often comes at personal physical risk, primarily through Peeta and then again through Mags and Johanna Mason. In *Catching Fire*, Collins introduces readers to Finnick's two closest friends among the fellow Victors who could not be more different from one another in appearance or temperament. Mags is an eighty-year-old woman from District 4 with a speech impediment and walking cane who volunteers for an unstable and hysterical young woman while Johanna Mason is a brutal, manipulative character from District 7 who admits to only caring about her own safety and well-being. Despite their differences, both characters help further our understanding of how relationships and sacrificial actions affect and influence personal agency. While Mag's character, like Peeta's, supports how sacrificial actions benefit agency, Johanna's character warns against the weakness that comes from lacking relationships for both her well-being and agency.

Mags closely aligns her identity to that of Peeta Mellark's character through her sacrificial actions. Considering Mag's age, she was alive during the first rebellion in which the Capitol supposedly destroyed District 13 before taking over the remaining twelve districts. Mags was approximately five years old when the Capitol initiated the first Hunger Games. Based on the timeline, the Capitol reaped Mags sometime between the 12th and 18th Hunger Games. By the time that Katniss volunteers for the 74th Hunger Games, the District surrounding the Capitol (Districts 1, 2, and 4) are known as Career districts where tributes eagerly volunteer for the honor and glory involved in winning the Games.

Nevertheless, it is conceivable that, due to the recentness of the first rebellion, District 4 had not yet accepted the Career-mindset and as such, Mags most likely did not volunteer for her Games. Indeed, it is more likely that during those first years, the Capitol rigged the reaping to intentionally draw the names of children whose families had been intricately involved in the rebellion. Various scholars have evaluated the "odds" within the Hunger Games and have determined that the Capitol most likely chooses its tributes intentionally as opposed to randomly.[7] Whether Mags volunteered or was reaped is an important distinction as it illuminates the intentions behind Mag's action on the reaping day of the 3rd Quarter Quell. Mags volunteers, not for district pride or for a chance to re-enter the Games as other Career Tributes like Brutus and Enobaria do, but rather so that she can die for another to live.

While it might seem that Mag's actions place her firmly under the Capitol's control, they represent her strength and her power over the system. On the surface, it appears that the Capitol holds Mags captive as they force her to once again participate within the Games. However, the only reason why they can place her in the arena at all is because Mags willingly chooses to go. In volunteering, knowing that she was signing her own death warrant, Mags removes the Capitol's power by exerting her own over the circumstances even though her sacrifice threatens her well-being.[8] Through her actions, Mags demonstrates how agency affects well-being and how well-being is not always the focus of agency. At times, agency may require the sacrifice of personal safety.

Indeed, when it comes to agency, Mags' well-being almost always comes in second after her desire to help others. If we remember from the introduction, according to the philosopher Amartya Sen, this is not uncommon: "People have aspects other than well-being. Not all their activities are aimed at maximizing well-being (nor do their activities always contribute to it), no matter how broadly we define well-being within the limits of that general concept. There are goals other than well-being, and values other than goals."[9] While Mags may not want to die a horrible death within the Games, she is not opposed to it if it means she can achieve her ultimate goal of defying the Capitol and protecting her valued loved ones. Undoubtedly, Mags is just as aware as Finnick of the rebel's plan to rescue the Victors from the arena. Therefore, Mag realizes that she does not have to be the last Victor standing, she just needs to survive long enough for the rebellion to save her. However, as seen through her earlier actions, Mag's goal is not solely focused on personal survival.

Mags actions circulate around agency based on the value of others and, very often, away from well-being. When the poisonous fog comes during the first night of the 3rd Quarter Quell and Finnick must choose between carrying Mags or Peeta, Mags willingly runs into the fog and commits suicide so as to remove the difficult choice from Finnick. In a moment that only takes seconds, Mags exerts her final effort of agency that carries through her death. While the Capitol was only ever concerned with her dying, Mag's only concern was with the other Victors living. Mags dies so that Finnick can be freed from the Capitol's enslavement, so that Peeta can stir a nation with his words, and so that Katniss can become the Mockingjay that the rebellion needs. In surrendering her own life, not running from the fog but walking directly into it, Mag's completely ignores her own well-being and seemingly grants the Capitol what they want, her death. However, the Capitol's victory is hollow as it was not their actions that brought about her death, but rather her own.

We have discussed numerous times agency and suicide in previous chapters. As stated, suicide, when running from confronting emotions or reality, often negates agency. However, in this case, Mags' suicide is based on exerting agency over outside constraints. In committing intentional suicide, Mags does what Katniss threatened to do in the 74th Hunger Games with the berries. Mags denies the Capitol any victory over her life as she not only protects her loved ones and furthers the rebellion, but she also robs the Capitol of any satisfaction in her death. Mags, like Peeta, achieves agency through the exclusion of well-being and the inclusion of self-sacrifice.

Johanna Mason—Isolation, Solitude and Suffering

Contrarily, Collins' depiction of Johanna Mason sets up in direct opposition to Mags' and Peeta's sacrificial natures as Johanna displays the consequences that a lack of relationships can bring to personal agency. It may seem that a lack of relationships is beneficial for the individual because there is no one worth sacrificing personal well-being for. For example, if Katniss did not love Prim she would not have volunteered for the Games, if Peeta did not love Katniss he would not have been beaten by the Capitol when he warned her of the incoming bombs, if Finnick did not love Annie or Mags then the Capitol could not force him into sex slavery. Johanna, seeing how the Capitol manipulates relationships, avoids them at all cost to maintain her individual well-being. However, Johanna's damaged agency and identity at the conclusion of the trilogy adamantly argues against using such strategies.

From the very beginning, Johanna displays her detachment from forming relationships. While in the 3rd Quarter Quell, Johanna enters into the wedge of the island previously inhabited by jabberjays which mimic the sounds of the Victor's loved one's tortured screams. Although Katniss warns her against entering, Johanna shakes her off, saying, "They can't hurt me. I'm not like the rest of you. There's no one left that I love."[10] These three short sentences reveal more about Johanna's character than the rest of the books combined. These sentences hint that, like Haymitch, Johanna lost her family and friends to the Capitol due to either a stunt pulled in the Games or her unwillingness to comply to Capitol obligations (such as Finnick's sexual enslavement). As Katniss repeatedly mentions Johanna's Games and her tactic of first appearing weak, it seems that the Capitol does not censor her Games as they do Haymitch's after he embarrassed them by using the force field. This means that Johanna's crime against the Capitol most likely occurred outside of the Games. From this, we can deduce that Johanna's focus on her own well-being most likely cost her the lives of her loved ones after she refused to comply with the Capitol's demands.

Having lost those who meant everything to her, Johanna attempts to view her isolation as beneficial as it means that there is no one left that the Capitol can use to manipulate her choices or threaten her well-being. Subsequently, she believes that she is set apart from the other Victors, stronger, due to her segregation from others. However, when President Snow announces the 3rd Quarter Quell, Johanna has the odds stacked against her as she remains the only female Victor from District 7. There is no one to volunteer to take her place, there is no other name that could be called, and the Capitol forces her back into the arena. Her lack of relationships does not protect her from re-entering the arena, torture from the Capitol, or the following Post Traumatic Stress Disorder (PTSD) that she develops. Johanna's isolation only leaves her lonely and broken.

Even in *Mockingjay*, Johanna returns to the narrative in full force, broken, bald, and with the same bad attitude as she continuously pushes aside any opportunity to form relationships, clinging to the idea that solitude will protect her well-being from external manipulation. This self-imposed seclusion excludes her from the other Victors. After failing her training due to her trauma that impedes her ability to act calmly, Johanna must remain in District 13 while the other Victors travel to the Capitol as part of the Star Squad. Johanna fails at forming stabilizing relationships as she still believes that they might threaten her independence. Even her friendships with Katniss and Finnick are strained at best. In the end, when Johanna votes yes in continuing the Hunger Games using the children of the Capitol, Collins presents her character as bitter, broken, and continuously alone. After the meeting, nothing further is said about Johanna and readers can only guess at her fate.

While Johanna survives the narrative and Mags does not, Mags clearly possesses more agency within the trilogy than Johanna. Johanna lives, but at what cost? Running from relationships that could possibly jeopardize her self-sufficiency, Johanna simply exists. While she desires to go to war, District 13 denies her request due to her lack of mental stability. Although Johanna desires a continuation of the Hunger Games, she is in no position to make that a reality. Repeatedly, external forces block Johanna's intentions and unfulfilled desires. On the other hand, Mag's desires repeatedly come to fruition. While Johanna would sacrifice her independence for no one, Mags and Peeta willingly obliterate their own well-being for the sake of others and are constantly rewarded within the narrative with agency for their efforts. Through these three characters, Collins highlights that while well-being plays a role in agency, individuals cannot obtain agency if well-being is the sole focus. Personal agency often requires personal sacrifice as autonomy flourishes within relationships and withers away within solitude.

Beetee—Power, Intelligence and (Human) Error

When first introduced, Beetee is part of a pair, he is "Volts" to his district partner Wiress' "Nuts." Together, they are "Nuts and Volts"—the Victor pair chosen from District 3 to participate in the 3rd Quarter Quell, and both are highly intelligent. Although the two seem inseparable, they are quickly parted within the Quell when Cashmere slits Wiress' throat early on during the Games. Surprisingly, Beetee is not overly distraught by her death, tears do not threaten his eyes as they do Finnick's after Mag's death. Almost mechanically, Beetee's fingers play over his spool of wire as he accepts that the odds did not favor Wiress' survival. Indeed, it seems that Beetee's closest companion in life was not his human partner, but rather the technology that he is able to manipulate—wire not Wiress.

Beetee wields his intelligence with technology just as Gale wields his cleverness with hunting and trapping. Beetee's intellect allows him to exercise agency by transforming his intentions and ideas into literal and practical applications. However, much like Gale who acts first without considering the consequences, Beetee focuses on what he *can* do as opposed to what he *should* do, often negatively impacting his agency as he allows his actions to take precedent over reasoning in which his inventions are used against him. During the training for the 3rd Quarter Quell, Beetee talks to Katniss about a sewing device that "Automatically ... rules out human error."[11] Ironically, Beetee prefers technology to humanity because he believes technology is foolproof unlike mankind with their various shortcomings. As humans are flawed, Beetee places his trust in and agency on technology. Throwing himself into his work, Beetee often focuses on the how instead of the why. Consequently, and perhaps ironically, Beetee brings his own human error into the technology that he creates. This focus on eliminating human error damages Beetee in the same way that Gale's focus on how to acquire power destroys his agency.

The shared desires for advancement through either intelligence or power drive Beetee and Gale away from moral concerns as demonstrated by their technological creations devised during the rebellion. In *Mockingjay*, in Special Forces of District 13, Beetee studies the aerodynamics of hummingbirds, hoping to mimic their flight patterns. When Katniss arrives, his mind shifts and asks if she would be able to shoot one with an arrow to which she replies she has never tried as there is not much meat on them. While conceding to this point, Beetee insists, "I bet they'd be hard to shoot, though."[12] Immediately, Gale too becomes captivated with the idea and wonders whether he could accomplish the action, not bothering with the why. He suggests that they could capture the birds in a net and then kill them. This small, seemingly inconsequential moment depicts both Beetee's and Gale's mentality of "could I" not "should I" which is more harmful to each of their agencies than beneficial.

Furthermore, like Gale, Beetee's accumulation of power, in the form of perfecting technological advancements, injures not only his own desires but also those around him. For instance, Beetee's interactions with technology are successful in the creation of a tool, but the tool often blocks his own ability to act. While living as a Victor underneath the Capitol's authority, Beetee practically redesigned the transmitting network for Panem Television. In the film adaptations,[13] Beetee expands on his involvement, confessing that he increased the security within the Capitol's airwaves not out of a sense of duty toward the Capitol or even because he was afraid of the Capitol's wrath, but because he wanted to see how far he could perfect the system. Beetee admits, "I can't find my way through it. Guess I did my job too well. At the time, I was just thinking of the science of it all."[14] In a sense, Beetee must battle against his past self to accomplish his present goals during the revolution. Throughout *Mockingjay*, Beetee admits that the casualties of war could prove problematic in sustaining a surviving population. Logically, Beetee is aware that the rebellion must preserve as many lives as possible and yet, simultaneously he works alongside Gale to create a two-timed bomb that creates mass casualties of not only combatants but also of innocent bystanders because he is interested in the design.

However, Beetee does differ from Gale in one important way, he acknowledges his own human errors before it is too late. When confronted by Katniss about the morality of the bomb, Gale is defiant but Beetee begins to doubt. It is this doubt and Beetee's own understanding that humans are erred that directs Beetee away from Gale's outcome. By the end of the trilogy, Gale, although humbled by Prim's death, is still Gale and only regrets that the bomb killed Prim, not that the bomb was created. However, Beetee realizing the horror that his technology can cause realizes that he must change his way of thinking. At the last meeting of the Victors, when asked to vote on the continuation of the Hunger Games, Beetee responds, "No.... It would set a bad precedent. We have to stop viewing one another as enemies. At this point, unity is essential for our survival. No."[15] No doubt, had Gale been a part of this group, fueled by his rage over Prim's death, he would have voted yes and waited contently to watch the slaughter of innocent Capitol-born children pay the penalties of their parents. In voting no, Beetee separates himself from Gale and from their combined desire to act instead of think. Most likely, Beetee's mind would have enjoyed the complexities of creating and executing a new arena as Head Gamemaker, but it is his restraint that demonstrates how Beetee's agency evolves by the end of the narrative. While Beetee is initially similar to Gale in the way that they act, interested in how to accomplish the action itself without thinking whether they should, he is entirely different at the end of the trilogy. Through this pair, Collins' narrative displays intentionality and thought behind agency. It is not enough to act, but agency requires action with proper motivation.

Sonder

While none of these characters, Finnick, Mags, Joanna, or Beetee, take one of the major roles in the narrative, their characters resonate with readers all across the globe who demand back stories and spin-offs on each of them. What fan does not want to read about Finnick and Annie's love story? *Forbes* recently released an article stating that Suzanne Collins new book coming out in 2020 will be a prequel novel in *The Hunger Games* series. According to the press release, recorded in *Forbes* article, "The untitled Panem novel 'will revisit the world of Panem sixty-four years before the event of *The Hunger Games*, on the morning of the reaping of the Tenth Hunger Games.'"[16] Will readers perhaps get to see a young Mags? Will we finally know whether she volunteers or is reaped? The announcement of a new book only highlights the effect that Collins' trilogy has on her audiences. Collins' complex creation of each character as highly individualized causes readers to crave more. Although Collins introduces Finnick, Mags, Johanna, and Beetee halfway through the trilogy, each of these characters demonstrate identities that are as complex as the identities that the major three characters present throughout each book. Individually, these minor characters struggle to discover, maintain, and enact personal agency within their circumstances and restrictions.

Unlike many traditional dystopian, Collins' side characters are not merely fodder for the plot line, but rather, each person actively affects reader understanding of the novels and agency. Additionally, these characters help support the discoveries made about their major counterparts. Both Finnick and Katniss illustrate the ability to exercise limited agency through one's body even when held hostage and susceptible to outside influences. Also, they each reclaim the agency of fallen tributes, highlighting the attainability of agency even after death. Between Peeta, Mags, and Johanna, readers can come to understand that well-being is not always the primary factor in obtaining and establishing own's own agency. Indeed, both Peeta and Mags, who constantly sacrifice their well-being, conclude their individual stories with far more personal power than Johanna Mason has throughout the entire trilogy. Lastly, both Beetee and Gale allow their personal desires for perfection and power to infect the ways in which the act. While Gale serves as a warning against the corrupting nature of power on agency, Beetee offers hope for an individual who has strayed to return to an uncontaminated state of agency.

We do not only analyze these characters for what they can individually teach readers, but also for what they represent as a collective. Collins' intricate presentation of minor characters not only supports the current discussions on agency but also creates a feeling of sonder within the reader. Coined by John Koenig in 2012 in his project *The Dictionary of Obscure Sorrows*, sonder is used to describe "the realization that each random passerby is living a life as vivid and complex as your own—populated with their own ambitions, friends, routines, worries and inherited craziness—an epic story that continues invisibly around you … thousands of other lives that you'll never know existed."[17] In other words, sonder forces an individual to look outward at the millions of other stories that surround them instead of only looking inward. In current society, adolescents have access to the lives of millions around them through Facebook, Instagram, Twitter, etc., and yet many still only focus on their own personal stories, often forgetting that there are others out there living as intensely as they are. Collins' inclusion of minor characters that are just as complex as Katniss, Peeta, and Gale ought to compel readers to consider more than their own profile.

Within *Catching Fire*, at the initiation of the 3rd Quarter Quell, readers are prepared to root against the other Victor-tributes, particularly those that hail from the Career Districts, and to cheer on their deaths as they hope for Katniss' and Peeta's survival. Contrary to these expectations, readers are surprised by Collins' inclusion and descriptions of characters such as Finnick, Mags, Johanna, and Beetee. Technically speaking, Finnick, Mags, and Beetee all originate from Career Districts in which the tributes are more likely to be trained for the Games. Due to the first book's emphasis on the antagonist aspects of Career Tributes, Collins conditions readers to automatically hate the Victor-tributes originating from such districts. In the second book, Collins could have created allies for Katniss and Peeta from any of the other districts and yet, she intentionally chose Victors from the despised, Capitol-loving districts instead. Repeatedly, Collins confronts reader expectation by not only incorporating Career Victor-tributes as allies but also as victims of the system.

Readers come to understand that these characters are not simply stock villains, but rather, each of these Victors is given a backstory and a life as real as Katniss' or Peeta's. Finnick is not only the sex-symbol of Panem, but also a man deeply in love with an unstable girl from his home district. Mags is not only an old, decrepit Victor, but also extremely capable of crafting beautiful fish hooks out of nothing. Johanna is not only a brutal killer, but also a woman broken from trauma. Beetee is not only a genius, but also someone who can translate the gibberish of his mentally unstable partner with unending patience. Collins' inclusion of these minute details helps to flesh out these characters until readers no longer view them as only opponents. With the recognition of these characters as separate individuals, Collins encourages readers to recognize the same importance of strangers within their own societies. Collins' characters not only display individual agency, but also demonstrate to readers how agency is available to every individual, not only themselves. In understanding how anyone can have agency and how everyone wants agency, readers are encouraged to look not only inward, but to look outward as well.

TEN

"I took over as head of the family"

Agency and Problematic Parental/Surrogate Figures

A theme common within most twenty-first century literature, although more prevalent in dystopian, is the overwhelming absence of strong parental guidance. In the early twenty-first century, the top three young adult dystopian series included: *The Hunger Games* trilogy, the *Divergent* series, and *The Maze Runner* novels. In each of these series, parental presence is nearly intangible. In *Divergent,* society expects children to choose their own faction (sub-society) that will determine the rest of their lives and often separates them from their families. Even those who remain within their original factions must act apart from their familiar bonds, not as children but as members on equal footing with their parents: *Faction before blood.*[1] The main protagonist, Tris, reunites with her parents at the end of the first novel only to watch as both her mother and father are killed before her eyes. In *The Maze Runner* series there is simply no biological parental presence at all and most adults fill the roles of antagonists and villains. Thomas, the main protagonist, and the rest of the boys are forced to become adults within the Glade, unable to even remember their parents or the adult-scientists who are watching how they respond to pain and death.[2]

This trend of parental absence continues within *The Hunger Games* trilogy as well with the initial death of Mr. Everdeen and the subsequent let-down of parental and surrogate figures such as Mrs. Everdeen, Haymitch, Cinna, Mr. & Mrs. Mellark, and Mr. & Mrs. Hawthorne. However, this theme of the absent parental figure is not new to twenty-first century young adult dystopia. It is not even new to the dystopian genre. Novels like *A Brave New World* and *Lord of the Flies* also illustrate a lack of adult influence over children's lives. However, it is Orson Scott Card's 1985 *Ender's Game* that best displays the connection between parental absence and individual agency for children and young adults in pre-twenty-first century dystopian fiction. Card's science-fiction, dystopian novel depicts a world in which only children can save mankind from their greatest enemy: buggers—a species from another planet intent on destroying Earth. Ender Wiggin, the main protagonist, is only *six years old* when his parents allow the government to ship Ender off to Battle School where he is isolated from his family and prevented from forming any relationships with others. Throughout this book, Colonel Graff—the main parental figure—forces Ender to endure the brutal training of Battle School alone without help or support from others to accelerate his maturity and tactical prowess.

The intentional vacuum caused by parental absence results in a need for something, or someone, to fill it. If young adults cannot rely on their parental figures, then they must rely on someone else. More than likely, that someone will be themselves as the young adult learns to rely on his/her own abilities. Colonel Graff from *Ender's Game* asserts, "Ender Wiggins must believe that no matter what happens, no adult will ever, ever step in to help him in any way. He must believe that to the core of his soul.... If he does not believe that, then he will never reach the peak of his abilities."[3] Likewise in Collins' *The Hunger Games* trilogy, parental absence is entirely necessary for the achievement of individual agency and Collins incorporates this theme to appeal to current young adult readers. Within dystopian literature, particularly young adult dystopian literature, parental absence is almost always intentional on the author's part as it enables the protagonist to claim center stage in their own story. Indeed, it is due to the inadequate assortment of parental and surrogate figures that young characters such as Katniss, Gale, and Peeta have no choice but to assume the role of adult figure in their own lives and in the lives of those around them.

Parental Absence

Within *The Hunger Games* trilogy, possible parental figures abound and subsequently, they all fail miserably in appropriately raising their adolescent charges due to death or their own inability. Interestingly, authors Carrie Hintz and Elaine Ostry, argue in their book *Utopian and Dystopian Writing for Children and Young Adults* that in most YA dystopias, young adolescents must overcome adult-generated problems.[4] Indeed, the first problem that each YA protagonist must overcome is either the absence or incompetency of their own biological guardians. The adolescents in YA dystopian literature are left to defend themselves and the idea that help only comes to those who help themselves is consistently reinforced throughout such narratives.

For instance, *The Hunger Games* trilogy illustrates the lack of parental support present in current dystopian literature. In each of the novels, adult figures swarm around the adolescent protagonists and yet, for all their involvement, they prove ineffective as parental guides. Mr. Everdeen and Mr. Hawthorne play similar roles in the lives of their children: Katniss and Gale. Both fathers, although working to provide for their families, die in a mining accident while their children are still too young to provide for themselves according to social standards. While the two fathers may act as metaphorically superior parents, especially as Katniss often reminiscences of her father with rose-colored glasses, their absence is undeniable as they are unable to support their children after death.

Mrs. Everdeen and Mrs. Hawthorne vary greatly in their responses to their husbands' deaths, yet both still prove fruitless in caring for their eldest children. Mrs. Everdeen, who falls into a catatonic depressive state, is both physically and emotionally absent from her children after their father's death. On the day of the mining accident that kills Mr. Everdeen and Mr. Hawthorne, Katniss collects Prim from school and together they find their mother at the accident site clenching the rope, oblivious to her children. When looking back, Katniss thinks, "Why were we looking for her, when the reverse should have been true?"[5] Mrs. Everdeen, although the mother of Katniss and Prim, cannot help but to place her own hysteria above the emotional distress of her children even before falling into a depressed state after losing her husband. While Mrs. Everdeen is a healer and able to pass that trait on to Prim whom she mothers from time to time, she is never able to re-establish her role as mother to Katniss.

Katie Arosteguy, in her essay "Transformative Motherhood and Maternal Influence," discusses the complex presentation of mothering and "othermothering." Specifically looking at Katniss' relationship with Mrs. Everdeen, Arosteguy states, "Even though Katniss attempts to reject and cast aside her mother in *The Hunger Games*, Collins resists the urge to follow the typic YA narrative conventions of mother-daughter relations. Instead, Katniss needs and desires her mother's [healing and plant life] knowledge.... In this way, Collins insists on making Katniss' mother present."[6] Indeed, at times, specifically in the first arena, Katniss wishes for the same healing capabilities as her mother and Prim. However, another reading might argue that while Katniss may desire a reconciliation with her mother, that physical event never takes place. Mrs. Everdeen may be present, but she is not reliable or beneficial in any way.

Even after Prim's death at the end of *Mockingjay*, when Katniss and her mother are all that remain of their family unit, Mrs. Everdeen does not accompany her daughter in her exile to District 12. For Mrs. Everdeen, returning would be "too painful to bear"[7]; reinforcing how her own emotional pain is more focal to her than that of her child's and revealing her ineffectual status as mother. Arosteguy argues, "Casting her mother aside ... is not an option for this modern-day heroine [Katniss] who ultimately must reconcile with her mother in order to save herself and those around her from the perils of the Capitol."[8] Perhaps there is indeed reconciliation with her mother at the end of the series, as Katniss finally calls her mother and together they grieve over Prim's death. However, the physical distance between the two women continuously displays the emotional gap that never seems to heal due to Mrs. Everdeen's initial abandonment.

Our heroine is not the only character within the series to suffer from the family dysfunction that runs prevalent throughout Panem like a fire. In the same district, the Hawthorne and Mellark families present similar struggles of physical and/or emotional abandonment or neglect. Unlike Mrs. Everdeen who instantly deteriorates after her husband's death, Mrs. Hawthorne immediately sets out to find work and attempts to fulfill the role of parent even as she is in her last weeks of pregnancy. However, due to her numerous children apart from Gale, two sons and the infant daughter, Mrs. Hawthorne is unable to provide for her family alone. Not only his siblings' survival but also his mother's survival requires Gale's attention and efforts.

Katniss clearly indicates that regardless of Mrs. Everdeen's and Mrs. Hawthorne's involvement, both women depend on Katniss and Gale in the same manner than children rely on their parents. According to Katniss, "You may as well throw in our mothers, too, because how would they live without us? Who would fill those mouths that are always asking for more?"[9] The biological parental figures for both Katniss and Gale fail in their ability to act as parents with the fathers' deaths and the mothers' inabilities to provide adequate support for their families. In the reversal of roles, the mothers assume the position of children while their eldest children assume the responsibility of parent.

Within the Mellark family, both parents are alive and well and physically present for the first two novels, and yet, they prove to be useless at best and damaging at worst. Mrs. Mellark is an abusive mother who verbally and physically mistreats her children as is evident by her calling Peeta a "stupid creature" and leaving a "red welt" on his face that later evolves into a blackened eye when he is still a child.[10] Mr. Mellark seems to cower is his wife's shadow as readers never see him addressing the abuse that Mrs. Mellark commits on their children. While Mr. Mellark may not physically abuse his sons, he neglects his responsibilities as both husband and father by remaining utterly passive throughout the narrative. Although Collins rarely mentions Peeta's home life within the trilogy, small moments are enough to paint the picture of a broken family.

If the physical abuse was not enough, the Games reveal the emotional abuse prevalent within the Mellark house as well. After being selected as tribute for the 74th Hunger Games, Peeta is sequestered away and allowed to say goodbye to his family. When Mrs. Mellark arrives, there is no encouragement or support, but rather her firm belief that Katniss might actually win the Games—leaving Peeta to be shipped home in a pine box. Even before Peeta's death, his mother has not only accepted it and moved forward, but implied to her son that he will not be missed, leaving Peeta to feel the full range of her rejection.

It comes as no surprise then that when Peeta manages to survive and return home, he does not return to his family. Instead, he takes up residence within Victory Village, alone. Although his family could live with him, as Katniss' family lives with her, Peeta's family remains physically and emotionally separated from him. While Peeta may occasionally speak with his father when in town, he never again mentions his mother. During a snowstorm, Peeta is the one who goes to check on his family instead of his parents checking on him, revealing where loyalties and love lie. While Peeta's parents may be physically present in his life and they do not require Peeta to provide for them, they are emotionally absent and devoid of key parental characteristics such as love and support.

Clearly, biological parents within dystopias are practically useless and, at times, damaging to their children mentally, emotionally, or even physically. Surrogate figures, like Effie, Cinna, and Haymitch in *The Hunger Games* trilogy make up potential parental figures who are nearly just as incompetent as their biological counterparts. Effie, the charismatic and entirely clueless Capitol escort for District 12, is awarded a much more-motherly role in the movie adaptations than the book series. In the films, Effie evolves from an ignorant Capitol citizen to an enlightened rebel who truly cares for Katniss' well-being. However, within the novels, Effie is hardly encouraging or rebellious. As this examination is focused primarily on the novels, that is the Effie we will be discussing in relation to parental figures. When Peeta paints a picture of Rue as his Victor-skill for the Gamemakers before the 3rd Quarter Quell, Effie reveals her own inability to clearly view reality and "looks a little misty [and asks] 'Was it a picture of Katniss?'"[11]

Even as Katniss and Peeta are being forced back into the arena yet again, even with the rebellious atmosphere in the districts, Effie still allows Capitol propaganda, such as the star-crossed lovers, to "mist over" her thoughts. For Effie, it is more romantic to believe that Peeta would paint a picture of Katniss than to think that Peeta rebelliously painted a picture of Rue lying dead wreathed in flowers. Indeed, in learning that it is the later, Effie nearly cries and says, "This is dreadful.... That sort of thinking.... It's forbidden."[12] Unlike the emotional and supportive Effie from the films that contradicts the books, the Effie within the novels is too careful and too self-absorbed to truly protect and care for Katniss or Peeta as a parental surrogate. For these reasons, Effie is primarily absent from the last novel and when she does return at the end, Collins describes her as "remarkably unchanged except for the vacant look in her eyes."[13] Similar to the earlier quote where Effie looks "misty," this quote notes the "vacant look" in her eyes. Ultimately, she is unchanged physically or emotionally, her clouded eyes portraying Effie's overall blindness to the events going on around her. Throughout the trilogy, Effie remains clueless to the cruelty of the Capitol, the rebellious motives of those around her, and is completely unable to fulfill the role of mother to Katniss.

Contrarily, Cinna nearly satisfies the father-role in Katniss life; however, much like Mr. Everdeen, death strips Cinna's presence from her life. In displaying fatherly actions, Cinna provides support, comfort, and guidance for Katniss while she is in the Capitol. While Mr. Everdeen taught Katniss the importance of hunting and music, Cinna teaches Katniss the importance of displaying inner strength through her physical appearance. Interestingly, both of these men, whom Katniss considers with utmost respect, teach Katniss not only about masculine traits such as strength and hunting, but also about feminine qualities such as music and fashion. In teaching these more feminine traits, both Mr. Everdeen and Cinna work to fulfill both the father and mother roles in Katniss' life. Nevertheless, both Mr. Everdeen and Cinna fail as father figures. Mr. Everdeen passes early on, and Cinna proves powerless in protecting Katniss from the Hunger Games while alive and because his guidance is no longer available after his untimely death. Both men create an absence in Katniss' life, not due to a lack of effort, but rather a lack of presence.

Unlike Mr. Everdeen or Cinna, Haymitch hardly ever fulfills the traditional roles of a father although he is in the perfect position to do so as Katniss' Mentor. Regardless of the opportunity, Haymitch is drunk and coarse; he can also be violent and ill-tempered. Within the first two novels, he withholds key information, lies to and otherwise deceives Katniss. Perhaps we could argue that Haymitch does offer guidance in the arenas, often encouraging Katniss to act in a certain way so that the sponsors will respond with generous gifts. However, these tit-for-tat exchanges echo more of a bartering system than that of a father providing for a daughter. While Haymitch does eventually demonstrate care for Katniss and provide comfort in *Mockingjay*, such as sharing her pain over Peeta, it is too little too late as his coarse nature continuously prevents him from engaging in a healthy father/daughter relationship. Haymitch's own vices, such as alcohol and lying, often blind him to Katniss' needs even after the war is over. When Katniss struggles to understand who set off the bomb that killed Prim, she goes to Haymitch, seeking guidance and reassurance. Drunk, he mocks her, asking if her problems revolve around "more boy trouble."[14] Ultimately, Haymitch proves to be more of an ally than a parent. By the time that Haymitch fully commits to his relationship with Katniss by volunteering to accompany her to District 12 in exile, Katniss no longer needs a parental figure having become her own.

Consequently Katniss, Gale, and Peeta all experience the same emptiness caused by a physical lack or ineffectual parental figures: biological or surrogate. According to Braithwaite, Hutton, and Miller, authors of "Family Ties? Parent-Child Relationships in a Selection of Young Adult Critical Dystopian Tests," "Critical dystopian texts for young adults demand a re-structuring of familial bonds, frequently with an emphasis on parent-child relationships."[15] However, as seen through *The Hunger Games* trilogy, dystopian texts do not merely require a re-structuring of parent-child relationships, but rather, it demands the *de-structuring* of parent-child relationships. Indeed, it is the physical and emotional separation from security offered by parental figures that prompts the young protagonist to seek power elsewhere. Therefore, the destruction of the family unit is entirely necessary to the achievement of agency in dystopian texts. When the parental figure is absent it disturbs the child's role from its intended position as dependent on another. The vacuum caused by parental absence requires that children forsake their childhoods and pushes them into early adulthood regardless of their physical age. Furthermore, it is the survival techniques that children learn within their broken childhood homes that later enable them to thrive as young adults.

Inherited Agency—A Product of Their Environment

While *The Hunger Games* is a series about children, there is nothing child-like about its content or its characters. Katniss, Gale, and Peeta may look like children at the beginning of their narratives, being respectively eleven, thirteen, and twelve years old when they lose parental guidance, Nevertheless, without the presence of strong parental figures, each of these children must abdicate their adolescence early on. Their childhoods are not filled with self-concern, but for the concern of others and how their actions might positively or negatively affect those whom they are now in charge of. The term "othermothering," highlighted by Arosteguy, applies to "characters who mother and act as mothers ... [and that *The Hunger Games*] broaden(s) societal discourse on what motherhood is and who can be a mother."[16] Katniss, Gale, and Peeta each enact othermothering to some extent and it is this role as surrogate adult-figures that cause such characters to quickly learn how to exert their own desires and transform them into intentional actions. In other words, the absent parental guide leads to an extreme need for personal agency influenced by personal experiences at a young age.

Both Katniss' and Gale's first sense of agency is based directly on the absence of parental figures within their lives and their own experiences with othermothering or "otherfathering" as it were. Within the opening pages of *The Hunger Games*, Katniss and Gale consider their odds of running away from District 12 and living happily in the woods. Gale admits, "We could do it…. If we didn't have so many kids."[17] Immediately, readers are made aware that Katniss' and Gale's actions are restricted by their obligations to their families. Not only that, but that Katniss and Gale accept without question that they are parents and as such, have restricted freedom concerning their own actions. There is no debate on whether they should simply flee without their kids. Much like a dedicated parent would abhor the idea of abandoning their children, Katniss and Gale accept their roles as other-mother and other-father to their siblings and mothers. Interestingly, while they are indeed two adolescents without any biological children, the idea of running off into the woods is pure fantasy while parenthood is their reality.

Additionally, both Katniss and Gale build their agency around what was deficient in their childhoods. In lacking both a father and a mother, Katniss must assume the role of both parents for the survival of her sister-child, Prim. In replacing the role of her father, Katniss finds strength and power in hunting. Although she is initially frightened by the woods, her love for her family and her need to provide for them overpowers her fear of injury or death. She also takes over as head of the household, not only in enacting the more traditionally male role of breadwinner, but also the stereotypical female role of comforter and nurturer. After all, it is Katniss who comforts and encourages Prim to stay strong on the reaping day, not Mrs. Everdeen. Due to the lack of physical or emotion support from her parents, Katniss sheds her childhood and becomes the adult figure, both father and mother, in not only Prim's life but in the lives of the innocents around her such as Rue, Bonnie, and Mags. Katniss' agency, affected by her childhood and based on the protection, provision, and care of others, follows her into her young adulthood. Her motherly nature compels her to care and comfort others like Rue, the tribute from District 11, and Bonnie, the runaway from District 8. Her fatherly characteristics encourage Katniss to fight against oppression, to even become violent if necessary, and to protect Peeta or her family by hunting others within the arena and during the rebellion.

Meanwhile, because Gale's father dies and his mother remains mostly intact, Gale focuses on assuming the role of father only, enacting a type of "otherfathering" just as Katniss endorses "othermothering." He must become the "man" of the household, relying entirely on his ability to bring home dinner—often shot in the woods—and work in the mines to provide for his family. Collins hyperbolizes Gale's maleness through his physicality as the tall, dark, handsome, traditional male protagonist of the young adult narrative. Katniss describes him as "good-looking, he's strong enough to handle the work in the mines, and he can hunt."[18] Gale, who attempts to fill the void left by his father's absence, discovers his worth in his ability to provide for his family and through his status as head of household—in other words, from his distinct "maleness."

The role that he is forced to assume influences how Gale exercises agency later in his adolescence. Gale's actions are primarily exaggerations of male physicality, violence, and spontaneity. According to Whitney Jones, "Collins' depiction of Gale is hyper-masculine; he is the emotionally-hardened warrior, hunter, provider, and overall alpha male."[19] Even at a young age, Gale takes to "rant[ing] about how the tesserae are just another tool to cause misery ... smoldering underneath his stony expression ... yelling about the Capitol in the woods."[20] Due to the absence of his father, Gale compensates by exaggerating many stereotypical male traits as he grows into adulthood. By the time the rebellion occurs, Gale's agency is influenced by his hot-temper, his assertive, take-control nature, and a tendency toward violence.

Different from both of the above characters, Peeta's parents are physically present in both his childhood and later adolescence; however, the negative actions of Mr. and Mrs. Mellark similarly affect and influence Peeta's development of agency. The lack in Peeta's home life stems from the absence of a compassionate, peaceful, and safe environment. While Peeta does not feel the need to fulfill the role of mother/father like Katniss, or father like Gale, an overwhelming desire for peace and non-violence influence Peeta's actions. As a child, Peeta takes the physical and verbal abuse from his mother without a single complaint, and yet, he does not allow the abuse to twist his own identity. He does not allow violence to corrupt his nature; but instead, it encourages him to become pacifistic.

Furthermore, although Peeta does not need to fill the role of parent, he does assume more domestic characteristics when compared to Gale's masculinity, reflecting the larger gap left by his mother as opposed to his father. Unlike Gale who hunts and works in the mines, Peeta paints and stays home in the kitchen and bakes. Although Peeta does not take over the mother's role, it is interesting that Peeta's actions are more stereotypically female when analyzed alongside Gale's masculine traits.[21] This is most likely attributed to Mrs. Mellark's deficiencies as a traditional and loving mother. In response to her faults, Peeta bases his agency in domesticity and non-violence. Like Katniss, Peeta engages in acts of "othermothering" through the way he cares for others, even his "opponents" within the Games. Essentially, Peeta becomes a calm, steady, reliable, and peaceful character because that is what he lacked most in his childhood.

Braithwaite, Hutton, and Miller, scholars of YA literature, assert, "For the young adult protagonist at least in this genre [young adult dystopian], that parents can be alive, dead, ineffectual or selfish, but they remain a powerful influence which must be negotiated for young adult protagonists to achieve true agency."[22] Consequently, within these narratives, parents that are alive, dead, and/or ineffectual highly affect the ways in which Katniss, Gale, and Peeta act out their own agency. Constantly, their actions are influenced by childhood experiences and restrictions placed on their freedom due to parental involvement or neglect. The absence of parental guidance eventually results in the destruction of childhood as children must evolve quickly into mature adulthood for their sakes and the sake of others. Furthermore, while the parents may be absent or ineffectual, their actions still influence the ways in which their children develop and grow into maturity. While the children can evolve into their new roles as mother, father, and protector in order to fill a gap, the lack of parental guidance is still reflected in their emotional instability.

The Need for Another

Regardless of their maturity and the adult-roles that they are able to assume, biologically Katniss, Gale, and Peeta are still children and perhaps this is why each character suffers a mental breakdown of sorts through the course of their narratives. For instance, after the explosion in the Capitol, after watching Prim burn to death, Katniss becomes "trapped for days, years, centuries maybe. Dead, but not allowed to die. Alive, but as good as dead."[23] Peeta, too, is stuck in a type of mental hysteria for months after the Capitol's hijacking as he is unable to distinguish reality from falsity, resulting in several breakdowns. While both of these characters have striven to fill the void lefts by their absent parental figures, and each have gained and exercised agency to some degree, there is still the recognition of the need for outside assistance. No matter how strong Katniss and Peeta have become, neither of these characters can survive or heal on their own.

These young adult characters, completely bereft of parental leadership, find support and family within their friendships and relationships. For instance, Katniss and Peeta do not heal through the efforts of an adult, but through the presence of an adolescent with similar experiences. Katniss, having lost Prim, essentially loses her purpose in life. Having cared for Prim since Katniss was eleven, Katniss has grown content with her role of mother and nurturer. Without Prim, Katniss' agency flounders for purchase and finds a new foundation with Peeta. Likewise, Peeta who once based his agency on non-violence finds that his identity has been torn apart and has transformed him into a man who has committed murder multiple times. However, in returning to District 12 and offering to plant primroses for Katniss, Peeta slowly returns to his original agency based on peace. With Peeta's family dead and Katniss' mother absent (again), Peeta and Katniss find strength in one another when "he clutches the back of a chair and hangs on until the flashbacks are over [and when Katniss] wake[s] screaming from nightmares of mutts and lost children."[24] Collins demonstrates that their agency, founded at a young age and tested by fire, can only be reignited by someone who has experienced similar loss and accomplishment.

Furthermore, through Collins' narrative, it is arguable that agency, influenced by filling the voids left in own childhood homes, follows the individual into parenthood. Some readers and viewers find Collins' epilogue with Katniss the Mother as extremely problematic. Sian Gaetano, of *The Horn Book*, criticizes, "Four movies. *Four.* Of strength and wit and sacrifice and crushing defeats and women enacting world-changing events. All to bring us to one final scene: Katniss the Mother. It devastates me that this ending was so misrepresented."[25] Indeed, any movie-goer who has not read the books may not understand how Katniss the Mother is actually the greatest representation of Katniss' strength. Having children returns Katniss to her initial sense of agency founded on her desire to nurture. Becoming a mother does not detract from Katniss' strength or individuality; rather it displays her healing and self-sufficiency.

Additionally, unlike their own parents, Katniss and Peeta do everything within their power to allow their children to remain children throughout their adolescence. In concluding the trilogy, Katniss thinks, "My children, who don't know they play on a graveyard. Peeta says it will be okay. We have each other.... We can make them understand in a way that will make them braver."[26] Together, Katniss and Peeta will raise children who are aware of social injustices; however, their children will not be expected to face the weight of the world on their own as Katniss and Peeta were forced to do. In acknowledging the power behind unity, Katniss and Peeta will break the cycle of problematic parental figures and usher in a new generation that can face the future because they have a record of the past. Through Katniss' and Peeta's decision to be honest with their children, Collins reinforces her own ideas that children should not be sheltered. Books are meant to challenge the young mind, and to bring about enlightenment and truth. This enlightenment of the real world is not supposed to be hidden by parents, but rather explained by them, so that they can help guide their children and teach them how to navigate such a society. In this way, Katniss and Peeta become the ideal image of what Collins desires for the parents of those children who read her books.

Interestingly, of the three major characters, Gale does not undergo a mental breakdown at the end of *Mockingjay* although he too has undergone various traumatic experiences. Perhaps on the surface this suggests that Gale is too strong, too adult to break, as he is at an adult age by the end of the trilogy. However, because Gale does not allow himself to break, he also cannot heal. In the end, he does not reach out to another for healing as Katniss and

Peeta do. Instead, he exits the narrative quietly and moves on to work a job in District 2. Perhaps we can hope that Gale is able to heal on his own, but his self-imposed isolation from the rest of the characters suggests otherwise.

Young Adult Dystopian Agency

Throughout the series, there is an abundance of mutilation, death, and destruction. Avoxes have their tongues cut out while tributes are torn apart piece by piece by fluffy carnivorous squirrels. In such a series, it follows that the family unit would also suffer physical mutilation that impacts every member: adults, adolescents, and children. Braithwaite, Hutton, and Miller state it best: "When the [family] structure is damaged, fragmented, or simply absent, the individual must behave in a way conducive to his or her own success, or in more extreme cases posited in dystopian test, his or her very survival."[27] In other words, when parental figures come up lacking in dystopian societies, the children must react quickly and effectively to survive. This reaction often comes in the shape of agency, formed at a young age because of and despite their childhood home environment. Parental figures must fall in dystopian literature so that the adolescent can rise and claim agency. However, that does not mean that the protagonist will discover agency easily or escape confrontation with challenges as seen by the various mental breakdowns that Katniss and Peeta endure. While the young adults' rising can be unstable at times, it does not diminish the fact that they do indeed rise.

Personal obstacles, social injustices, and traumatic experiences await the adolescent and young adult in the twenty-first century. *The Hunger Games* series follows a theme of parental absence similar to that of other YA dystopias such as *Ender's Game*, *The Maze Runner*, and *Divergent*. However, it is this trilogy that best dramatizes the negative effects of a broken family unit and places further emphasis on how individuals can discover their own maturity and agency due to the absence of parental support or guidance. Parental absence becomes an ever-more prevalent predicament of the twenty-first century, causing narratives such as *The Hunger Games* to becoming increasingly more common and relevant. In such narratives, young protagonists are often physically smaller and less powerful than the adult antagonists to encourage its readers in discovering their own strengths and capabilities. While protagonists like Katniss may feel abandoned by their parents and left to struggle on their own, they survive and establish agency all their own. With novels such as these, the adolescent or young adult reader is left with Katniss, Peeta, and Gale as examples for how to approach their own societies: to develop your own agency, to fight to fill the void in your own life, and to create a better world for the next generation.

ELEVEN

"The promise that life can go on.... That it can be good again"

Agency and 21st Century Readers

Suzanne Collins published the first installment of *The Hunger Games* trilogy in 2008. Since then, Collins' books have captured the minds and hearts of audiences all over the globe. Even twelve years after their publication, the trilogy remains popular in both the scholarly and non-scholarly realms, and there is no sign that its status will lessen any time soon with the news of an upcoming prequel to debut in 2020. *The Hunger Games* trilogy has taken its place among top dystopian novels, often studied in the classroom, like *Nineteen Eighty-Four*, *Brave New World*, and *A Handmaid's Tale* that reflect their individual societal concerns. Likewise, in many ways the nation of Panem intentionally reflects our own twenty-first century and hyperbolizes current concerns. Just as Huxley, Orwell, and Atwood wrote about issues regarding their own societies, Collins' trilogy is a response and critique of the violence of war, the national state of anxiety, and the callousness of twenty-first century viewers as evidenced by reality television and other media outlets.

The Hunger Games trilogy is an unflinching examination of the social issues that many twenty-first century readers face in their lives. In her trilogy, Collins provides readers with an opportunity to vicariously experience personal dilemmas and communal complications within the safety of their own bedrooms and libraries. Melissa Ames, a scholar of adolescent dystopias, notes that twenty-first century young adults "often turn to the safe confines of fiction to wrestle with them [political themes and concerns]."[1] Although, Collins' dystopian novels follow the dystopian genre (such as the three traditional dystopias mentioned above), she departs from them in a specific and significant way as her main characters overcome the oppression of their society. Indeed, Collins characters, both major and minor, are able to reject traditional dystopian endings through personal and cooperative agency, a theme seen repeatedly through the actions of Katniss, Peeta, Gale, Haymitch, Cinna, Prim, Finnick, Mags, Johanna, and Beetee. Consequently, based on previous discussions as seen throughout this book, readers can see that Collins' positive illustration of agency in a dystopian society separates her trilogy from other YA dystopian literature. Collins characters, plot, and hopeful conclusion appeal directly to a twenty-first century society in need of honesty, intentionality, and encouragement.

Closer to Panem Than You Think

A large part of reader fascination with *The Hunger Games* series comes from the similarities, although hyperbolized, that the books share with our own twenty-first century society. All over the world, people are bombarded by warfare, either in person or on a screen. Viewers across the globe have access to graphic images of war and death, not only on the nightly news, but also on social media outlets such as Facebook and Instagram. Reality television transforms real-life dystopian issues into forms of entertainment. Within the world of Panem, the Capitol's form of entertainment comes from the Hunger Games. Within the world of the twenty-first century reader, entertainment can be found in adopting more serious issues into competitions.

The idea of watching contestants struggle to survive is not a new one in our society with shows literally titled *Survivor* that find their basis in history with events such as the colosseum and gladiators. While show contestants do not attempt to slaughter one another, they do lie, steal, and cheat. In fact, producers encourage such actions if the contestants really want to win. Our society does not seem so very different from that of Panem when we consider the reality television show proposed in 2016. Indeed, only one year after *Mockingjay Part 2* was released in theaters, Russian entrepreneur Yevgeny Pyatkovsky planned the ultimate reality survival show titled "Games: Winter2" which the media referred to as the "real-life Hunger Games" of the twenty-first century. In anticipation of this proposed reality television show, hopeful participants from around the globe submitted their profiles and online videos, hoping to garner a fan base that would vote them into participating in the Games and later sponsor them by sending gifts.

Once chosen, these participants—tributes—would be shipped off to the Russian wilderness, equipped with a body camera, and expected to last nine months without any outside help. The area—or arena—would supposedly be surveilled with over two-thousand cameras to capture footage 24/7 that audience members would have constant access to after paying a small fee. When the media first announced the Winter Games, Pyatkovsky received backlash over his one rule: "Everything is allowed. Fighting, alcohol, murder, rape, smoking, anything."[2] Although the participants were not encouraged to fight, rape, or kill, they would not be stopped by the organizers of the Games.[3] Regardless of this controversial quote, participants from all over the world volunteered with the hopes of being chosen. Women, men, young and old all looked forward to testing their survival skills and of course, winning the million-dollar prize which was to be split between the remaining contestants at the end of the nine months.

Contestants' dreams were dashed in June 2017 however, when reports revealed that Yevgeny Pyatkovsky had fabricated the entire thing, the website was taken down and contestants were told that the entire project was only a stunt, "a fake to help my [Pyatkovsky's] market research."[4] Perhaps what is even more disturbing than the fact that so many people willingly signed up for this experience, is how many people were outraged when they learned it was a fake. Contestants called Pyatkovsky a cheat and a swindler as they were robbed of their chance to compete in the Games: Winter2. Even those who had no desire to participate themselves were disappointed by the fact that they could never watch these Games online. While the show never came to fruition, its popularity soared as audiences around the world prepared themselves to watch twenty-four-hour footage of contestants struggling against nature and each other to win the ultimate prize. Like Capitol citizens, viewers had already begun to vote on which contestants they wanted to see in the Games and who they would willingly sponsor with gifts of food and supplies. The similarities between the world of Panem and our own twenty-first century society are eerily obvious when we consider how easily audiences were drawn into a seemingly real version of the Hunger Games.

Capitol Television

Perhaps some, similar to those in the districts, are appalled by the possibility of our own Hunger Games, but even then, they are not safe from the images blasted through social outlets. Like those in the districts, whom the Capitol forces to watch beatings and public executions, viewers across the nation are bombarded with violent images on almost every screen. Nightly news covers domestic and foreign terror attacks, such as the Las Vegas Shooting of 2017, and repeatedly replayed the associated graphic and disturbing images and videos. In April of 2013, the terrorist group Islamic State in Iraq and the Levant (known to many as ISIL or ISIS) began leaving bloody footprints throughout the news. As of 2018, ISIS had commenced 142 attacks in twenty-nine different countries killing more than 2,000 people.[5] Some of their tactics are unnervingly similar to those shown in Collins' series as ISIS has been known to air videos of the beheading and/or torture of American and British hostages such as James Foley and Alan Henning in 2014. While several nations such as the United States, France, the United Kingdom, Russia, and other Arab nations have united against ISIS, such gruesome acts and images will most likely continue to reappear nightly on televisions throughout the nations.

Not only are viewers exposed to violence through news, but also through social media where they are not prepared for the continuous and surprising onslaught of traumatic images. In 2017, unsuspecting Facebook viewers, including young children, watched a video in which a mentally unstable man, Steve Stephens, approached an unarmed, elderly man name Robert Godwin on the streets of Ohio City. Although the two did not know each other, Stephens posted a live video of him killing Godwin by shooting him directly in the head. Long before Facebook was aware and removed the video, viewers across the globe had witnessed the event with the blood splattered image ingrained in their minds. In another circumstance, students posted videos on Facebook and Snapchat of themselves hiding or running during the 2018 Stoneman Douglas High School shooting. These videos included the images of dead students. It is no longer surprising that social media is filled with images just as graphic, if not more so, as the news. As society becomes more contorted and corrupted, so too does social media, resulting in a blanket of fear and anxiety that oozes out into the community.

Today, young adults live in an anxiety-riddled society in which they feel unprepared and ill-equipped to exercise their own agency and accomplish their own ambitions based on intention. Mark Borg, Jr., a psychologist and psychoanalyst, studies the "pure war" mentality, which was revitalized in the psychological practice after 9/11, in which individuals live in a constant state of anxiety. This "pure war" mentality, he explains, "becomes an internal condition, a perpetual state of preparation for absolute destruction and for personal, social, and cultural death ... pure war obliterates the distinction between soldier and citizen."[6] In other words, this mentality, re-initiated after 9/11 and strengthened by recent events, such as ISIS, domestic terrorism, etc., on social media and news has resulted in blanketed fear even amongst civilians. According to a study in the *Psychiatric Annals*, conducted in 2007, "[Children's] opportunities for personal development are intimately linked to their social environment ... fear is a major and intentional outcome of war and terrorism."[7] This fear is prevalent in the twenty-first century as 6.3 million teens reported having an anxiety-related disorder in 2015 and this number is only likely to have grown since.[8]

Having taken all of the above into consideration, is it any surprise that adolescents within the twenty-first century feel connected to the characters found within current young adult dystopian stories? Just as the survivors from District 12 are stripped of their citizenship and re-titled as "Soldiers" within District 13, young adults of the twenty-first century feel that they are entering into a battle field in which their only option is to be afraid of everything or else to become desensitized to anything. In such a society, where the adolescent "craves more power and control, and feels the limits on his or her freedom intensely," they are drawn toward literature which grants them strength and encouragement.[9] It is this draw toward literature that Collins' trilogy fulfills.

A Different Dystopia

Within Collins' trilogy there is a shift between traditional dystopian novels that only warn against a detrimental future and twenty-first century dystopias that both warn and offer hope to readers. In traditional twentieth century dystopias such as *Brave New World, Nineteen Eighty-Four,* and *A Handmaid's Tale,* protagonists are unable to overcome restrictions placed on them by their corrupt societies/authorities. In *Nineteen Eighty-Four,* George Orwell addresses the circulating fears of surveillance and omnipresent governmental presence that demeans the individual. Main protagonist, Winston Smith, attempts to rebel against Big Brother only to be tortured and eventually succumbing to their methods and ideology, forfeiting his body, mind, and soul to love only Big Brother. Aldous Huxley, author of *Brave New World,* responds to the technological advancements of his time and the fear of unethical manipulation of technology. In his narrative, John the Savage, the only character to exist apart from the immoral society, eventually commits suicide as self-punishment for allowing the World State to compromise his agency.

Continuously, Margaret Atwood's novel, *The Handmaid's Tale,* which was recently re-introduced as a Hulu series, explores the revival of conservative values in the West during the 1960s and 70s and the fear that religious extremists would eliminate newly established women's rights by portraying a society that values women only for their reproductive capacities. In Atwood's narrative, Offred's fate is left up to interpretation as she is led away by agents of the Eye with no action on her part except to not resist arrest. Throughout such novels, authors like Orwell, Huxley, and Atwood portray protagonists who, if ever able to experience agency, ultimately lose control to the authoritarian government after sacrificing their own abilities to think, feel, or act.

Unlike her dystopian predecessors, Collins challenges readers to consider human agency, or one's ability to act, as a never-ending battle. Collins uses not only her main protagonist, Katniss Everdeen, as a soldier, but also a myriad of characters to illustrate how agency is continuously achievable even after having lost it. Indeed, Collins' focus on the hope of regaining agency is partially responsible for the rise in popularity of dystopian literature for the twenty-first century reader. One journalist, Debra Donston-Miller, asserts that the upsurge in young adult dystopian literature is due to "uncertain times" and in response to "deep-seated social need or anxiety."[10] Like the traditional dystopias of the twentieth century, Collins' *Hunger Games* reproduces the concerns of the current context, particularly in response to the anxieties caused by a society focused on calloused entertainment and plagued by domestic and foreign terrorist attacks. Both adults and adolescents must endure these social anxieties and mindsets caused by traumatic experiences. Unlike the twentieth century dystopian authors, Collins offers hope to her readers.

The *Hunger Games* trilogy combats the "pure war" mindset described by Mark Borg, Jr., and the social uncertainties of the twenty-first century by portraying a hopeful ending in a catastrophic world. The stories of Katniss, Peeta, Gale, Haymitch, Cinna, Prim, Finnick, Mags, Johanna, and Beetee are not only reiterations of their personal journeys with agency, but they form the reassuring narrative of redemption that twenty-first century readers are craving. At the end of *Mockingjay*, Katniss chooses Peeta, claiming that what she needs is the "dandelion in the spring. The bright yellow that means rebirth instead of destruction. The promise that life can go on, no matter how bad our losses. That it can be good again."[11]

Indeed, Collins' trilogy itself becomes that dandelion, the bright yellow, the promise for twenty-first century readers that regardless of how bad society becomes life can be good again. Collins' trilogy does not ignore the trauma of reality as both Katniss and Peeta are heavily scarred, physically, mentally, and emotionally by the end of the narrative. Through her characters, Collins starkly depicts the consequences of a calloused and violent society: injury, separation, trauma, and death. However, in offering hope, unlike Huxley, Orwell, or Atwood, Collins' novels encourage readers to seek agency, regardless of the obstacles. Agency within Panem becomes a roadmap for agency within the twenty-first century as Collins' characters provides lessons for the young adult reader to follow. It accepts the possibility of pain and suffering, but also declares that agency is still obtainable regardless of any injury or authority.

Agency for the Twenty-First Century Reader

As stated at the opening, the purpose of this book was to discuss what human agency looks like, how it is discovered, tested, enacted, lost, and regained particularly within a dystopian society such as *The Hunger Games* as readers can relate to one or another of its diverse cast of characters. In the introduction, I laid out a simple definition of agency as being the ability to act intentionally based on desire while working either with or against internal and external constraints. As seen through Collins' trilogy, a plethora of inside and outside forces can and will affect and manipulate agency. Throughout her novels, Collins leaves her readers with something to think about and to be encouraged by.

Undeniably, through these characters, readers such as yourself, can come to realize many things such as the importance of your body, not only in how it is perceived by others but especially how you perceive yourself. In particular, this lesson is predominantly potent for young readers, target audiences of Collins, who find themselves attempting to discover who they are through the outward portrayal of their bodies. However, it is crucial that this portrayal not be consumed by another's desires, but rather displayed through their own intentions so as to gain personal autonomy. Katniss Everdeen can only be the Mockingjay and can only possess that strength when her actions and desires are authentic and genuine. Katniss, for whom the odds never favored, may have fallen from her status of hero in *Mockingjay*, but she does not allow even her failures to destroy her agency. Through relationships, Katniss finds strength and the ability to go on. Likewise, young readers must find their own way to rise after they fall, as they will fall often, through forming relationships with others in their own lives.

Additionally, readers may find themselves challenged by the lives of Peeta Mellark and Gale Hawthorne for whom both struggle with finding themselves once corrupted by outside forces. Through these boys, readers must question their own values and intentions. What within you is shaping your desires and actions? How do you form your own identity? Will you be like Peeta who always finds his way back to his true nature, or will you end up like Gale, corrupted by his chase after something "more"? Characters like Cinna and Haymitch work to display the significance of shared agency, intentionality, and visibility. Lovely Primrose Everdeen holds the dandelion of hope that keeps the fires of rebellion warm. Her innocence and positive attitude prompts readers like yourself to find the light in the darkness. Characters such as Finnick, Mags, Johanna, and Beetee remind us that no matter how small our story, our actions are enormous and impact the lives of those around us. Lastly, each of these characters remind readers that our lives are not the only ones affected by the issues of society. There is a whole world, filled with minor characters, whose lives are just as intricate as our own.

Therefore, dear readers, you may feel that your world is slipping into dystopia and as such, you may feel that you lack individual power to do anything to save yourself or others. However, all individuals, regardless of their circumstances, possess the capability to discover, exercise, maintain, and grow agency. This is the lesson that is inscribed and explored throughout Collins' book and the lesson that we strive to understand through our examination of Collins' characters. Agency is humanity's greatest gift and humanity's greatest struggle. Agency is the antidote for the dystopian society. The lessons that readers, such as ourselves, can learn from this series will stick with each of us for the rest of our lives. While I know that I may never hear the Mockingjay's melody in the trees of Big Bear, it will not stop me from returning time and time again to whistle Rue's four notes in a salute to Suzanne Collins and her myriad of characters who taught us so much about what it means to be human.

Appendix A: Character List and Terminology

Character List

- **Alma Coin (President)**—is the leader of District 13 who initially appears as an ally to the districts. However, Coin's harsh, ulterior motives are quickly discovered as she proves to be just as ruthless as President Snow. Using the districts for fodder, Coin is able to gain control of Panem without achieving any major losses for herself or her people. Ultimately revealing herself as yet another tyrant, Coin is killed by Katniss Everdeen at the end of *Mockingjay*.

- **Annie Cresta**—is chosen as tribute during the reaping of the Quarter Quell; however, she is rescued from re-entering the Games by Mags, (see below) who volunteers to take her place. Annie is considered mentally unstable and madly in love with Finnick Odair (see below) whom she later marries and has a child with. She votes no against President Coin's proposition to hold a final Hunger Games as one of the few surviving Victors.

- **Atala**—is first seen in *The Hunger Games* at the Training Center. There, she gives instructions to the tributes who are allowed to train for three days before the Games.

- **Aurelius (Doctor)**—appears toward the end of *Mockingjay* as the psychologist who treats Katniss after Prim's death and acts as Katniss' star-witness during her trial for killing President Coin. He proves to be a relatively useless influence in Katniss' healing until he supports her idea to write a book in remembrance of all those who have died. He remains alive at the end of the novel.

- **Beetee**—is the male Victor-tribute from District 3 for the Quarter Quell. His intelligence is reflected in his fidgety fingers which long to manipulate wire into inescapable traps. Humbled by his creation of the bomb which possibly killed Prim, Beetee voted no against President Coin's proposition for a final Hunger Games.[1] He remains alive at the end of the series, though confined to a wheelchair.

- **Blight**—is the male Victor-tribute from District 7 chosen for the 3rd Quarter Quell. Blight dies the first night of the Quarter Quell when blinded by blood-rain and electrocuted by the force field.

- **Boggs (Commander)**—although he initially appears as the forty-something, blue-eyed, muscled-lackey of President Coin, Boggs swiftly becomes one of Katniss' allies, both protecting and supporting her. Most importantly, Boggs warns Katniss of President Coin's dissatisfaction with Katniss' loyalty. Also, Boggs transfers his Holo to Katniss after having his legs blown off on the Capitol streets and his subsequent death which proves vital to Katniss' survival.

- **Bonnie**—is a young girl fleeing from District 8 after a failed uprising who meets Katniss Everdeen by the lake outside of District 12. She is traveling with Twill, a middle-aged woman from District 8. Both women are considered to have died in the woods, never having reached District 13.

- **Bristel**—is one of Gale's coal-mining crewmates in District 12. Bristel provides a stretcher for Gale after his whipping by Romulus Thread (see below). She is presumed dead, having perished in the fire-bombing of District 12.

- **Brutus**—unlike the majority of Victors, Brutus volunteers to be the male tribute for the 3rd Quarter Quell. While in the arena, Brutus allies with the Career pack and forms the primary opposition to Katniss' allied pack. Brutus is killed by Peeta, and as such, is the only tribute confirmed to be intentionally killed by Peeta in the Games.

- **Buttercup**—is Prim's cat. Several scholars have noted Buttercup's importance; indeed, for a more cohesive analysis of Buttercup as representing Katniss' feral and wild personality please see Valerie E. Frankel's *Katniss the Cattail*.[2] In *Mockingjay*, Buttercup proves crucial to Katniss' healing process as his appearance triggers her emotional revival. It is likely that Buttercup died naturally between the last chapter and the epilogue of *Mockingjay*.

- **Caesar Flickerman**—appearing in all three novels, Caesar Flickerman is the host of the Hunger Games, interviewing the tributes and narrating the Games. While he is friendly and helpful toward the tributes, he clearly sides with the Capitol during the war. It is unknown whether or not he survived the war although it is likely that he did.

- **Cashmere**—is the female Victor-tribute from District 1 chosen to compete in the Quarter Quell. She is often referred to alongside her brother Gloss who work as a team with Brutus and Enobaria to take out their fellow tributes within the arena. Cashmere is killed by Johanna Mason (see below).

- **Castor**—is most often referred to alongside his twin brother Pollux. Castor, a Capitol-born citizen flees to District 13 to help film and produce the propos (see below under terminology) for the rebellion. Castor follows Katniss and the Star Squad into the Capitol and is killed by the lizard-mutts.

- **Cato**—is the volunteer, male-tribute from District 2 for the 74th Hunger Games. He is the leader of the Career Tributes and represents the most brutal type of tribute who eagerly volunteers for a chance to murder others. Cato is the last tribute remaining apart from Katniss and Peeta in the 74th Hunger Games. He is mutilated by the wolf-muttations (see below under terminology) before Katniss' ends his suffering with an arrow.

- **Cecelia**—is a mother of three kids and the female Victor-tribute from District 8 for the Quarter Quell Hunger Games. Cecelia dies in the initial bloodbath of the Games.

- **Chaff**—is the male Victor-tribute from District 11 chosen as tribute for the Quarter Quell. He is mentioned to be one of Haymitch's (see below) closest friends. Described as a humorous and self-deprecating character, he is most remembered for kissing Katniss full on the mouth after the chariot ride as a joke. Chaff survives most of the Quarter Quell, most likely aware of the rebel's plan to rescue the Victors; however, he is killed by Brutus (see above) only moments before the arena walls are blown apart.

- **Cinna**—is the Capitol stylist for District 12 tributes, specifically the female tributes. During his debut year in the Games, Cinna styles both Katniss and Peeta. As Katniss' close friend in the Capitol, Cinna nearly becomes a surrogate father-figure to Katniss.[3] Due to his rebellious actions, Cinna is killed moments before the beginning of the Quarter Quell.[4] However, Cinna's presence is still felt by Katniss in *Mockingjay* through his sketches and the Mockingjay armor.

- **Claudius Templesmith**—Capitol-born citizen, Claudius Templesmith is best known for his voice. Not only does he count down the start of each Hunger Games but he also makes announcements to the tributes during the Games such as the opportunity to attend a Feast (see below under terminology).

- **Clove**—is the girl tribute from District 2 who is particularly skilled at throwing knives. She is not named until halfway through *The Hunger Games*. Clove nearly kills Katniss at the Feast (see terminology below); however, due to her hubris she is instead killed by Thresh (see below) who believes he is avenging Rue's (see below) death.

- **Coriolanus Snow (President)**—is the primary antagonist throughout the entire series and the President of Panem. Intelligent and cruel, President Snow constantly works to manipulate those around him and poisons others when necessary. Ultimately, when captured, President Snow reveals to Katniss who was behind the bombing that killed Prim. Although he was supposed to be executed by Katniss, President Snow most likely dies of asphyxiation from choking on blood while laughing after Katniss kills President Coin.

- **Cray**—is the head Peacekeeper of District 12 during *The Hunger Games* and the beginning of *Catching Fire*. He is particularly known for preying on the starving women of District 12 by paying for sex. It can be assumed that he was killed by the Capitol for his incompetence when he was replaced by Romulus Thread (see below).

- **Cressida**—is the female director, born and raised in the Capitol, who flees to District 13 to direct Katniss' camera crew in *Mockingjay*. Cressida's camera often forces Katniss to confront reality. Cressida survives the descent into the Capitol and supposedly is alive at the end of the trilogy.

- **Dalton**—first appears toward the beginning of *Mockingjay* as a refugee from District 10 who fled to District 13.

- **Darius**—is a young, redheaded Peacekeeper in District 12 who was on friendly terms with many of the citizens, often visiting the Hob (see in Terminology). In *Catching Fire*, Darius attempts to stop Gale's whipping and is punished for his actions and transformed into an Avox (see in terminology). In *Mockingjay* it is revealed that Darius was tortured, with beatings and the cutting off of body parts, in front of Peeta. Eventually Darius succumbed to his torture.

- **Delly Cartwright**—originally described as a merchant kid from District 12 with blond hair (often curled) and excess weight in *The Hunger Games*, she first makes a physical appearance in *Mockingjay*. Delly is one of the few survivors from District 12 who made it to District 13. Delly is instrumental in Peeta's recovery process as she provides a real, yet safe, connection to his past. Delly is presumed to have survived the war and might have been included in the group of

District 12 survivors who returned to rebuild their district at the end of the war.

- **Eddy**—is a young, injured boy from District 8 whom Katniss visits on her first outing as the Mockingjay. He is assumed dead, killed by the Capitol's hovercrafts which return to murder the innocent and injured gathered in a makeshift hospital.

- **Effie Trinket**—is the handler for the District 12's tributes. She is a Capitol-born and bred woman with high taste and vain mannerisms. She is charged with choosing the tributes at the yearly reaping, escorting her tributes to the Games and managing their appearances along the Victory Tour. Surprisingly, she survives the rebellion, and is presumed alive at the end of the series.

- **Enobaria**—is the female, Victor-tribute from District 2 and is partners with Brutus. Enobaria is described as barbaric with teeth filed to points and tipped with gold. Kept alive during the rebellion by the Capitol and saved by the Mockingjay Pardon, Enobaria survives the trilogy and is presumed alive.

- **Mr. Everdeen**—is the father of both Katniss and Primrose Everdeen and husband to Mrs. Everdeen. He first appears posthumously within the first few pages, introducing trauma to the novel. He was killed during a mining accident and buried alive when Katniss was only eleven years old. Although rarely described physically, Mr. Everdeen's voice is repeatedly mentioned and described within the trilogy as the first connection to the Mockingjay (see below in Terminology).

- **Mrs. Everdeen**—is the mother of both Katniss and Primrose Everdeen and wife to Mr. Everdeen. Having fallen into a depression after her husband's death, Mrs. Everdeen is initially distrusted by Katniss (although Katniss attempts to bridge this gap later on). Throughout the trilogy, Mrs. Everdeen is presented as an unsatisfactory parental figure[5] who must be shielded from bad news and secrets. While Mrs. Everdeen survives the trilogy, she remains separated from Katniss, preferring to live outside of District 12.

- **Finnick Odair**—is the male, Victor-tribute for the 3rd Quarter Quell and first appears during the chariot scene in *Catching Fire*. He is the sex-icon of Panem. However, he soon reveals himself to be kind, humorous, and tortured by his love for Annie (see above) and his sexual enslavement. Finnick becomes one of Katniss' greatest allies in *Mockingjay*. While Finnick is granted a small amount of happiness in marrying Annie, it is short lived when he is killed by lizard-mutts in the Capitol sewers.

- **Flavius**—is a male member of Katniss' prep team within the Capitol. Often described with his corkscrew hair and purple lipstick, Flavius is ill-prepared for life in District 13—where he is transferred during the rebellion. He, along with Octavia and Venia, form the team that styles Katniss during the rebellion. They are presumed alive at the end of the series.

- **Foxface**—is the female tribute for the 74th Hunger Games. Never named, readers only know her as "Foxface," the nickname given to her by Katniss. Foxface is tricked by Peeta's own ignorance and accidentally consumes poisoned berries known as Nightlock (see in Terminology).

- **Fulvia Cardew**—is the female assistant to Plutarch Heavensbee (see below). She comes up with the idea of doing a "Tribute to the Tributes" in which individual propos (see in Terminology) focus on the lives of fallen tributes. She is presumed alive at the end of the trilogy.

- **Gale Hawthorne**—is a male resident of District 12 and Katniss' best friend and hunting partner. Gale is a skilled trapper and is often consumed with his anger directed at the Capitol. Although he is romantically interested in Katniss, she does not share his feelings as she is more concerned with a rebellion than with romance. He eagerly joins the rebellion and often crosses moral boundaries for the sake of the greater good. He unintentionally creates the two-timed bomb responsible for killing Primrose Everdeen. He is presumed alive at the end of the series and working in District 2.

- **Glimmer**—is the female tribute for District 1 in the 74th Hunger Games. She is killed by a swarm of Tracker Jackers which Katniss drops on the Career pack during the Games.

- **Gloss**—is the male, Victor-tribute for District 1 during the 3rd Quarter Quell. He is the brother to Cashmere, who is also chosen for the Quarter Quell. Together they team up with Brutus and Enobaria to form the Career Pack. Gloss kills Wiress and is immediately killed after by Katniss.

- **Goat Man**—is known only as the "Goat Man," this resident of District 12 manages goats and sells milk to make a living. He sells Prim her goat after the animal is mauled by a dog. He is presumed to have died during the firebombing of District 12.

- **Greasy Sae**—is a female resident of District 12 who is often found in the Hob (see in Terminology) cooking various stews. She is one of the few residents of District 12 to survive both the firebombing of 12 and the rebellion. She returns to District 12 with her granddaughter and watches over Katniss, cooking and cleaning her house.

- **Haymitch Abernathy**—is the only surviving Victor of District 12 when the story takes place. He was the Victor of the 2nd Quarter Quell in which forty-eight children were sent into the arena. He is infamous for his drunken behavior. However, he is also a rebel and intricately involved in the revolution to overthrow the Capitol. As Mentor to both Katniss and Peeta, Haymitch manipulates and guides his tributes throughout the trilogy. He survives the rebellion and spends his days raising geese in District 12.

- **Homes**—is a resident of District 13 and a member of Squad Four-Five-One, also referred to as the Star Squad (see below in Terminology). Homes follows Katniss into the descent into the Capitol and is killed by the lizard-mutts.

- **Jackson**—is a native of District 13 and Boggs' second-in-command on the Star Squad. Jackson initially challenges Katniss' mission to assassinate President Snow. However, she concedes and aids Katniss in their descent into the Capitol. Jackson is killed holding off the lizard-mutts at the Meat Grinder (see in Terminology) in the Capitol's sewers.

- **Johanna Mason**—is the female, Victor-tribute of District 7 chosen for the 3rd Quarter Quell. Well-known for playing weak before revealing herself as a brutal killer and often stripping down naked, Johanna proves to be an unlikely ally to Katniss. Johanna's morals remain questionable at the end of *Mockingjay* as she votes "yes" on continuing the Hunger Games using the Capitol's children. Although Johanna survives the trilogy, not much is known about her life after President Coin's death.

- **Katniss Everdeen**—is the main, female protagonist of the entire series. Katniss is sixteen at the beginning of the trilogy and a resident of District 12. As a hunter, she is particularly skilled with the bow and arrow. She volunteers to take her sister's place in the Hunger Games after Prim's name is called. Within the Games, Katniss rebels against the Capitol's design by threatening to commit suicide if she and Peeta (see below) were not both allowed to live. Due to her actions, a revolution is ignited. Katniss evolves into the figurehead of the rebellion as the Mockingjay. In the end, she is mentally, physically, and emotionally damaged living in District 12. She finds healing through Peeta and together they settle down, rebuild District 12, and have children.

- **Lady**—is the name given to Prim's goat.
- **Lavinia**—is the female, red-headed Avox (see below in Terminology) assigned to the District 12 tributes while in the Capitol. Katniss recognizes Lavinia from her past when Katniss and Gale were hunting in the woods. Lavinia and an unnamed boy came running through the trees, followed by a hovercraft, that swiftly speared the boy and captured Lavinia. Katniss remembers her specifically as she called for Katniss' help. Although Katniss assumes Lavinia would hate her, Lavinia proves to be a source of comfort before both the 74th and 75th Hunger Games. In *Mockingjay*, it is made known that Lavinia, along with Darius (see above), were tortured in front of Peeta to break him. Lavinia was electrocuted to death.
- **Leeg 1 & Leeg 2**—natives of District 13, these sisters are in their early twenties and described as so similar that it is difficult to tell them apart. Both are initial members of the Star Squad. Leeg 2 is killed when a metal dart strikes her brain during a propo and is replaced in the group by Peeta. Leeg 1 is killed by the "Meat Grinder" in the sewers beneath the Capitol.
- **Leevy**—is a young resident of District 12 who finds Hazell and tells her of Gale's whipping. Presumed to be killed during the firebombing of District 12.
- **Lyme**—is a middle-aged, female Victor from District 2 who leads the rebellion's efforts against the Nut (see below in Terminology).
- **Madge Undersee**—is daughter to the mayor of District 12 and friend to Katniss Everdeen. She is responsible for giving Katniss the Mockingjay pin (see below in Terminology) that becomes the rebel's symbol. She is killed in the fire-bombing of District 12.
- **Mags**—is the female, eighty-year-old Victor-tribute from District 4 for the 3rd Quarter Quell and partners with Finnick Odair (see above). She volunteers to take the place of Annie Cresta (see above) and willingly sacrifices herself to save Peeta Mellark (see below).
- **Martin**—is a young, mentally disabled boy in District 11 who is killed for taking a pair of night-vision glasses to play with.
- **Marvel**—is the male tribute for District 1 in the 74th Hunger Games. His weapon of choice is a spear which he uses to kill Rue (see below). He is killed with an arrow by Katniss Everdeen (see above).
- **Maysilee Donner**—is one of the female tributes from District 12 for the 2nd Quarter Quell and aunt to Madge (see above). Within the Games, she teams up with Haymitch Abernathy, but is later killed

by birds that skewer her neck with long beaks. She was the original owner of the Mockingjay pin (see below).

- **Mellark Family**—the Mellark family consists of Mr. Mellark, Mrs. Mellark, Peeta (see below), and his two older brothers. They all work in District 12's bakery. Mr. Mellark is described as a quiet man, Mrs. Mellark is an abusive woman, and Peeta's two older brothers are hardly ever mentioned and never seen.

- **Messalla**—first appears in *Mockingjay* as Cressida's (see above) assistant. He is described as a young man with several piercings in both his ears and tongue. Messalla is killed during the descent into the Capitol within the sewers, having been caught in a beam that melts the flesh from his bones.

- **Mitchell**—is a member of Squad Four-Five-One, also referred to as the Star Squad (see below in Terminology). Mitchell dies during the filming of a propo after Peeta throws him in a maniacal rage onto a pod which triggers a net that encases Mitchell in barbed wire. Although Gale tries to rescue him, Mitchell is suffocated by the black wave of goo that is triggered by Capitol Gamemakers.

- **Morphlings** (District 6)—refers to the male and female Victor-tributes from District 6 chosen for the 3rd Quarter Quell. Both are masters of camouflage and self-medicate on a drug called "morphling" (see below in Terminology). The female Victor sacrifices herself to save Peeta's life from the "Monkee-mutations" (see below in Terminology).

- **Octavia**—is the youngest member of Katniss Capitol, stylist prep team. Her entire body is dyed green. She, along with Flavius and Venia, are the only prep team to remain alive at the end of the trilogy.

- **Paylor** (Commander)—described as being in her early thirties, Commander Paylor leads the rebellion in District 8. Described as authoritarian, yet compassionate, Commander Paylor assumes leadership after President Coin's (see above) assassination.

- **Peeta Mellark**—is the male tribute from District 12 chosen to participate in the 74th Hunger Games with Katniss Everdeen. In love with Katniss, Peeta attempts to keep her alive throughout the Games and after, during the Victory Tour. He later volunteers to participate in the 3rd Quarter Quell so that he can go back into the arena with Katniss. When he is captured by the Capitol following the Quarter Quell, his mind is hijacked and he is turned into a twisted version of himself. By the end of *Mockingjay*, Peeta is primarily healed, but still suffers from PTSD.

- **Plutarch Heavensbee**—is first introduced as the Head Gamemaker to replace Seneca Crane (see below). He secretly works alongside the rebellion to break the Victors out of the 3rd Quarter Quell and is in charge of creating media propaganda using the Mockingjay during the revolution.

- **Pollux**—is most often referred to alongside his twin brother Castor. Pollux is a Capitol-born citizen who was punished for some crime by being turned into an Avox (see in terminology). His years of imprisonment in the Capitol's sewers proved instrumental in helping navigate the Star Squad. He survives the rebellion.

- **Portia**—is the head stylist for Peeta Mellark. She is partners with Cinna. She is assumed dead, killed by the Capitol during the rebellion.

- **Posy Hawthorne**—is the youngest of the Hawthorne children and the only girl. She is assumed alive at the end of the trilogy although she is not mentioned by Katniss.

- **Primrose Everdeen**—is the first character named within the trilogy, even before the narrator. The fact that she is named in the second sentence of *The Hunger Games*, even before Katniss, displays Prim's primary importance to Katniss who values her sister over herself. Described as blue-eyed and blonde haired, Prim is often depicted as small, young, and innocent. Prim proves to be the crux of the entire trilogy as Katniss might never have undergone the Games— never have sparked a rebellion—if not for Prim's name being reaped. Throughout the novels, Prim provides motivation for Katniss' actions and, towards the end, stability for Katniss' deteriorating mental state. Prim's death in *Mockingjay* generates controversy between readers who argue where the blame should be applied: to Gale, the Capitol, or President Coin. While Prim does not physically survive the trilogy, her influences over Katniss can be seen even after death in the epilogue of *Mockingjay*.

- **Purnia**—is a peacekeeper from District 12 who was friendly with Katniss and Gale. It is unknown whether she was killed in the firebombing or for her lax attitude toward punishment in District 12 or if she survived the trilogy.

- **Ripper**—is a native of District 12 who illegally sells alcohol, specifically to Haymitch. She is presumed to be dead, killed by the firebombing of District 12.

- **Romulus Thread**—replaces the old Head Peacekeeper of District 12 in *Catching Fire*. He is particularly brutal and breaks in his new reign by whipping Gale for poaching. He is presumed to have returned to the Capitol when District 12 was firebombed but it is unknown whether he survived the war.

- **Rooba**—is the butcher of District 12 who lives in the Seam. She often buys meat from Katniss and Gale and is partially responsible for Prim receiving her goat, Lady (see above). She is presumed to have died in the firebombing.

- **Rory Hawthorne**—is the second oldest Hawthorne boy after Gale. He is presumed to be alive at the end of the trilogy.

- **Rue**—is the young tribute from District 11 who is reaped for the 74th Hunger Games. She is particularly skilled at climbing through trees and remaining hidden. Rue forms an alliance with Katniss, gives significance to the Mockingjay pin, and is the originator of the four-note whistle found throughout the series. Rue is killed by Marvel with a spear.

- **Seeder**—is the female, Victor-tribute from District 11 reaped for the 3rd Quarter Quell. She was killed, presumably by Career Tributes, during the initial bloodbath of the Games.

- **Seneca Crane**—is the Head Gamemakers for the 74th Hunger Games. He allowed both Katniss and Peeta to win as co-Victors which resulted in his own hanging.

- **Tax**—is one of the trainers for the 3rd Quarter Quell who, noticing Katniss' talent, began to launch plastic birds in the air for her to shoot.

- **Thom**—first appears in *Catching Fire* as one of Gale's crewmates in the mines. He does not reappear until the end of *Mockingjay* having returned to District 12. Thom works to gather the remains and bury them in the meadow.

- **Thresh**—dark-skinned and towering over the majority of the tributes, Thresh is described as a silent, but deadly powerhouse. While he is absent for the majority of the Games, hiding out in the tall grasses, he is responsible for saving Katniss' life from Clove as repayment for her care of Rue. Although he makes it to the final five tributes toward the end of the 74th Hunger Games, he is killed by Cato.

- **Tigris**—was once a stylist from the Games. However due to the extreme body modification that she used on herself to make herself look more like a Tiger, she was banned from the Games. Bitter at Snow, Tigris hides Katniss, Gale, Peeta, and the remainder of the Start Squad (see below in Terminology) in her basement.

- **Titus**—is mentioned posthumously before the 74th Hunger Games in Katniss' thoughts. He originated from District 6 as the male tribute in the Games a few years ahead of Katniss. Katniss assumes that Titus was intentionally killed by engineered avalanche within the Games as Titus' cannibalism did not sit well with the Capitol citizens.

- **Twill**—is a middle-aged woman running away from District 8 with Bonnie (see above). Together, they are fleeing from an uprising gone wrong and seeking shelter at District 13. She is presumed to have died in the wilderness never having made it to District 13.

- **Mayor & Mrs. Undersee**—Mr. Undersee is the mayor of District 12 and his daughter, Madge (see above) is friends with Katniss Everdeen. Mrs. Undersee was the twin sister to Maysilee Donnor (see above) and is haunted by her sister's death, Mrs. Undersee suffers from migraines. Both Mr. and Mrs. Undersee died in the firebombing of District 12.

- **Venia**—is one of the three stylists who make up Katniss' prep team and work under Cinna (see above). She is often level-headed and takes charge after Cinna's death. She is alive at the end of the trilogy.

- **Vick Hawthorne**—is the youngest Hawthorne son.

- **Wiress**—is the female, Victor-tribute from District 3 reaped for the 3rd Quarter Quell. While Wiress seems mentally unstable she is keen enough to realize that the arena is designed as a clock with traps in each hour. She is killed by Gloss.

- **Woof**—is the male, Victor-tribute from District 8 for the 3rd Quarter Quell. He is senile in his old age and is killed quickly within the Games.

- **York**—is a native of District 13 who is in charge of training soldiers. Soldier York trains both Katniss and Johanna. Her fate is unknown.

For more in-depth discussions of the meanings behind character names consider reading Valerie E. Frankel's *Katniss the Cattail: An Unauthorized Guide to Names and Symbols in Suzanne Collins' The Hunger Games.*[6]

Terminology

- **Airtime Assault**—refers to the propos created by District 13 and Plutarch (see above in Character List) with the intent of persuading the districts to either start or continuing rebelling.

- **Avox**—is the title given to traitors of the Capitol who have been captured and tortured. Their tongues have been mutilated to the point where they are unable to speak. Avoxes live their lives as servants for those in the Capitol. While there are several nameless Avoxes in the trilogy, the three Avoxes most known to readers are: Lavinia, Darius, and Pollux (see above in Character List).

- **Beauty Base Zero**—refers to the physical appearance of a person, most likely a tribute, whose imperfections (such as dirt, leg hair, arm hair, etc.) have been erased and who have been polished to a natural beauty before applying more blatant cosmetic changes.

- **Bloodbath**—refers to the opening battle at the onset of every Hunger Games in which tributes are drawn in by the tempting bounty placed within and around the Cornucopia. Often times, the highest number of deaths in one day occurs on the initial day during the bloodbath.

- **Canary**—is a small bird which was often brought down into mining shafts. When the canary stopped singing, the miners were alerted to bad air quality. Canaries served as warnings.

- **Capitol**—is the ruling authority of the nation of Panem. Situated within the twelve districts, the Capitol rules with violence and surveillance. The Capitol is a city of luxury and overabundance in which the citizens are glutinous and cheer on the deaths of children as entertainment.

- **Career Tributes**—these tributes most likely originate from the wealthier districts such as 1, 2, and 4 where children are trained to compete in the Games and often volunteer. Well-known Career Tributes within the series include: Cato, Clove, Marvel, Glimmer, Brutus, Enobaria, Finnick, Mags, Cashmere, and Gloss (see above in Character List).

- **City Circle**—refers to the outdoor stadium in the Capitol in which several pre–Game festivities take place such as the Chariot Ride.

- **Cornucopia**—is shaped similar to that of the Thanksgiving basket which overflows with fruit. It has a wide opening in the front and narrows down to a tail which curves up. At the beginning of every Hunger Games, tributes are strategically placed in a circle around the cornucopia which holds various objects ranging from survival tools and food to weapons. Due to this tempting and overflowing bounty, many tributes are drawn in at the onset of the Games and butchered in the following bloodbath (see above).

- **Feast**—within the Games, tributes may be called to a "Feast" in which the Capitol offers items desperately needed by the tributes like food, weapons, or medicine. In the 74th Hunger Games, Katniss goes to the feast to get medicine that can heal Peeta's blood poisoning.

- **Full-Body Polish**—refers to when a tribute's body is completely healed of all injuries after the Games. Even scars are removed from the body, giving the tribute a clear and healthy glow.

- **Gamemakers**—are in charge of designing, organizing, and running the Games smoothly; their primary concern is keeping the citizens of the Capitol entertained with constant violence within the Games, often coercing the tributes into fighting one another.

- **Hob**—is the black-market trading facility located in the Seam of District 12. Although the black market is technically illegal, peacekeepers are also seen buying items from the Hob such as fresh meat and alcohol. The Hob is where Katniss does most of her trading. The people of the Hob such as Greasy Sae (see in Character List) collected a sum of money to help support Katniss in the 74th Hunger Games. The Hob is set on fire in *Catching Fire* after the arrival of Romulus Thread (see in Character List) which foreshadows the eventual fire-bombing of District 12.

- **Holo**—is an electronic map. Every commander of District 13 possesses a Holo as they attempt to navigate the streets of the Capitol. The Holo does not only show streets, but it also displays the activated pods (see below) hidden on or below the streets. It is activated by the Commander's voice and has the ability to self-destruct, exploding everything within a five-yard radius.

- **Hovercraft**—is a type of flying vehicle, similar to that of a helicopter or plane. They can be transport vehicles or they can be armed as weapons.

- **Hunger Games**—are gladiator-styled competitions in which twenty-four tributes, one boy and one girl from each district, must battle it out to the death until only one remains. The Games are televised and treated as spectacle[7] by citizens of the Capitol while they are used as punishment for the citizens of the districts. There are seventy-five Hunger Games in total, with three particularly gruesome Games referred to as Quarter Quells (see below). These Games are hosted in arenas that present artificial outdoor wildernesses such as deserts, jungles, forests, ruined cities, etc.

- **Justice Building**—is the primary government building of each district where public events (such as the Reaping—see below) take place.

- **Katniss Root**—is a plant with leaves shaped like an arrowhead and edible, potato-like roots. Mr. Everdeen (see above) named Katniss after these roots.

- **Launch Room (Stockyard)**—is the room which houses individual tributes minutes before the Games. In this room they are dressed and prepared for the Games. Katniss refers to the rooms as a stockyard as the tributes are about to be sent up into the arena for slaughter.

- **Meadow**—is a piece of land situated between the Seam and the woods (although separated from the woods by a gate which is at times electrified). The Meadow is seen as the gateway to survival as Katniss first forages for dandelions in the Meadow before venturing into the woods. The Meadow is repeatedly seen as a positive image as Katniss sings about the dream of a meadow where Rue can rest safely in death and again in *Catching Fire*, Katniss wonders if there is a place such as The Meadow where Peeta's hypothetical children could safely play. Ironically, there is. At the end of *Mockingjay*, Peeta and Katniss' children play in The Meadow, which is now the burial ground for the majority of District 12's citizens.

- **Meat Grinder**—is a pod (see below) created by Gamemakers and placed underground in the Transfer (see below). Activated by weight, the Meat Grinder is depicted as a pit filled with "a poisonous brew of human waste, garbage, and chemical runoff … parts of the surface are on fire, others emit evil-looking clouds of vapor" (*M* 310). The meat grinder claims several lives of both rebels and peacekeepers.

- **Mockingjay (bird)**—is a hybrid of Jabberjays (see below) and Mockingjays. While the birds lost the ability to speak, they can repeat sounds and melodies. The birds often listen to anyone with a beautiful voice. They can also sense an incoming hovercraft.

- **Mockingjay (pin)**—is a golden pin that displays a Mockingjay with its wings outstretched inside of a circle. Madge once owned this pin but later gave it to Katniss when she volunteered for the 74th Hunger Games. The pin became the symbol of the rebellion.

- **Muttations (mutts)**[8]—are genetically altered or engineered animal-like creatures, created by the Capitol to physically or mentally attack their enemies.

  ○ **Jabberjays**—are genetically engineered birds that can record entire conversations and repeat them. These birds were designed by the Capitol during the first rebellion. However, when they were found faulty, the Capitol left them to die in the wilderness.

  ○ **Tracker Jackers**—are a type of wasp-like creature whose stings produce unbearable pain, hallucinations, and in some cases, death. They hone in on their prey, often following them for long distances, in order to exact their revenge.

° **Tribute Wolves**—at the climax of the 74th Hunger Games, these creatures that resemble ginormous wolves force Cato, Katniss, and Peeta to fight on top of the Cornucopia (see above). Each wolf represents a fallen tribute as their fur matches that individual's hair color, they each have the eyes of their tribute, and a number from that tribute's district inlaid their collar.

° **Carnivorous Squirrels**—these muttations appear in the 2nd Quarter Quell where everything looks beautiful but is dangerous. They look like normal squirrels except slightly bigger and more dangerous.

° **Stinging Butterflies**—these muttations appear in the 2nd Quarter Quell where everything looks beautiful but is dangerous. The butterflies possess a sting similar to that of Tracker Jackers (see above).

° **Monkees**—these muttations appear in the 3rd Quarter Quell. They are genetically engineered to be faster, stronger, and more aggressive than normal monkeys.

° **Lizard Peacekeepers**—never given a specific name, Katniss describes them as "white, four-limbed, about the size of a full-grown human … naked, with long reptilian tails, arched backs, and heads that jut forward," and smelling like Snow's artificial roses (*M 309*). They appear in *Mockingjay* and are programmed to hunt down Katniss, although they will kill anyone in their path. They are responsible for killing Homes, Castor, and Finnick.

• **Nightlock** (berries)—are poisonous berries present in the 74th Hunger Games. The berries themselves are inconsequential apart from Katniss' and Peeta's bluff to use them to commit suicide at the end of the Games. "The handful of berries" becomes a symbol of the rebellion to the districts.

• **Nightlock** (pill)—named after the berries, Nightlock in pill form was created by District 13 for the rebels to consume should they be captured.

• **Panem**—is what remains of North America after it is plagued by natural disasters such as floods, fires, and earthquakes.[9] Once made up of thirteen districts, Panem consists of only twelve districts at the beginning of the series, having supposedly destroyed District 13 (which is later discovered to be false).

• **Peacekeepers**—are the police force within the nation of Panem. They are primarily made up of District 2 citizens and Capitol-citizens with unpaid debts.

- **Pods**—are booby-traps placed within the Games in *The Hunger Games* and *Catching Fire*. One example is in *The Hunger Games* when Katniss activates the pods that shoot fireballs at her as she runs. The pods are usually rigged to attack only in certain areas. In *Mockingjay* the Capitol arms its abandoned streets with pods that activate when soldiers come within range resulting in: toxic gas, tracker jackers (see above under "muttations"), mines, and more.

- **Propos**—"propaganda spots" created by Plutarch and Fulvia.
    - ° *We Remember*—consists of a set of propos intended as "a tribute to your tributes" (*M* 109). Each propo targets a specific district by remembering one of their fallen tributes such as Rue from District 11 and Mags from District 4.

- **Quarter Quell**—every 25 years the President reads a card that changes a rule in the Hunger Games making that year's Games particularly heinous.
    - ° 25th Quarter Quell—this year all of the Districts had to choose which tributes they would be sending into the Hunger Games.
    - ° 50th Quarter Quell—this year all of the Districts had to sacrifice double the amount of tributes; forty-eight tributes instead of twenty-four.
    - ° 75th Quarter Quell—this year, the tributes were reaped from the existing pool of Victors (most likely a tactic to insure Katniss' death).

- **Reaping Day**—this day takes place during the summer season. By law, all citizens are required to participate either as possible tributes or spectators. All children between twelve and eighteen are accounted for and divided into sections designated by age. On this day, a boy and girl tribute are chosen at random via lottery to compete in the yearly Hunger Games.

- **Remake Center**[10]—is the initial drop-off spot for all tributes once they enter the Capitol. Here they are stripped, cleaned, and groomed by their prep teams before meeting their stylists.

- **Seam**—refers to the poorest housing section of District 12. Both Katniss and Gale live within the Seam.

- **Special Defense**—is one of the lowest levels of District 13 where the rebellion designs and creates weapons for war. Beetee and Gale (see above) can often be found in Special Defense; it is there that they created the two-timed bomb that killed Prim (see above).

- **Sponsors**—refers primarily to rich Capitol citizens who donate money and gifts toward the tributes in the arenas to purchase needed items such as food, medicine, protection, etc. While citizens from the districts can be sponsors, such as the Hob gathering a collection for Katniss in the 74th Hunger Games, most sponsors are assumed to be Capitol-born.

- **Star Squad**—also known as Squad Four-Five-One, it is the "on-screen" representation of the rebellion. Made up of Katniss, Gale, Finnick, Boggs, Jackson, Leeg 1 and Leeg 2, Homes, Mitchell, and later Peeta, this squad was never meant for real combat; rather, it was intended to be used for propaganda shots.

- **Tesserae**—is the unfair system in which children between twelve and eighteen can submit their name in the reaping pool an additional time each month for food and grain.

- **Training Center**—before the Games, all tributes go to the Training Center where they are taught basic survival and self-defense tactics.

- **Transfer**—is the underground network of tunnels beneath the Capitol that directly mirror the aboveground streets. The Star Squad uses the Transfer and various tunnels to descend into the Capitol.

- **Treaty of Treason**—this document was constructed by the Capitol after the first rebellion. This treaty states that due to the district's rebellion they will sacrifice one male and one female tribute each year to the Hunger Games as payment for their actions.

- **Tributes**—echoing the term used to describe bounty offered up to appease angry gods, Tributes are the name given to the boys and girls from each district who are chosen at random to participate in the Hunger Games.

- **Victory Tour**—six months after every Hunger Games, the Victor tours through each of the districts, giving speeches and reminding everyone about the Capitol's power.

- **Victor's Village**—in every district there is a section of fine, luxurious houses set aside for Victors to live in.

Appendix B:
Recommended Reading

Henthorne, Tom. *Approaching* The Hunger Games *Trilogy*. McFarland, 2012. $29.

In this book, Henthorne takes a comprehensive look at *The Hunger Games* trilogy with particular emphasis on Katniss Everdeen. Although other scholarly books will attempt to open their works with a biography of Suzanne Collins, Henthorne is perhaps the most successful in his attempt as he thoroughly narrates important aspects of Collins' life such as her militaristic/historic upbringing, career in television, role in children's stories such as *Clifford's Puppy Days*, major publications including *The Underland Chronicles* and *The Hunger Games*, and her subsequent reclusive nature. Henthorne's chapters are devoted to investigating the literary production of the novels, identity, gender, and transgression within Katniss' character, conflict and activism, ethics, reality television, trauma and recovery, and the novels interactivity with readers as a digital text. His chapter "Making War, Not Love: Conflict, Representation and Activism" is a particularly interesting examination of morality within the trilogy. Filled with discernment and fluid writing, Henthorne's book is ideal as a foundation of information for a reader interested in scholarship on *The Hunger Games* series. Also, at the back of the book, Henthorne includes Appendix C: Questions for Further Study. This portion of the book is brimming with academic inquiries meant to initiate the reader's own study and analysis.

Frankel, Valerie Estelle. *Katniss the Cattail: An Unauthorized Guide to Names and Symbols in Suzanne Collins'* The Hunger Games. CreateSpace, 2012. $7.

This short work is divided into four primary sections: "Big Three," "The Names of Panem," "Symbols," and "Allusions to Literature and Life." Valerie Estelle Frankel, author of numerous articles and nonfiction books on young adult literature, does a superb job at investigating the possible meanings and allusions of character names to both plant-based interpretations and relation to historical influences such as Rome, Mythology, and American battle history. While her assumptions have not been confirmed by Collins, Frankel makes a compelling case for each of the names that she inspects, repeatedly supported by additional scholarship. Both sections "Symbols" and "Allusions" are sufficient for her chosen topics. Readers who are interested in a thorough examination of the hidden meanings behind Collins' characters and symbols will find explanation in Frankel's short book. In fact, Frankel's concise discussions concerning symbols and allusions provide the perfect foundation for readers who are interested in expanding upon and adding to the ideas already presented. For instance, Frankel briefly relates *The Hunger Games* to the dystopian genre—specifically referencing George Orwell's dystopian words. Readers can build upon this connection in their own research to further discuss the ways in which classical dystopian literature relates to more contemporary dystopian young adult texts.

Garriott, Deidre A. E., Whitney Elaine Jones, and Julie Elizabeth Tyler. *Space and Place in* The Hunger Games. McFarland, 2014. $30.

Published by McFarland, this collection of twelve critical essays approaches the popular *Hunger Games* trilogy in new and exciting ways with special emphasis on space and place. In their introduction, editors claim the book is "about how space can be used politically and socially to wield power and create social hierarchies. It is about safe places and dangerous places" (12). The chapters contained in this book vary in subject from arguing that *The Hunger Games* series can be used as a way to discuss the Holocaust, to the different spaces inhabited by gender, to whether the series itself is a prediction of future similar "spaces." The five parts of this book are split into: I. Identifying and Challenging Narrative Space, II. Provoking Change and Creating Radical Spaces, III. Experiencing Trauma in Safe Spaces, IV. Popular Responses in Actual Spaces, and V. Envisioning Future Spaces. Three chapters are of specific interest for the study found in *Agency in* The Hunger Games. Anne Canavan's and Sarah Petrovic's essay "Tipping the Odds Ever in Her Favor" explores Katniss' agency through looking at her roles as mother, daughter, tribute, lover, and Girl on Fire. Whitney Elaine Jones' "Katniss and Her Boys" dissects the love triangle between Katniss, Peeta, and Gale based on gender and identity. Lastly, Katie Arosteguy's "I have a kind of power I never knew I possessed" investigates the mother/daughter relationship between Mrs. Everdeen and Katniss Everdeen with emphasis on the idea of "othermothering." Each of the three articles above help to influence and develop ideas present in *The Agency Games*.

Pharr, Mary F., and Leisa A. Clark (Eds.). *Of Bread, Blood and* The Hunger Games: *Critical Essays on the Suzanne Collins Trilogy.* McFarland, 2012. $10.

Published by McFarland, this collection of critical essays contains twenty-one shrewd and inclusive articles on *The Hunger Games* trilogy encompassing a diverse range of topics. In section one, authors Bill Clemente, Anthony Pavlik, Valerie E. Frankel, Tina L. Hanlon, and Max Despain discuss history, politics, economics and culture within the trilogy. In section two, authors Guy Andre Risko, Tammy L. Grant, Kathryn Wright, Sharon D. King, Ellyn Lem, Holly Hassel, and Jennifer Mitchell examine ethics, aesthetics, identity, and gender roles within the series. For the reader interested in the gender discussion, Lem's "'Killer' Katniss and 'Lover Boy' Peeta," along with Mitchell's "Of Queer Necessity" provide excellent commentary on the roles of gender and the subsequent fusing of such roles. In section three, authors Amy L. Montz, Kelley Wezner, Shannon R. Mortimore-Smith, and Helen Day address themes relating to the female body, power through surveillance and the spectacle of the Games. Amy L. Montz, in her article "Costuming the Resistance: The Female Spectacle of Rebellion," takes a controversial stance on her depiction of Cinna as a manipulator rather than friend to Katniss. In the fourth and last section, authors Catherine R. Eskin, Rodney M. DeaVault, Sarah Murphy, Amanda Firestone, and Mary F. Phar create unique comparisons between *The Hunger Games* trilogy and literary works such as Shakespeare's *Henriad*, *Ender's Game*, *Twilight*, and *Harry Potter*. Such a collection, covering a multitude of topics, is necessary for any reader who wishes to gather research on various aspects of *The Hunger Games*.

Dunn, George A., and Nicolas Michaud (Eds.). The Hunger Games *and Philosophy: A Critique of Pure Treason*. John Wiley & Sons, 2012. $13.

Published by John Wiley & Sons, this philosophical collection contains nineteen scholarly-crafted chapters that range from discussing science, gender, morality, and politics. Brian McDonald starts off Part One on art and beauty with a discussion of "Mimetic and Monstrous Art" in the series. Authors such as George A. Dunn, Joseph F. Foy, and Louis Melancon ask the big questions in relation to war, violence, and morality. Nicolas Michaud's examination of Peeta Mellark is particularly relevant to this book's analysis of Peeta's character in chapter 6. For scholars concerned with gender in Panem, look no further than Part Four wherein authors Abigail E. Myers, Jessica Miller, and Lindsey Issow Averill talk about love, the politics of gender, and feminism. Pulling on well-know and insightful philosophers such as Aristotle, Plato, Immanuel Kant, David Hume, and Zeno of Citium, this collection of essays approaches the familiar series in unexpected ways filled with ancient wisdom.

Arrow, V. *The Panem Companion: An Unofficial Guide to Suzanne Collins'* Hunger Games. Smart Pop, 2012. $11.

V. Arrow, a specialist of children and pop literature, addresses various themes in her unofficial guide which range from world building to fan fiction.

Arrow's first three chapters are devoted to exploring the world of Panem, as constructed by Collins and interpreted by readers, in which she attempts to map the geography of Panem, delves into race and ethnicity as displayed by particular districts and socioeconomics of the tesserae system. A few chapters address and even attempt to validate fan fiction such as Prim being the Baker's biological daughter, who architected the rebellion, and Cinna's sexual relationship with Finnick. While such discussion proves interesting, it is Arrow's more academically-based chapters that provide important scholarship for readers. In fact, Arrow's analyses of "The Games as Exploitation, Exploitation as Entertainment" and "Accountability for Acts of War in the Hunger Games" each offer insightful, yet open-ended conclusions for readers to interpret and answer through their own research. While some chapters deviate from accepted, academic scholarship by entertaining fan fiction, Arrow's unofficial guide presents unique, colorful observations that intrigue readers to approach the trilogy in new and unprecedented ways.

Chapter Notes

Preface

1. A more thorough definition and explanation of human agency can be found in the Introduction.

2. For a more comprehensive look at the literature conducted on *The Hunger Games* trilogy, please see Appendix B at the back of the book.

3. Tom Henthorne, *Approaching* The Hunger Games *Trilogy* (McFarland, 2012).

4. Jessica Miller, "'She has no idea. The effect she can have': Katniss and the Politics of Gender," in *The Hunger Games and Philosophy: A Critique of Pure Treason*, ed. George Dunn and Nicolas Michaud (Wiley & Sons, 2012), 145–61.

5. Ellyn Lem and Holly Hassel, "'Killer' Katniss and 'Lover Boy' Peeta: Suzanne Collins's Defiance of Gender-Genred Reading," *Of Blood, Bread, and* The Hunger Games, ed. Mary F. Pharr and Leisa A. Clark (McFarland, 2012), 118–27.

6. A "motif" refers to a reoccurring distinctive feature or dominant idea in a piece of literature.

7. Brian McDonald, "'The Final Word on Entertainment': Mimetic and Monstrous Art in *The Hunger Games*," in *The Hunger Games and Philosophy: A Critique of Pure Treason*, ed. George A. Dunn and Nicolas Michaud (John Wiley & Sons, 2012).

8. Susan Tan, "Burn with Us: Sacrificing Childhood in *The Hunger Games*." *Lion and the Unicorn* 37, no. 1 (2013), 54–73, https://dx-doi org.libproxy.calbaptist.edu/10.1353/uni.2013.0002.

9. Michael Macaluso and Cori McKenzie, "Exploiting the Gaps in the Fence: Power, Agency, and Rebellion in *The Hunger Games*," in *The Politics of Panem*, ed. Sean P. Connors (Sense Publishers, 2014): 103–24.

10. Anne Canavan and Sarah Petrovic are an exception to this statement as they are included in the few authors who discuss Katniss' agency intentionally and in its correlation to teen readers in their essay "Tipping the Odds Ever in Her Favor: An Exploration of Narrative Control and Agency in the Novel and Film."

Introduction

1. Suzanne Collins, *The Hunger Games* (New York: Scholastic, 2008), 56.

2. See Appendix A "Terminology" for more on the muttations of Panem.

3. "The Hunger Games Total Franchise Revenue," Statistic Brain Research Institute, last modified April 17 2017, https://www.statisticbrain.com/hunger-games-total-franchise-revenue/.

4. Suzanne Collins, *The Hunger Games* (New York: Scholastic, 2008), 70.

5. Tim Challies. "What Makes *The Hunger Games* So Popular?" *Challies*, April 5, 2012, https://www.challies.com/articles/what-makes-the-hunger-games-so-popular/.

6. Jeff Goins, "Why *The Hunger Games* Is the Future of Writing," *Goins, Writer*, accessed December 5, 2017, https://goinswriter.com/hunger-games/.

7. Gilad Feldman. "Making Sense of Agency: Belief in Free Will as a Unique and Important Construct," *Social and Personality Psychology Compass* (2016): 1–15.

8. Amartya Sen. "Well-Being, Agency and Freedom: The Dewey Lectures 1984," *The Journal of Philosophy*, 82, no. 4 (1985): 183–221, http://www.jstor.org/stable/2026184?origin=JSTOR-pdf.

9. Andrew Eshleman, "Moral Responsibility,"

The Stanford Encyclopedia of Philosophy, last modified December 21, 2016, https://plato.stanford.edu/entries/moral-responsibility/.

10. Susan Dominus, "Suzanne Collins's War Stories for Kids," *New York Times*, April 8, 2011, https://www.nytimes.com/2011/04/10/magazine/mag-10collins-t.html.

11. "The Hunger Games Reaches Another Milestone: Top 10 Censored Books," TIME, last modified April 10, 2012, http://entertainment.time.com/2011/01/06/removing-the-n-word-from-huck-finn-top-10-censored-books/.

12. Heba Hasan, "*The Hunger Games* Trilogy Climbs on List of Most-Challenged Book," *Time*, last modified April 10, 2012, http://newsfeed.time.com/2012/04/10/the-hunger-games-trilogy-climbs-on-list-of-most-challenged-books/.

13. Susan Dominus, "Suzanne Collins's War Stories for Kids," *New York Times*, April 8, 2011, https://www.nytimes.com/2011/04/10/magazine/mag-10collins-t.html.

14. Michel Foucault, a French philosopher, historian, social theorist, and literary critic, is perhaps most known for his theories on power and knowledge.

15. Suzanne Collins, *Mockingjay* (New York: Scholastic, 2010), 352.

16. Sir John Dalberg-Acton, an English Catholic historian, politician, and writer, was best known for his above quote which was taken from a letter written to an Anglican bishop in 1887.

17. "Lord Acton Writes to Bishop Creighton," Online Library of Liberty, accessed January 12, 2018, http://oll.libertyfund.org/quote/214.

Chapter One

1. Suzanne Collins, *Catching Fire* (New York: Scholastic, 2009), 252.

2. Suzanne Collins, *The Hunger Games* (New York: Scholastic, 2008), 58.

3. Naomi Jacobs, "Dissent, Assent, and the Body in Nineteen-Eighty-Four," *Utopian Studies*, 18, no. 1 (2007): 3–20, Jstor.

4. Pamela Cooper, "'A Body Story with a Vengeance': Anatomy and Struggle in *The Bell Jar and The Handmaid's Tale*," *Women's Studies*, 26, no. 1 (July 1997): 89–123, Taylor & Francis Online.

5. Gregory Claeys, "News from Somewhere: Enhanced Sociability and the Composite Definition of Utopia and Dystopia," *Wiley Online Library*, 98, no. 330 (2013), https://doi.org/10.1111/1468-229X.12005.

6. "Tesserae," Online Etymology Dictionary.

7. Susan Tan is a scholar of *The Hunger Games* series. Her articles have been featured in other scholarly collections such as *The Politics of Panem* edited by Sean P. Connors.

8. Susan Tan, "Burn with Us: Sacrificing Childhood in The Hunger Games," *Lion and the Unicorn* 37, no. 1 (2013): 54–73, https://dx-doi org.libproxy.calbaptist.edu/10.1353/uni.2013.0002.

9. Suzanne Collins, *The Hunger Games* (New York: Scholastic, 2008), 26.

10. *Ibid.*, 9.

11. *Ibid.*

12. Foucault's book, *Discipline and Punish*, opens up with a vivid description of the torture of Robert-François Damiens who was executed in the mid-18th century. In this book, Foucault discusses the changes that took place in the Western penal system concerning torture, punishment, discipline, and prison. In particular, Foucault's discussions on governmental control are crucial for the discussion of bodies and agency in Panem.

13. Michel Foucault, *Discipline and Punish* (New York: Vintage Books, 1995), 138.

14. "Panem et circenses," Online Etymology Dictionary, accessed January 12, 2016, https://www.etymonline.com/word/panem%20et%20circenses.

15. Michel Foucault, *Discipline and Punish* (New York: Vintage Books, 1995), 49.

16. Suzanne Collins, *The Hunger Games* (New York: Scholastic, 2008), 19.

17. Michel Foucault, *Power and Knowledge* (New York: Vintage Books, 1980), 152.

18. *Ibid.*, 155.

19. Suzanne Collins, *The Hunger Games* (New York: Scholastic, 2008), 81.

20. Michel Foucault, *Discipline and Punish* (New York: Vintage Books, 1980), 58.

21. *Ibid.*

22. Suzanne Collins, *The Hunger Games* (New York: Scholastic, 2008), 6.

23. Michael Macaluso and Cori McKenzie's article "Exploiting the Gaps in the Fence: Power, Agency and Rebellion in *The Hunger Games*" explores the physical fence that separates District 12 from the woods with particular emphasis on the presence of the gap through which Katniss can go-between each world.

24. *Ibid.*, 52.
25. Suzanne Collins, *The Hunger Games* (New York: Scholastic, 2008), 5.
26. Michel Foucault, *Discipline and Punish* (New York: Vintage Books, 1995), 138.
27. Suzanne Collins, *The Hunger Games* (New York: Scholastic, 2008), 140.
28. *Ibid.*, 23.
29. Anne Canavan and Sarah N. Petrovic, "Tipping the Odds Ever in Her Favor: An Exploration of Narrative Control and Agency in the Novel and Film," in *Space and Place in* The Hunger Games: *New Readings of the Trilogy*, ed. Deidre Garriot, Whitney Jones, and Julie Tyler (McFarland, 2014), 57.
30. Suzanne Collins, *The Hunger Games* (New York: Scholastic, 2008), 61.
31. Michel Foucault, *A History of Sexuality* (New York: Vintage Books, 1990), 140.
32. Suzanne Collins, *The Hunger Games* (New York: Scholastic, 2008), 18.
33. *Ibid.*, 234.
34. *Ibid.*, 236.
35. *Ibid.*, 237.
36. *Ibid.*, 242.
37. *Ibid.*, 339.
38. *Ibid.*, 340.
39. *Ibid.*, 344.
40. Suzanne Collins, *Catching Fire* (New York: Scholastic, 2009), 20.
41. *Ibid.*, 41.
42. Anthony Pavlik, "Absolute Power Games," in *Of Bread, Blood and* The Hunger Games, ed. Mary F. Pharr and Leisa A. Clark (McFarland, 2012), 30–38.
43. Suzanne Collins, *Catching Fire* (New York: Scholastic, 2009), 22.
44. Michel Foucault, *Power and Knowledge* (New York: Vintage Books, 1980), 59.
45. Suzanne Collins, *Catching Fire* (New York: Scholastic, 2009), 75.
46. *Ibid.*, 122.
47. *Ibid.*, 244.
48. *Ibid.*, 252.
49. Suzanne Collins, *Mockingjay* (New York: Scholastic, 2010), 59.
50. *Ibid.*, 90.
51. *Ibid.*

Chapter Two

1. Suzanne Collins, *The Hunger Games* (New York: Scholastic, 2008), 23–4.
2. Benjamin Kunkel, "Dystopia and the End of Politics," *Dissent*, 55, no. 4 (January 2008): 89–98, http://dx.doi.org/10.1353/dss.2008.0072.
3. David Dreyer, "War, Peace and Justice in Panem: International Relations and the Hunger Games Trilogy," *European Political Science*, 15 (November 2015): 251–265, http://dx.doi.org/10.1057/eps.2015.68.
4. Suzanne Collins, *Mockingjay* (New York: Scholastic, 2010), 223.
5. Aristotle, *The Poetics of Aristotle*, trans. S. H. Butcher (Gutenberg, 2008), 9, https://www.amherst.edu/system/files/media/1812/The%252520Poetics%252520of%252520Aristotle%25252C%252520by%252520Aristotle.pdf.
6. *Ibid.*, 15.
7. Michel Foucault, a French philosopher, historian, social theorist, and literary critic of the twentieth century, is perhaps most known for his theories on power and knowledge.
8. Michel Foucault, *A History of Sexuality* (New York: Vintage Books, 1990), 27.
9. *Ibid.*, 30.
10. Whitney Jones, "Katniss and Her Boys: Male Readers, the Love Triangle and Identity Formation," in *Space and Place in the Hunger Games: New Readings of the Trilogy*, ed. Deidre Garriot, Whitney Jones, and Julie Tyler (McFarland, 2014), 75.
11. Suzanne Collins, *Mockingjay* (New York: Scholastic, 2010), 330.
12. Political Realism focuses more intensely on what is considered the natural conflicting disposition of international relationships as opposed to cooperation. Realism considers human beings to be inherently self-serving.
13. Julian Korab-Karpowicz, "Political Realism in International Relations," The Stanford Encyclopedia of Philosophy, ed. Edward Zalta, last modified on May 24, 2017, https://plato.stanford.edu/entries/realism-intl-relations/.
14. Suzanne Collins, *The Hunger Games* (New York: Scholastic, 2008), 40.
15. *Ibid.*, 142.
16. *Ibid.*, 142.
17. Andrew Fiala, "Pacifism," The Stanford Encyclopedia of Philosophy, ed. Edward Zalta, last modified on September 15, 2018, https://plato.stanford.edu/entries/pacifism/.
18. Suzanne Collins, *The Hunger Games* (New York: Scholastic, 2008), 142.
19. *Ibid.*, 209 and 299.
20. *Ibid.*, 183.

21. *Ibid.*, 186.

22. *Ibid.*, 232.

23. Although two other tributes, Glimmer and the girl tribute from District 4, have died as a result of Katniss' actions at this point, Marvel is the first tribute she has actively and intentionally killed.

24. *Ibid.*, 243.

25. *Ibid.*, 341.

26. Michel Foucault, *A History of Sexuality* (New York: Vintage Books, 1990), 28.

27. Suzanne Collins, *Catching Fire* (New York: Scholastic, 2009), 172.

28. *Ibid.*, 243.

29. *Ibid.*, 377.

30. Suzanne Collins, *Mockingjay* (New York: Scholastic, 2010), 31.

31. *Ibid.*, 205.

32. *Ibid.*, 23.

33. *Ibid.*, 203.

34. *Ibid.*, 209.

35. *Ibid.*, 212.

36. *Ibid.*, 232.

37. Brian McDonald, "'The Final Word on Entertainment': Mimetic and Monstrous Art in the *Hunger Games*," In *The Hunger Games and Philosophy: A Critique of Pure Treason*, ed. George A. Dunn and Nicolas Michaud (John Wiley & Sons, 2012), 22.

38. Suzanne Collins, *Mockingjay* (New York: Scholastic, 2010), 234.

39. Interestingly, this provides another comparison to Greco-Roman mythology (the first being Theseus and the Minotaur). Having to retreat underneath the city and into the sewers, the Star Squad must travel underground. By forcing her characters underground, Collins offers up the Greco-Roman understanding of the underworld in which the main protagonist encounters and faces off with death. Several characters must remain in the underworld as death claims them.

40. *Ibid.*, 314.

41. *Ibid.*, 252 and 350.

Chapter Three

1. Susan Dominus, "Suzanne Collins's War Stories for Kids," *New York Times Magazine*, April 8, 2011, https://www.nytimes.com/2011/04/10/magazine/mag-10collins-t.html.

2. Caroline Framke, "Why *Mockingjay*, the messiest and most ambitious *Hunger Games* book, needed to get out of Katniss Everdeen's head," *Vox*, November 24, 2015, https://www.vox.com/2015/11/24/9792300/hunger-games-mockingjay-finnick-johanna.

3. Bill Clemente, "Panem in America: Crisis Economics and a Call for Political Engagement," in *Of Bread, Blood and The Hunger Games*, ed. Mary F. Pharr and Leisa A. Clark (McFarland, 2012), 20–29.

4. In dystopias, and in most twenty-first century young adult literature, it is quite common that the main character be orphaned or have absent parental figures. This allows the protagonist the opportunity to mature quickly and make decisions uninhibited by parental influence. The separation between parent and child is necessary in order for the protagonist to claim center stage in their own story.

5. Laurie Vickroy, *Trauma and Survival in Contemporary Fiction* (Charlottesville: University of Virginia Press, 2002), 24, 26.

6. Joshua Pederson, "Speak, Trauma: Toward a Revised Understanding of Literary Trauma Theory," *Narrative* 22, no. 3 (October 2014): 334, https://doi.org/10.1353/nar.2014.0018.

7. Suzanne Collins, *Mockingjay* (New York: Scholastic, 2010), 250–51.

8. Laurie Vickroy, *Trauma and Survival in Contemporary Fiction* (Charlottesville: University of Virginia Press, 2002), 32.

9. Suzanne Collins, *Mockingjay* (New York: Scholastic, 2010), 350.

10. Suzanne Collins, *The Hunger Games* (New York: Scholastic, 2008), 70.

11. Suzanne Collins, *Mockingjay* (New York: Scholastic, 2010), 252.

12. *Ibid.*, 367.

13. *Ibid.*, 389.

14. Michelle Balaev, "Trends in Literary Trauma Theory," *Mosaic*, 21, no. 2 (June 2008): 164, Literature Online.

15. Suzanne Collins, *Mockingjay* (New York: Scholastic, 2010), 370.

16. *Ibid.*, 367.

17. Tom Henthorne, *Approaching The Hunger Games Trilogy* (McFarland, 2012), 134.

18. Suzanne Collins, *Mockingjay* (New York: Scholastic, 2010), 373.

19. *Ibid.*, 377.

20. Laurie Vickroy, *Trauma and Survival in Contemporary Fiction* (Charlottesville: University of Virginia Press, 2002), 24, 26.

21. Suzanne Collins, *The Hunger Games* (New York: Scholastic, 2008), 211.

22. *Ibid.*, 301.
23. Suzanne Collins, *Mockingjay* (New York: Scholastic, 2010), 376.
24. *Ibid.*, 376.
25. *Ibid.*, 377.
26. *Ibid.*, 386.
27. Joshua Pederson, "Speak, Trauma: Toward a Revised Understanding of Literary Trauma Theory," *Narrative*, 22, no. 3 (October 2014): 338, https://doi.org/10.1353/nar.2014.0018.
28. Suzanne Collins, *Mockingjay* (New York: Scholastic, 2010), 387.
29. Tom Henthorne, in the book *Approaching* The Hunger Games *Trilogy*, mentions that Collins' series itself works as a collection of survivor stories. Survivor stories are often recollections of those who have endured trauma, survived it, and record it for their own healing or even for the sake of another.
30. Judith Herman, *Trauma and Recovery* (New York: Basic, 1992) quoted in Laurie Vickroy, *Trauma and Survival in Contemporary Fiction* (Charlottesville: University of Virginia Press, 2002), 22.
31. Suzanne Collins, *Mockingjay* (New York: Scholastic, 2010), 387.
32. *Ibid.*, 389.
33. Susan Tan, "Burn with Us: Sacrificing Childhood in The Hunger Games," *Lion and the Unicorn* 37, no. 1 (2013): 59, https://dx-doi-org.libproxy.calbaptist.edu/10.1353/uni.2013.0002.
34. Suzanne Collins, *Mockingjay* (New York: Scholastic, 2010), 390.

Chapter Four

1. James Tyner, "Self and Space, Resistance and Discipline: A Foucauldian Reading of George Orwell's 1984," *Social & Cultural Geography* 5, no. 1 (March 2004): 133, Taylor & Francis Group.
2. Collins, *Mockingjay* 270.
3. Collins, *The Hunger Games* 32.
4. Suzanne Collins, *The Hunger Games* (New York: Scholastic, 2008), 95.
5. *Ibid.*, 141.
6. *Ibid.*, 142.
7. *Ibid.*, 437.
8. Suzanne Collins, *Catching Fire* (New York: Scholastic, 2009), 53.
9. *Ibid.*, 54.
10. *Ibid.*, 49.
11. *Ibid.*, 59.
12. *Ibid.*, 104.

13. For more on this book, please see Appendix B "Suggested Readings."
14. V. Arrow, *The Panem Companion* (Smart Pop, 2012), 73.
15. Suzanne Collins, *Catching Fire* (New York: Scholastic, 2009), 243.
16. *Ibid.*, 277.
17. Suzanne Collins, *Mockingjay* (New York: Scholastic, 2010), 24.
18. *Ibid.*, 23.
19. *Ibid.*, 134.
20. Nicolas Michaud, "Who is Peeta Mellark? The Problem of Identity in Panem," in *The Hunger Games and Philosophy: A Critique of Pure Treason*, ed. George A. Dunn and Nicolas Michaud (John Wiley & Sons, 2012), 193.
21. *Ibid.*, 202.
22. Suzanne Collins, *Mockingjay* (New York: Scholastic, 2010), 189.
23. Whitney Jones, "Katniss and Her Boys: Male Readers, the Love Triangle and Identity Formation," in *Space and Place in the Hunger Games: New Readings of the Trilogy*, ed. Deidre Garriot, Whitney Jones, and Julie Tyler (McFarland, 2014), 75.
24. Suzanne Collins, *The Hunger Games* (New York: Scholastic, 2008), 141.
25. Suzanne Collins, *Mockingjay* (New York: Scholastic, 2010), 297.
26. *Ibid.*, 370.
27. *Ibid.*, 373.
28. *Ibid.*, 388.
29. *Ibid.*, 388.

Chapter Five

1. Suzanne Collins, *Mockingjay* (New York: Scholastic, 2010), 205.
2. "Lord Acton Writes to Bishop Creighton." *Online Library of Liberty*. Liberty Fund, 2018, http://oll.libertyfund.org/quote/214.
3. See chapter three for more on Katniss' morality.
4. See chapter five for more on Peeta's identity as Savior.
5. Suzanne Collins, *The Hunger Games* (New York: Scholastic, 2008), 111.
6. *Ibid.*, 12.
7. *Ibid.*
8. Whitney Jones, "Katniss and Her Boys: Male Readers, the Love Triangle and Identity Formation," in *Space and Place in* The Hunger Games: *New Readings of the Trilogy*, ed. Deidre Garriot, Whitney Jones, and Julie Tyler (McFarland, 2014), 74.

9. Suzanne Collins, *The Hunger Games* (New York: Scholastic, 2008), 111.

10. Suzanne Collins, *Mockingjay* (New York: Scholastic, 2010), 329.

11. *Ibid.*

12. Suzanne Collins, *Catching Fire* (New York: Scholastic, 2009), 12.

13. Suzanne Collins, *Mockingjay* (New York: Scholastic, 2010), 7.

14. *Ibid.*, 207.

15. *Ibid.*, 64.

16. *Ibid.*, 118.

17. *Ibid.*

18. "Lord Acton Writes to Bishop Creighton," Online Library of Liberty, accessed January 12, 2018, http://oll.libertyfund.org/quote/214.

19. Suzanne Collins, *Mockingjay* (New York: Scholastic, 2010), 186.

20. "Lord Acton Writes to Bishop Creighton," Online Library of Liberty, accessed January 12, 2018, http://oll.libertyfund.org/quote/214. *Sic.*

21. Suzanne Collins, *Mockingjay* (New York: Scholastic, 2010), 209.

22. Whitney Jones, "Katniss and Her Boys: Male Readers, the Love Triangle and Identity Formation," in *Space and Place in* The Hunger Games: *New Readings of the Trilogy*, ed. Deidre Garriot, Whitney Jones, and Julie Tyler (McFarland, 2014), 74.

23. Suzanne Collins, *Mockingjay* (New York: Scholastic, 2010), 384.

24. *Ibid.*, 209.

Chapter Six

1. Susan Bordo received her Ph.D. from the State University of New York and is a professor of Gender and Women's Studies. She has written various books and articles on feminism, the female body, the male body, and culture.

2. Susan Bordo, *Unbearable Weight: Feminism, Western Culture, and the Body* (Berkley: University of California Press, 2005), xvii.

3. Suzanne Collins, *The Hunger Games* (New York: Scholastic, 2008), 35.

4. Abigial Williams, "These Sparkly Geode Lips Are About to Rock Your World," *Huffpost,* September 22, 2016, https://www.huffingtonpost.ca/entry/crystal-geode-lips-makeup-trend_n_57e3c563e4b08d73b82fb1e3.

5. Nordstrom, "Beauty Inspiration: The Hunger Games," *The Thread*, November 22, 2019. Blogs.nordstrom.com/beauty.

6. Susan Bordo, *Unbearable Weight: Feminism, Western Culture, and the Body* (Berkley: University of California Press, 2005), 165.

7. Chad Timm, "Class Is In Session: Power and Privilege in Panem," in *The Hunger Games and Philosophy: A Critique of Pure Treason*, ed. George A. Dunn and Nicolas Michaud (John Wiley & Sons, 2012), 279.

8. Suzanne Collins, *The Hunger Games* (New York: Scholastic, 2008), 3, emphasis mine.

9. *Ibid.*, 63.

10. *Ibid.*, 64.

11. Abraham Roth, "Shared Agency and Contralateral Commitments," *The Philosophical Review* 113, no. 3 (July 2004): 360, https://www.jstor.org/stable/4147974.

12. Amy Montz, "Costuming the Resistance: The Female Spectacle of Rebellion," in *Of Blood, Bread, and* The Hunger Games, ed. Mary F. Pharr and Leisa A. Clark (McFarland, 2012), 145.

13. Suzanne Collins, *The Hunger Games* (New York: Scholastic, 2008), 56.

14. *Ibid.*, 56.

15. *Ibid.*, 70.

16. *Ibid.*, 128.

17. Amy Montz, "Costuming the Resistance: The Female Spectacle of Rebellion," in *Of Blood, Bread, and* The Hunger Games, ed. Mary F. Pharr and Leisa A. Clark (McFarland, 2012), 145.

18. Suzanne Collins, *The Hunger Games* (New York: Scholastic, 2008), 121.

19. *Ibid.*, 355.

20. *Ibid.*, 205.

21. Amy Montz, "Costuming the Resistance: The Female Spectacle of Rebellion," in *Of Blood, Bread, and* The Hunger Games, ed. Mary F. Pharr and Leisa A. Clark (McFarland, 2012), 145.

22. *Ibid.*

23. Suzanne Collins, *Catching Fire* (New York: Scholastic, 2009), 253.

24. *Ibid.*, 254.

25. *Ibid.*, 262.

26. Suzanne Collins, *Mockingjay* (New York: Scholastic, 2010), 43.

27. *Ibid.*

Chapter Seven

1. Collins, *The Hunger Games* 135.

2. Rick Margolis, "A Killer Story: An

Interview with Suzanne Collins, Author of "The Hunger Games," *School Library Journal*, last modified September 1, 2008, https://www.slj.com/?detailStory=a-killer-story-an-interview-with-suzanne-collins-author-of-the-hunger-games.

3. Suzanne Collins, *The Hunger Games* (New York: Scholastic, 2008), 134.

4. *Ibid.*, 19.

5. Suzanne Collins, *Catching Fire* (New York: Scholastic, 2009), 197.

6. Suzanne Collins, *Mockingjay* (New York: Scholastic, 2010), 172.

7. *Ibid.*, 172.

8. Suzanne Collins, *The Hunger Games* (New York: Scholastic, 2008), 56.

9. Eric Deggans, "Reality TV Is What We Make of It," *New York Times*, October 21, 2012, https://www.nytimes.com/roomfordebate/2012/10/21/are-reality-shows-worse-than-other-tv/reality-tv-is-what-we-make-of-it.

10. Suzanne Collins, *The Hunger Games* (New York: Scholastic, 2008), 46.

11. Suzanne Collins, *Catching Fire* (New York: Scholastic, 2009), 386.

12. Suzanne Collins, *The Hunger Games* (New York: Scholastic, 2008), 169.

13. Suzanne Collins, *Catching Fire* (New York: Scholastic, 2009), 178.

14. Suzanne Collins, *Mockingjay* (New York: Scholastic, 2010), 370.

15. *Ibid.*, 25.

16. For more in-depth discussions on shared agency, please see previous chapter.

17. Suzanne Collins, *Mockingjay* (New York: Scholastic, 2010), 216.

18. *Ibid.*, 216.

19. *Ibid.*, 370.

20. *Ibid.*, 387.

Chapter Eight

1. Suzanne Collins, *The Hunger Games* (New York: Scholastic, 2008), 22.

2. Ellyn Lem and Holly Hassel, "'Killer' Katniss and 'Lover Boy' Peeta: Suzanne Collins's Defiance of Gender-Genred Reading," in *Of Blood, Bread, and* The Hunger Games, ed. Mary F. Pharr and Leisa A. Clark (McFarland, 2012), 118–27.

3. Suzanne Collins, *The Hunger Games* (New York: Scholastic, 2008), 3.

4. *Ibid.*, 36.

5. *The Hunger Games.* DVD. Directed by Francis Lawrence. New York: Lionsgate Entertainment, 2012.

6. Suzanne Collins, *The Hunger Games* (New York: Scholastic, 2008), 57.

7. *Ibid.*, 233.

8. Suzanne Collins, *Catching Fire* (New York: Scholastic, 2009), 122.

9. *Ibid.*, 346.

10. Suzanne Collins, *Mockingjay* (New York: Scholastic, 2010), 181.

11. *Ibid.*, 150.

12. *Ibid.*, 349.

13. While the language of flowers has been a part of various cultures, *Dictionnaire du langage des fleurs* written by Joseph-HammerPurgstall in 1809 is accredited with being the first published list associating flowers with symbolic definitions. It is his definition that is used in the above analysis.

14. Launa Herrmann, "Primrose—'I can't live without you,'" *Daily Republic*, March 24, 2013, https://www.dailyrepublic.com/all-dr-news/solano-news/local-features/local-lifestyle-columns/primrose-i-cant-live-without-you/.

Chapter Nine

1. Through presenting Finnick as a male rape victim instead of using a female tribute, Collins challenges social constructs in which society views rape as something that can only happen to females and is only done by males. Through Katniss' own thoughts, Collins displays how easily one can slide into victim-blaming based on an individual's gender, attitude, appearance, etc. Collins intentionally uses Finnick to rebel against twenty-first century ideas concerning sex slavery.

2. Rue is also related to nature. Collins most likely uses this to connect her to Katniss and display Rue's own identity.

3. Suzanne Collins, *Catching Fire* (New York: Scholastic, 2009), 307.

4. *Ibid.*, 208.

5. Suzanne Collins, *Mockingjay* (New York: Scholastic, 2010), 172.

6. *Ibid.*, 72.

7. There are many articles that touch of the "random" aspect of the reaping and how it is most likely rigged. For more on this topic see Appendix A: Suggested Readings.

8. Well-being within this chapter referring specifically to the individual's physical safety from external forces.

9. Amartya Sen, "Well-Being, Agency

and Freedom: The Dewey Lectures 1984," *The Journal of Philosophy*, 82, no. 4 (1985): 186, http://www.jstor.org/stable/2026184? origin=JSTOR-pdf.

10. Suzanne Collins, *Catching Fire* (New York: Scholastic, 2009), 347.

11. *Ibid.*, 227.

12. *Ibid.*, 65.

13. Although this discussion intends to stay as closely to the written narrative as possible, there are moments of film, approved by Suzanne Collins, that do not conflict with the novels and help give depth to minor characters that are worth mentioning in our study.

14. *Mockingjay*. DVD. Directed by Francis Lawrence. New York: Lionsgate Entertainment, 2015.

15. Suzanne Collins, *Mockingjay* (New York: Scholastic, 2010), 370.

16. Rachel Bussel, "New Suzanne Collins Prequel Novel in *The Hunger Games* Series Coming In 2020," *Forbes*, June 17, 2019, https://www.forbes.com/sites/rachelkramerbussel/2019/06/17/new-suzanne-collins-prequel-novel-in-the-hunger-games-series-coming-in-2020/#6649671d1df0.

17. John Koenig, "Sonder," The Dictionary of Obscure Sorrows, last modified 2012, www.dictionaryofobscuresorrows.com/post/23536922667/sonder.

Chapter Ten

1. Veronica Roth, *Divergent* (New York: HarperCollins, 2011), 43.

2. Dashner, James. *The Maze Runner* (New York: Penguin Random House, 2009).

3. Orson Card, *Ender's Game*. (New York: Tor Books, 1992).

4. Carrie Hintz and Elaine Ostry, "Introduction," in *Utopian and Dystopian Writing for Children and Young Adults* (New York: Taylor and Francis Books, 2003).

5. Suzanne Collins, *Mockingjay* (New York: Scholastic, 2010), 208.

6. Katie Arosteguy, "'I have a kind of power I never knew I possessed': Transformative Motherhood and Maternal Influence," in *Space and Place in* The Hunger Games: *New Readings of the Trilogy*, ed. Deidre Garriot, Whitney Jones, and Julie Tyler (McFarland, 2014), 161.

7. Suzanne Collins, *Mockingjay* (New York: Scholastic, 2010), 364380.

8. Katie Arosteguy, "'I have a kind of power I never knew I possessed': Transfor-

mative Motherhood and Maternal Influence," in *Space and Place in* The Hunger Games: *New Readings of the Trilogy*, ed. Deidre Garriot, Whitney Jones, and Julie Tyler (McFarland, 2014), 161.

9. Suzanne Collins, *The Hunger Games* (New York: Scholastic, 2008), 9.

10. *Ibid.*, 30.

11. Suzanne Collins, *Catching Fire* (New York: Scholastic, 2009), 240.

12. *Ibid.*

13. Suzanne Collins, *Mockingjay* (New York: Scholastic, 2010), 364.

14. *Ibid.*, 362.

15. Elizabeth Braithwaite, Rebecca Hutton, and Alyson Miller, "Family Ties? Parent-Child Relationships in a Selection of Young Adult Critical Dystopian Texts," *Interjuli* 2012, no. 2 (2012): 93, http://hdl.handle.net/10536/DRO/DU:30048285.

16. Katie Arosteguy, "'I have a kind of power I never knew I possessed': Transformative Motherhood and Maternal Influence," in *Space and Place in the Hunger Games: New Readings of the Trilogy*, ed. Deidre Garriot, Whitney Jones, and Julie Tyler (McFarland, 2014), 160.

17. Suzanne Collins, *The Hunger Games* (New York: Scholastic, 2008), 9.

18. *Ibid.*, 10.

19. Whitney Jones, "Katniss and Her Boys: Male Readers, the Love Triangle and Identity Formation," in *Space and Place in* The Hunger Games: *New Readings of the Trilogy*, ed. Deidre Garriot, Whitney Jones, and Julie Tyler (McFarland, 2014), 74.

20. Suzanne Collins, *The Hunger Games* (New York: Scholastic, 2008), 14.

21. In the article, "Katniss and Her Boys: Male Readers, the Love Triangle and Identity Formation," Jones Whitney dives into discussing the portrayal of gender differences between Gale and Peeta. She argues that Gale's masculinity and Peeta's femininity help to inform Katniss' own gender identity.

22. Elizabeth Braithwaite, Rebecca Hutton, and Alyson Miller, "Family Ties? Parent-Child Relationships in a Selection of Young Adult Critical Dystopian Texts," *Interjuli* 2012, no. 2 (2012): 106, http://hdl.handle.net/10536/DRO/DU:30048285.

23. Suzanne Collins, *Mockingjay* (New York: Scholastic, 2010), 349.

24. *Ibid.*, 388.

25. Sian Gaetano, "Mockingjay, Part 2: Let's Talk about that Epilogue," The Horn Book, last modified 2015, https://www.hbook.com/mockingjay-part-2-lets-talk-about-that-epilogue/.

26. Suzanne Collins, *Mockingjay* (New York: Scholastic, 2010), 390.

27. Elizabeth Braithwaite, Rebecca Hutton, and Alyson Miller, "Family Ties? Parent-Child Relationships in a Selection of Young Adult Critical Dystopian Texts," *Interjuli* 2012, no. 2 (2012): 105, http://hdl.handle.net/10536/DRO/DU:30048285.

Chapter Eleven

1. Melissa Ames, "Engaging "Apolitical" Adolescents: Analyzing the Popularity and Educational Potential of Dystopian Literature Post-9/11," *The High School Journal* 97, no. 1 (January 2013): 7, https://doi.org/10.1353/hsj.2013.0023.

2. "'Everything is allowed. Fighting, alcohol, murder, rape, smoking, anything,'" *The Siberian Times*, December 15, 2016, https://siberiantimes.com/other/others/news/n0820-everything-is-allowed-fighting-alcohol-murder-rape-smoking-any thing/.

3. According to Pyatkovsky, what he meant by this quote was that the organizers were located too far away from the arena to stop anyone from committing heinous acts, but that they would be held punishable by law once the authorities arrived.

4. "Anger as controversial Siberian 'Hunger Games' creator claims his idea was a 'fake,'" *The Siberian Times*, June 1, 2017, https://siberiantimes.com/other/others/news/anger-as-controversial-siberian-hunger-games-creator-claims-his-idea-was-a-fake/.

5. Tim Lister, Ray Sanchez, Mark Bixler, Sean O'Key, Michael Hogenmiller, and Mohammed Tawfeeq, "ISIS Goes Global: 143 Attacks in 29 Countries Have Killed 2,043," *CNN World*, July 25, 2016, https://www-m.cnn.com /2015/12/17/world/mapping-isis-attacks-around-the world/index.html?r=https%3A%2F%2Fwww.google.com%2F.

6. Mark Borg, Jr., "Psychoanalytic Pure War: Interactions with the Post-Apocalyptic Unconscious," *Journal for the Psychoanalysis of Culture and Society* 8, no. 1 (Spring 2003): 57, http://muse.jhu.edu/article/40697/pdf.

7. Anas Alkhatib, Judy Regan, and Donna Barrett, "The Silent Victims: Effects of War and Terrorism on Child Development," *Psychiatric Annals* 37, no. 8 (2007): 588, PsycINFO.

8. Susanna Schrobsdorff, "Teen Depression and Anxiety: Why the Kids Are Not Alright," *TIME*, October 27, 2016, https://time.com/4547305/november-7th-2016-vol-188-no-19-u-s/.

9. Carrie Hintz and Elaine Ostry, "Introduction," in *Utopian and Dystopian Writing for Children and Young Adults* (New York: Taylor and Francis Books, 2003), 10.

10. Debra Donston-Miller, "Why Young Adults 'Hunger' For The Hunger Games and Other Post-Apocalyptic Dystopian Fiction," *Forbes*, November 20, 2014, https://www.forbes.com/sites/sungardas/2014/11/20/why-young-adults-hunger-for-the-hunger-games-and-other-post-apocalyptic-dystopian-fiction/#4b1d90d4ef0e.

11. Suzanne Collins, *Mockingjay* (New York: Scholastic, 2010), 388.

Appendix A

1. For more on Beetee's morality and agency please see Chapter Ten: "You can't put everyone in here": Agency and Those that Should Not be Forgotten.

2. For more information on Frankel's book please see Appendix B.

3. For more on Cinna as father-figure please see Chapter Nine "I took over as head of the family": Agency and Problematic Parental/ Surrogate Figures.

4. For more on Cinna the rebel please see Chapter Seven "I always channel my emotions into my work": Cinna's Embellished Agency.

5. See Chapter Nine "Agency and the Problematic Parental/ Surrogate Figures" for more on the importance of withholding or providing names for parental figures.

6. For more information on Frankel's book see Appendix B.

7. See Chapter One "Agency and the Body" for more on this idea of the Games as spectacle.

8. For more information regarding muttations consider reading Jason T. Eberl's article "'No Mutt is Good'—Really? Creating Interspecies Chimeras." This article can be found in *The Hunger Games and Philosophy*, see Appendix C for more on this collection of articles.

9. See V. Arrow's *The Panem Companion* for the Unofficial Map of Panem.

10. Brian McDonald, author of "'The Final Word on Entertainment': Mimetic and and Monstrous Art in the Hunger Games," has an interesting commentary on the "Remake Center" borrowing the term *de-creation* from philosopher Phillip Rieff. See Appendix B for more information on McDonald's article.

Bibliography

Alkhatib, Anas, Judy Regan, and Donna Barrett. "The Silent Victims: Effects of War and Terrorism on Child Development." *Psychiatric Annals* 37, no. 8 (2007): 586–89. PsycINFO.

Ames, Melissa A. "Engaging 'Apolitical' Adolescents: Analyzing the Popularity and Educational Potential of Dystopian Literature Post-9/11." *The High School Journal* 97, no. 1 (January 2013): 3–20. https://doi.org/10.1353/hsj.2013.0023.

"Anger as controversial Siberian 'Hunger Games' creator claims his idea was a 'fake.'" *The Siberian Times,* June 1, 2017. https://siberiantimes.com/other/others/news/anger-as-controversial-siberian-hunger-games-creator-claims-his-idea-was-a-fake/.

Aristotle. *The Poetics of Aristotle.* Translated by S. H. Butcher. Gutenberg, 1961, https://www.amherst.edu/system/files/media/1812/The%252520Poetics%252520of%252520Aristotle%25252C%252520by%252520Aristotle.pdf.

Arosteguy, Katie. "'I have a kind of power I never knew I possessed': Transformative Motherhood and Maternal Influence." In *Space and Place in* The Hunger Games: *New Readings of the Trilogy,* edited by Deidre Garriot, Whitney Jones, and Julie Tyler, 157–70. Jefferson, NC: McFarland, 2014.

Arrow, V. *The Panem Companion.* Smart Pop, 2012.

Balaev, Michelle. "Trends in Literary Trauma Theory." *Mosaic* 21, no. 2 (June 2008): 149–65. Literature Online.

Bordo, Susan. *Unbearable Weight: Feminism, Western Culture, and the Body.* Berkley: University of California Press, 2005.

Borg, Mark, Jr. "Psychoanalytic Pure War: Interactions with the Post-Apocalyptic Unconscious." *Journal for the Psychoanalysis of Culture and Society* 8, no. 1 (Spring 2003): 57–67. http://muse.jhu.edu/article/40697/pdf.

Braithwaite, Elizabeth, Rebecca Hutton, and Alyson Miller. "Family Ties? Parent-Child Relationships in a Selection of Young Adult Critical Dystopian Texts." *Interjuli* 2012, no. 2 (2012): 92–108. http://hdl.handle.net/10536/DRO/DU:30048285

Bussel, Rachel K. "New Suzanne Collins Prequel Novel in *The Hunger Games* Series Coming In 2020." *Forbes,* June 17, 2019. https://www.forbes.com/sites/rachelkramerbussel/2019/06/17/new-suzanne-collins-prequel-novel-in-the-hunger-games-series-coming-in-2020/#6649671d1df0.

Canavan, Anne M., and Sarah N. Petrovic. "Tipping the Odds Ever in Her Favor: An Exploration of Narrative Control and Agency in the Novel and Film." In *Space and Place in* The Hunger Games: *New Readings of the Trilogy,* edited by Deidre Garriot, Whitney Jones, and Julie Tyler, 56–70. Jefferson, NC: McFarland, 2014.

Card, Orson S. *Ender's Game.* Tom Doherty Associates, 1992.

Challies, Tim. "What Makes the Hunger Games So Popular?" *Challies,* April 5, 2012. https://www.challies.com/articles/what-makes-the-hunger-games-so-popular/.

Claeys, Gregory. "News from Somewhere: Enhanced Sociability and the Composite Definition of Utopia and Dystopia." *Wiley Online Library* 98, no. 330 (2013), https://doi.org/10.1111/1468-229X.12005.

Clemente, Bill. "Panem in America: Crisis Economics and a Call for Political Engagement."

In *Of Bread, Blood and* The Hunger Games, edited by Mary F. Pharr and Leisa A. Clark, 20–29. New York: McFarland, 2012.

Collins, Suzanne. *Catching Fire.* New York: Scholastic, 2009.

_____. *The Hunger Games.* New York: Scholastic, 2008.

_____. *Mockingjay.* New York: Scholastic, 2010.

Cooper, Pamela. "'A Body Story with a Vengeance': Anatomy and Struggle in *The Bell Jar* and *The Handmaid's Tale.*" *Women's Studies,* 26 no. 1 (July 1997): 89–123. Taylor & Francis Online.

Dashner, James. *The Maze Runner.* New York: Random Penguin House, 2009.

Deggans, Eric. "Reality TV Is What We Make of It." *New York Times,* October 21, 2012. https://www.nytimes.com/roomfordebate/2012/10/21/are-reality-shows-worse-than-other-tv/reality-tv-is-what-we-make-of-it.

Dominus, Susan. "Suzanne Collins's War Stories for Kids." *New York Times,* April 8, 2011. https://www.nytimes.com/2011/04/10/magazine/mag-10collins-t.html.

Donston-Miller, Debra. "Why Young Adults 'Hunger' For *The Hunger Games* and Other Post-Apocalyptic Dystopian Fiction." *Forbes,* November 20, 2014. https://www.forbes.com/sites/sungardas/2014/11/20/why-young-adults-hunger-for-the-hunger-games-and-other-post-apocalyptic-dystopian-fiction/#4b1d90d4ef0e.

Dreyer, David R. "War, Peace and Justice in Panem: International Relations and the Hunger Games Trilogy." *European Political Science,* 15 (November 2015): 251–265. http://dx.doi.org/10.1057/eps.2015.68.

Eshleman, Andrew. "Moral Responsibility." The Stanford Encyclopedia of Philosophy. Last modified December 21, 2016. https://plato.stanford.edu/entries/moral-responsibility/.

"'Everything Is Allowed. Fighting, Alcohol, Murder, Rape, Smoking, Anything.'" *The Siberian Times,* December 15, 2016. https://siberiantimes.com/other/others/news/n0820-everything-is-allowed-fighting-alcohol-murder-rape-smoking-anything/.

Feldman, Gilad. "Making Sense of Agency: Belief in Free Will as a Unique and Important Construct." *Social and Personality Psychology Compass* (2016): 1–15.

Fiala, Andrew. "Pacifism." The Stanford Encyclopedia of Philosophy, edited by Edward Zalta. Last modified on September 15, 2018. https://plato.stanford.edu/entries/pacifism/.

Foucault, Michel. *Discipline and Punish.* New York: Vintage Books, 1995.

_____. *A History of Sexuality.* New York: Vintage Books, 1990.

_____. *Power and Knowledge.* New York: Vintage Books, 1980.

Framke, Caroline. "Why Mockingjay, the Messiest and Most Ambitious Hunger Games Book, Needed to Get Out of Katniss Everdeen's Head." *Vox,* November 24, 2015. https://www.vox.com/2015/11/24/9792300/hunger-games-mockingjay-finnick-johanna.

Gaetano, Sian. "Mockingjay, Part 2: Let's Talk About That Epilogue." The Horn Book, last modified 2015. https://www.hbook.com/mockingjay-part-2-lets-talk-about-that-epilogue/.

Goins, Jeff. "Why *The Hunger Games* Is the Future of Writing." *Goins, Writer,* accessed December 5, 2017. https://goinswriter.com/hunger-games/.

Hasan, Heba. "The *Hunger Games* Trilogy Climbs on List of Most-Challenged Books." TIME. Last modified April 10, 2012. http://newsfeed.time.com/2012/04/10/the-hunger-games-trilogy-climbs-on-list-of-most-challenged-books/.

Henthorne, Tom. *Approaching* The Hunger Games *Trilogy.* Jefferson, NC: McFarland, 2012.

Herman, Judith. *Trauma and Recovery.* New York: Basic, 1992.

Herrmann, Launa. "Primrose—'I Can't Live Without You.'" *Daily Republic,* March 24, 2013. https://www.dailyrepublic.com/all-dr-news/solano-news/local-features/local-lifestyle-columns/primrose-i-cant-live-without-you/.

Hintz, Carrie, and Elaine Ostry. "Introduction." In *Utopian and Dystopian Writing for Children and Young Adults,* 1–22. New York: Taylor and Francis Books, 2003.

The Hunger Games. DVD. Directed by Francis Lawrence. New York: Lionsgate Entertainment, 2012.

"The Hunger Games Reaches Another Milestone: Top 10 Censored Books." TIME, last modified April 10, 2012. http://entertainment.time.com/2011/01/06/removing-the-n-word-from-huck-finn-top-10-censored-books/

Jacobs, Naomi. "Dissent, Assent, and the Body in *Nineteen-Eighty-Four.*" *Utopian Studies* 18, no. 1 (2007): 3–20. Jstor.

Jones, Whitney E. "Katniss and Her Boys: Male Readers, the Love Triangle and Identity Formation." In *Space and Place in* The Hunger Games: *New Readings of the Trilogy,* ed. by Deidre Garriot, Whitney Jones, and Julie Tyler, 71–93. Jefferson, NC: McFarland, 2014.

Koenig, John. "Sonder." *The Dictionary of Obscure Sorrows,* last modified 2012. www.dictionaryofobscuresorrows.com/post/23536922667/sonder

Korab-Karpowicz, W. Julian. "Political Realism in International Relations." The Stanford Encyclopedia of Philosophy, edited by Edward N. Zalta. Last modified May 24, 2017. https://plato.stanford.edu/entries/realism-intl-relations/.

Kunkel, Benjamin. "Dystopia and the End of Politics." *Dissent* 55, no. 4 (January 2008: 89–98. http://dx.doi.org/10.1353/dss.2008.0072.

Lem, Ellyn, and Holly Hassel. "'Killer' Katniss and 'Lover Boy' Peeta: Suzanne Collins's Defiance of Gender-Genred Reading." In *Of Blood, Bread, and* The Hunger Games, edited by Mary F. Pharr and Leisa A. Clark, 118–27. Jefferson, NC: McFarland, 2012.

Lister, Tim, Ray Sanchez, Mark Bixler, Sean O'Key, Michael Hogenmiller, and Mohammed Tawfeeq. "ISIS Goes Global: 143 Attacks in 29 Countries Have Killed 2,043." *CNN World,* July 25, 2016. https://www-m.cnn.com/2015/12/17/world/mapping-isis-attacks-around-the-world/index.html?r=https%3A%2F%2Fwww.google.com%2F.

"Lord Acton Writes to Bishop Creighton." Online Library of Liberty. Accessed January 12, 2018. http://oll.libertyfund.org/quote/214.

Macaluso, Michael and Cori McKenzie. "Exploiting the Gaps in the Fence: Power, Agency, and Rebellion in *The Hunger Games.*" In *The Politics of Panem,* edited by Sean P. Connors, 103–24. Sense Publishers, 2014.

Margolis, Rick. "A Killer Story: An Interview with Suzanne Collins, Author of "The Hunger Games." School Library Journal, last modified September 1, 2008. https://www.slj.com/?detailStory=a-killer-story-an-interview-with-suzanne-collins-author-of-the-hunger-games.

McDonald, Brian. "'The Final Word on Entertainment': Mimetic and Monstrous Art in the *Hunger Games.*" *The Hunger Games and Philosophy: A Critique of Pure Treason,* edited by George A. Dunn and Nicolas Michaud. 8–25. John Wiley & Sons, 2012.

Michaud, Nicolas. "Who is Peeta Mellark? The Problem of Identity in Panem." In *The Hunger Games and Philosophy: A Critique of Pure Treason,* edited by George A. Dunn and Nicolas Michaud, 193–205. John Wiley & Sons, 2012.

Miller, Jessica. "'She has no idea. The effect she can have': Katniss and the Politics of Gender." *The Hunger Games and Philosophy: A Critique of Pure Treason,* edited George Dunn and Nicolas Michaud, John Wiley & Sons, 2012, p. 145–61.

Mockingjay. DVD. Directed by Francis Lawrence. New York: Lionsgate Entertainment, 2015.

Montz, Amy L. "Costuming the Resistance: The Female Spectacle of Rebellion." In *Of Blood, Bread, and* The Hunger Games, edited by Mary F. Pharr and Leisa A. Clark, 139–147. Jefferson, NC: McFarland, 2012.

Nordstrom. "Beauty Inspiration: The Hunger Games." *The Thread,* November 22, 2019. Blogs.nordstrom.com/beauty

"Panem et circenses." Online Etymology Dictionary, accessed January 12, 2016. https://www.etymonline.com/word/panem%20et%20circenses.

Pavlik, Anthony. "Absolute Power Games." In *Of Bread, Blood and* The Hunger Games, edited by Mary F. Pharr and Leisa A. Clark, 30–38. Jefferson, NC: McFarland, 2012.

Pederson, Joshua. "Speak, Trauma: Toward a Revised Understanding of Literary Trauma Theory." *Narrative* 22, no. 3 (October 2014): 333–53. https://doi.org/10.1353/nar.2014.0018.

Roth, Abraham S. "Shared Agency and Contralateral Commitments." *The Philosophical Review* 113, no. 3 (July 2004): 359–410. https://www.jstor.org/stable/4147974.

Roth, Veronica. *Divergent.* New York: HarperCollins, 2011.

Schrobsdorff, Susanna. "Teen Depression and Anxiety: Why the Kids Are Not Alright." *TIME,* October 27, 2016. https://time.com/magazine/us/4547305/november-7th-2016-vol-188-no-19-u-s/.

Sen, Amartya. "Well-Being, Agency and Freedom: The Dewey Lectures 1984." *The Journal of Philosophy* 82, no. 4 (1985): 183–221. http://www.jstor.org/stable/2026184? origin=JSTOR-pdf.

Statistic Brain "The Hunger Games Total Franchise Revenue." Last modified April 17, 2017, https://www.statisticbrain.com/hunger-games-total-franchise-revenue/.

Tan, Susan S.M. "Burn with Us: Sacrificing Childhood in *The Hunger Games*." *Lion and the Unicorn* 37, no. 1 (2013): 54–73. https://dx-doi org.libproxy.calbaptist.edu/10.1353/uni.2013.0002.

Timm, Chad W. "Class Is in Session: Power and Privilege in Panem." In *The Hunger Games and Philosophy: A Critique of Pure Treason,* edited by George A. Dunn and Nicolas Michaud, 277–289. John Wiley & Sons, 2012.

Tyner, James A. "Self and Space, Resistance and Discipline: a Foucauldian Reading of George Orwell's *1984*." *Social & Cultural Geography* 5, no. 1 (March 2004): 129–49. Taylor & Francis Group.

Vickroy, Laurie. *Trauma and Survival in Contemporary Fiction.* Charlottesville: University of Virginia Press, 2002.

Williams, Abigail. "These Sparkly Geode Lips Are About to Rock Your World." *Huffpost,* September 22, 2016. https://www.huffingtonpost.ca/entry/crystal-geode-lips-makeup-trend_n_57e3c563e4b08d73b82fb1e3.

Index